ENTERPRISE
DATABASE
CONNECTIVITY

▼ ENTERPRISE
▼ DATABASE
▼ CONNECTIVITY

*The Key
to Enterprise Applications
on the Desktop*

Richard D. Hackathorn

JOHN WILEY & SONS, INC.
New York • Chichester • Brisbane • Toronto • Singapore

Publisher: Katherine Schowalter
Senior Acquisitions Editor: Diane Cerra
Associate Editor: Terri Hudson
Managing Editor: Jacqueline A. Martin
Composition: Rebecca Herr & Alan Bernhard, Argent Associates

This text is printed on acid-free paper.

Designations used by companies to distinguish their products are often claimed as trademarks. In all instances where John Wiley & Sons, Inc. is aware of a claim, the product names appear in Initial Capital or all capital letters. Readers, however, should contact the appropriate companies for more complete information regarding trademarks and registration.

Illustrations on pages 4 and 19 © Rich Tennant/Computerworld, used with permission.

Copyright © 1993 by John Wiley & Sons, Inc.
All rights reserved. Published simultaneously in Canada.

Reproduction or translation of any part of this work beyond that permitted by section 107 or 108 of the 1976 United States Copyright Act without the permission of the copyright owner is unlawful. Requests for permission or further information should be addressed to the Permission Department, John Wiley & Sons, Inc.

This publication is designed to provide accurate and authoritative information in regard to the subject matter covered. It is sold with the understanding that the publisher is not engaged in rendering legal, accounting, or other professional service. If legal advice or other expert assistance is required, the services of a competent professional person should be sought. FROM A DECLARATION OF PRINCIPLES JOINTLY ADOPTED BY A COMMITTEE OF THE AMERICAN BAR ASSOCIATION AND A COMMITTEE OF PUBLISHERS.

Library of Congress Cataloging-in-Publication Data

Hackathorn, Richard D.
    Enterprise database connectivity : the key to enterprise applications on the desktop / Richard D. Hackathorn.
       p.   cm.
    Includes bibliographical references and index.
    ISBN 0-471-57802-9 (alk. paper : pbk.)
    1. Data base management.   2. System design.   3. Application software.   I. Title.
QA76.9.D3H25   1993   92-40043
005.75'8—dc20   CIP

Printed in the United States of America
10 9 8 7 6 5 4 3 2 1

To Linda, Eric, and Robin,

my lifelong associates
whose love and patience have encouraged me

CONTENTS

ABOUT THE AUTHOR	xvii
FOREWORD	xix
PREFACE	xxi

1. INTRODUCTION — 1
- 1.1 Challenges of the 1990s — 2
  - 1.1.1 World turned upside down — 2
  - 1.1.2 Decline of IS corporate function — 3
  - 1.1.3 Disintegration of enterprise systems — 4
  - 1.1.4 Fragmentation of enterprise data — 5
- 1.2 Shifts in Fundamental Paradigms — 6
  - 1.2.1 The workgroup is the architecture — 6
  - 1.2.2 The network is the system — 7
  - 1.2.3 The desktop is the application — 7
  - 1.2.4 Process and data are the same — 8
- 1.3 Deploying Enterprise Applications to the Desktop — 11
  - 1.3.1 Some definitions — 11
  - 1.3.2 Development as analyzing, designing, and implementing — 14
  - 1.3.3 Deployment as installing, supporting, and maintaining — 14
  - 1.3.4 Sharing of data across the enterprise — 15
  - 1.3.5 Implications of federated databases — 16
- 1.4 Pursuit of Open Systems — 19
  - 1.4.1 The open systems approach — 20
  - 1.4.2 The elusive benefits of open systems — 21
  - 1.4.3 Standards, standards, standards . . . — 22
- 1.5 Enterprise Database Connectivity — 24
  - 1.5.1 Functional layers of EDC — 24
  - 1.5.2 Common architectures for EDC — 26

2. FUNDAMENTALS OF DATA MANAGEMENT — 29
- 2.1 Database Management Systems — 30

		2.1.1	Production versus decision support	31
	2.2	Data Models		33
		2.2.1	Historical perspective	34
		2.2.2	Relational data model	35
		2.2.3	Object-oriented data model	36
	2.3	SQL as a Connectivity Language		38
		2.3.1	Features for connectivity	39
	2.4	Database Programming Interfaces		40
		2.4.1	Basic distinctions	40
	2.5	Database Front-End Tools		47
		2.5.1	Categories	50
		2.5.2	API of front-end tools	51
		2.5.3	Desktop integration mechanisms	51
	2.6	Problems with Data Transparency		53
		2.6.1	Database interface	53
		2.6.2	Database connection	54
		2.6.3	SQL syntax and semantics	54
		2.6.4	System catalog tables	55
		2.6.5	Data types and encodings	56
		2.6.6	Status codes and messages	56
		2.6.7	Collating sequences	57
		2.6.8	Data semantics	57
3.	**FUNDAMENTALS OF PROCESS MANAGEMENT**			**61**
	3.1	Transaction Control		61
		3.1.1	What is a transaction?	61
		3.1.2	ACID properties	62
		3.1.3	COMMIT and ROLLBACK	63
		3.1.4	Short versus long transactions	64
		3.1.5	What really is a transaction?	67
	3.2	Concurrency Control		69
		3.2.1	Concurrency problems	69
		3.2.2	Pessimistic concurrency control	72
		3.2.3	Optimistic concurrency control	78
		3.2.4	Data uncertainty	79
	3.3	Security Control		80
		3.3.1	Database privileges	81
		3.3.2	GRANT and REVOKE	82
		3.3.3	View definition	82
		3.3.4	Stored procedures	83
	3.4	Problems with Process Transparency		84
		3.4.1	Transaction boundaries mismatch	85
		3.4.2	Isolation levels mismatch	86
		3.4.3	User identification and privileges	86

4. BUILDING CENTRALIZED SYSTEMS — 89
- 4.1 Why Centralized Systems? — 89
  - 4.1.1 Evolution of system architecture — 90
- 4.2 Data Objects and Presentation Objects — 91
  - 4.2.1 Sharing data objects — 93
- 4.3 Basic Application Structure — 94
  - 4.3.1 Presentation service — 95
  - 4.3.2 Presentation logic — 95
  - 4.3.3 Function Logic — 96
  - 4.3.4 Data logic — 96
  - 4.3.5 Data service — 96
- 4.4 Types of Linkages — 96
  - 4.4.1 Transaction linkage — 97
  - 4.4.2 Value linkage — 97
  - 4.4.3 Structure linkage — 97
- 4.5 Generic Linkage Techniques — 98
  - 4.5.1 Table viewing — 98
  - 4.5.2 Row viewing — 100
  - 4.5.3 Join path viewing — 101
- 4.6 Roles of Client and Server — 102

5. BUILDING DISTRIBUTED SYSTEMS — 105
- 5.1 Why Distributed Systems? — 105
  - 5.1.1 Advantages — 107
  - 5.1.2 Disadvantages — 108
  - 5.1.3 Summary — 111
- 5.2 Client-Server Architectures — 112
  - 5.2.1 Bilevel CSA — 113
  - 5.2.2 Multilevel CSA — 114
  - 5.2.3 Peer-to-peer CSA — 115
  - 5.2.4 Local and remote servers — 115
  - 5.2.5 Generic versus custom services — 118
- 5.3 Slicing the Basic Application Structure — 118
  - 5.3.1 Distributed database — 120
  - 5.3.2 CSA database — 120
  - 5.3.3 Enhanced CSA database — 120
  - 5.3.4 Application server — 121
  - 5.3.5 Enhanced presentation — 121
  - 5.3.6 Terminal emulation — 121
  - 5.3.7 General comparisons — 121
- 5.4 Ways of Distributing Data — 123
  - 5.4.1 What is a distributed database system? — 123
  - 5.4.2 Techniques for data distribution — 124
- 5.5 Ways of Distributing Process — 127

		5.5.1	Key aspects of distributing process	127
		5.5.2	Levels of distributing database transactions	128
		5.5.3	Remote procedure call	133
		5.5.4	Distributed transaction monitors	134

6. ARCHITECTURES FOR OPEN CONNECTIVITY — 137

6.1	Layered Architectures and OSI	138
6.2	Client-Server Architecture Revisited	141
6.3	Problems with Proprietary Architectures	144
6.4	The Three Basic Approaches	147
	6.4.1 Common-interface approach	148
	6.4.2 Common-gateway approach	152
	6.4.3 Common-protocol approach	155
	6.4.4 Some interesting combinations	157
6.5	Comparison Criteria	160
	6.5.1 Performance	160
	6.5.2 Transparency	161
	6.5.3 Openness	161
	6.5.4 Manageability	162
	6.5.5 Reliability	163
	6.5.6 Stability	163
	6.5.7 Permissiveness	164
	6.5.8 Summary of comparisons	164
6.6	Relation to EDC Functional Layers	165

7. ACCESS MANAGEMENT — 167

7.1	Allowing Direct SQL Access	168
7.2	Client-Server Networking	168
	7.2.1 Fitting the pipes together	169
	7.2.2 Client platform	170
	7.2.3 Server platform	172
	7.2.4 Plumbing in the middle	173
	7.2.5 Three basic routes	175
	7.2.6 Connecting Windows clients to DB2	177
	7.2.7 Requirement for network integration	179
7.3	INDEPTH: Microsoft Open Database Connectivity	182
	7.3.1 Windows open service architecture	183
	7.3.2 Examples of using ODBC	185
	7.3.3 Brief overview of ODBC programming	186
7.4	INDEPTH: Micro Decisionware Database Gateway	189
7.5	INDEPTH: IBM Distributed Relational Database Architecture	193
	7.5.1 DRDA components	195
	7.5.2 An example	197
	7.5.3 OS/2 distributed database connection services/2	207
7.6	INDEPTH: ISO Remote Database Architecture	210

			Contents ▼ xi

		7.6.1 SQL access group	212
	7.7	Comparison of IBM DRDA and ISO RDA	215

8. COPY MANAGEMENT — 221
- 8.1 Management of Copy Management — 222
- 8.2 Mechanics of Copy Management — 223
  - 8.2.1 Retrieval of copy set — 223
  - 8.2.2 Placement of copy sets — 224
  - 8.2.3 General case of copy management — 224
  - 8.2.4 Factors for evaluating copy management — 226
  - 8.2.5 Living without distributed updates — 229
- 8.3 Techniques for Simple Copy Management — 230
  - 8.3.1 Centralization — 230
  - 8.3.2 Partition — 230
  - 8.3.3 Simple extract — 232
  - 8.3.4 Timestamp extract — 233
  - 8.3.5 Checked extract — 233
  - 8.3.6 Refreshed extract — 234
  - 8.3.7 Periodic replica — 235
  - 8.3.8 Continuous replica — 236
  - 8.3.9 Check-out replica — 237
  - 8.3.10 Comparisons among techniques — 239
- 8.4 INDEPTH: MDI Database Gateway TRANSFER — 239
  - 8.4.1 Centralized database case — 240
  - 8.4.2 Simple extract case — 241
  - 8.4.3 Refreshed extract case — 243
  - 8.4.4 Periodic replica case — 245
  - 8.4.5 Continuous replica case — 246
  - 8.4.6 Final TRANSFER examples — 246
- 8.5 INDEPTH: Digital VAX Data Distributor — 247

9. WAREHOUSE MANAGEMENT — 251
- 9.1 What Is a Warehouse? — 251
  - 9.1.1 A definition — 252
  - 9.1.2 An example of a large warehouse — 254
  - 9.1.3 Some characteristics — 255
  - 9.1.4 Key issues — 258
- 9.2 INDEPTH: IBM Information Warehouse Framework — 263

10. ADMINISTRATION ISSUES — 267
- 10.1 The Sacred Seven — 268
- 10.2 Handling the Complexity of Technology — 270
  - 10.2.1 Riding the technology roller coaster — 270
  - 10.2.2 Diversity of technology — 271
  - 10.2.3 Fads versus concepts — 272

	10.2.4	Timing of adoption	273
	10.2.5	Assessing new technology	273
10.3	Dealing with Legacy Systems		274
10.4	Application Extensibility		276
10.5	INDEPTH: IBM DataHub		278
10.6	Action Planning		281
	10.6.1	Hedge your bets	281
	10.6.2	Action steps	282

APPENDIX A: ODBC Function Summary — **285**

APPENDIX B: Comparison of DRDA and RDA Commands — **291**

GLOSSARY — **293**

ACRONYMS — **307**

REFERENCES — **313**

INDEX — **319**

LIST OF FIGURES

1.1	The bewildered CIO	4
1.2	End-user computing and workgroup computing	6
1.3	Process and data as opposite sides of a coin	9
1.4	Federated databases versus distributed databases	17
1.5	Enterprise-to-workgroup distribution	17
1.6	Workgroup-to-enterprise distribution	18
1.7	Need more IT arrows?	19
1.8	EDC layers	25
1.9	EDC architectures	26
2.1	What is a DBMS?	31
2.2	Efficiency versus flexibility	32
2.3	Traditional database interfaces	40
2.4	Example of embedded SQL in COBOL	41
2.5	Processing embedded API	42
2.6	Example of call-level program in C	43
2.7	Binding times	44
2.8	Embedded versus call-level	45
2.9	Example of a stored procedure	47
2.10	Effort versus complexity	48
2.11	Power versus skill	50
3.1	Transaction boundaries: Classical case	65
3.2	Transaction boundaries: Short transaction	65
3.3	Transaction boundaries: Long transaction	66
3.4	Splintered transaction	68
3.5	Ultralong transaction	68
3.6	Concurrency problem: Dirty read	70
3.7	Concurrency problem: Nonrepeatable read	71
3.8	Concurrency problem: Phantom rows	71
3.9	Concurrency problem: Lost update	72
3.10	Concurrent transaction in deadlock	76

xiv ▼ List of Figures

3.11	Pessimistic versus optimistic controls	78
3.12	Stored procedures as a security control	84
3.13	Transaction boundaries mismatch	85
4.1	Evolution of system architecture	90
4.2	Data objects and presentation objects	92
4.3	Linking presentation objects and data objects	94
4.4	Basic application structure	95
4.5	Table viewing	99
4.6	Row viewing	100
4.7	Join path viewing	102
5.1	Process and data have conflicting trends	110
5.2	Simple client-server architecture	112
5.3	Bilevel client-server architectures	113
5.4	Multilevel client-server architecture	114
5.5	Peer-to-peer architecture	115
5.6	Local and remote servers	115
5.7	Slicing the BAS	119
5.8	Various BAS arrangements	119
5.9	Four levels of distributing transactions	128
5.10	Summary of the four levels	129
5.11	Two-phase commit	130
5.12	Remote procedure call	133
5.13	X/Open distributed transaction processing	135
6.1	Simple two-system interconnect	138
6.2	Two systems in a network	140
6.3	Conventional database architecture	141
6.4	Client-server architecture	142
6.5	Problems of proprietary interface	144
6.6	Additional problems with proprietary interface	146
6.7	Common interface: Client-side and client-owned	150
6.8	Common interface: Client-side and server-owned	150
6.9	Common interface: Server-side and client-owned	151
6.10	Common interface: Server-side and server-owned	151
6.11	Common gateway	153
6.12	Common protocol	155
6.13	Combination #1	157
6.14	Combination #2	158
6.15	Combination #3	159
6.16	Combination #4	159
7.1	Components of client-server networking	170
7.2	Connecting Windows clients to DB2	177
Table 7.1	Products that provide connectivity	179
7.3	New IBM SNA blueprint	181
7.4	Common interface and ODBC	183
7.5	Microsoft Windows Open Service Architecture	184

List of Figures ▼ xv

7.6	Examples of using ODBC	185
7.7	ODBC context hierarchy	186
7.8	ODBC one-time execution	187
7.9	ODBC repeated execution	188
7.10	Components of Database Gateway	190
7.11	Handling multiple clients and servers	191
7.12	Remote Sored Procedures and client services	192
7.13	DRDA architecture	193
7.14	DRDA combinations	195
7.15	DRDA components	196
7.16	DRDA DDM commands	197
7.17	Establish connection	203
7.18	Do bind processing	205
7.19	Terminate connection	206
7.20	Process query and retrieve results	207
7.21	DDCS/2 configurations	208
7.22	ISO RDA	211
7.23	RDA services	212
7.24	SAG membership list	213
7.25	ISO RDA and SQL access	214
7.26	Comparison of DRDA and RDA components	215
7.27	Migration paths for DRDA and RDA	219
8.1	Copy management, simple case	223
8.2	Copy management, general case	225
8.3	Well-behaved data volatility	228
8.4	Centralization	230
8.5	Partition	231
8.6	Simple extract	232
8.7	Timestamp extract	233
8.8	Checked extract	234
8.9	Refreshed extract	234
8.10	Periodic replica	235
8.11	Continuous replica	236
8.12	Check-out replica	237
8.13	Comparison of copy techniques	238
8.14	Database Gateway TRANSFER	250
9.1	Anatomy of a warehouse	253
9.2	Chaining of transformations	256
9.3	Enterprise and workgroup warehouses	262
9.4	Focus on IBM Information Warehouse	264
10.1	Fads versus concepts	272
10.2	Application extensibility	277
10.3	DataHub presentation of objects	279
10.4	Back to basics	281

ABOUT THE AUTHOR

Dr. Richard D. Hackathorn is a well-known innovator and educator in the database connectivity field with over twenty-five years of experience.

Dr. Hackathorn is founder and president of Bolder Technology, Inc., specializing in the emerging concepts and practices of Enterprise Database Connectivity. He is also an associate with DataBase Associates of Morgan Hill, California, and is associate editor of *InfoDB* and *Database Review,* leading professional publications in the database area.

In 1980, Dr. Hackathorn founded and remains active in Micro Decisionware, Inc., an international supplier of database connectivity products. At Micro Decisionware, he designed and developed the Database Gateway for DB2 as a joint project with Microsoft Corporation.

For over a decade, Dr. Hackathorn was a professor at the Wharton School of the University of Pennsylvania and then at the University of Colorado. He received his B.S. degree from the California Institute of Technology in Information Science and his M.S. and Ph.D. degrees from the University of California, Irvine, in Information Systems.

Dr. Hackathorn has published numerous articles in academic and trade publications and regularly presents at leading trade conferences. He is a member of Association of Computing Machinery, IEEE Computer Society, Society for Information Management, and a founding member of the International Conference on Information Systems.

▼ ▼ ▼ ▼ ▼ ▼

Bolder Technology, Inc. (BTI) offers a range of services from traditional consulting, informal workshops, insightful presentations, to innovative prototyping. The firm emphasizes close working relationships with a few leading-edge clients. To track the rapid developments in the industry, BTI offers various products and services to maintain current with the field of Enterprise Database Connectivity. For further information, BTI can be contacted at: 4740 Hancock Drive, Boulder, Colorado 80303 USA; 303-447-8677 voice; 303-727-6511 fax.

FOREWORD
by Herbert A. Edelstein

We are in the midst of a fundamental shift in the way organizations use data. No longer do we simply automate the transactions and the manual procedures that comprise the operations of a company, but we now use the information inherent in the data to monitor and analyze those operations, to forecast future requirements, and to provide a competitive edge.

To effectively implement this change requires moving from large, centralized computer systems to networks of computers that vary in size, operating system, and vendor; and from a few large databases to data dispersed throughout the organization on a variety of different DBMSs. Applications are moving from terminal oriented interfaces running on the mainframe to graphical user interfaces running in client-server environments. This distributed, interactive environment is the essence of enterprise computing.

Enterprise Database Connectivity is a welcome guide to many of the obstacles that have made this transition much more difficult than most people originally anticipated. New technologies and techniques are required to work together in order for an application to run in the enterprise computing environment. And since there is already a large installed base of computer systems and applications, the new applications must also integrate with the older "legacy" systems.

After an in-depth background, Dr. Hackathorn provides a valuable structure to help understand the problems of enterprise connectivity. His description of client-server computing distinguishes the different varieties that exist in practice and the design decision that will dictate your choice of a particular approach to client-server computing.

The explanation of competing connectivity technologies such as IBM's DRDA (Distributed Relational Data Access) and Microsoft's ODBC (Open Database Connectivity) helps clarify the different approaches and provide necessary information for access strategies to multiple server databases.

Many distributed applications for which today's fully distributed database technology is too cumbersome, slow, or expensive can be built by careful use of redundant data stored at multiple sites. The discussion of copy management is of particular value in building applications using this architecture.

The move to enterprise-wide computing systems requires tackling tough, gritty problems for which there are no elegant, off-the-shelf solutions. Consequently, many organizations have been slow to achieve the benefits such as they expected. The approach of this book is to examine the real-world problems that organizations are trying to solve and see how the new technologies can successfully be applied. Dr. Hackathorn gives pragmatic "how-to" coverage of client-server computing and distributing data that will help the reader escape potential problems by showing how to analyze particular situations. The reader will also avoid some unpleasant surprises by finding out where there are important gaps in vendor products.

Enterprise Database Connectivity has helped me solve some problems with my consulting clients, and explain some difficult issues to my seminar students. I think that it will be of similar value to the reader embarking on the move to enterprise connectivity.

PREFACE

This book is a bold attempt at integrating the current frenzy of the desktop with the principles of enterprise systems that have been painstakingly accumulated over several decades. I believe that the key factor is how we share data across the enterprise, especially as it relates to deploying enterprise applications on the desktop. Hence, the focus should be on connectivity among databases. Once considered distinct, database management has blended with data communications, creating a hybrid field called *Enterprise Database Connectivity*.

My initial bias with this book was towards conventional database management systems, which is my area of expertise. But writing is a learning process. I learned that my notions of database were too narrow to deal with the critical issues. I now believe that we must deal with information not only as data in its static nature, but also data in its dynamic nature. As endorsed by object-oriented proponents, a true melding of data and process is required. I have attempted to accomplish this objective by discussing data management in a parallel fashion with process management. In this book, I am elevating the concept of a database to that of a collection consisting of both data and process objects.

The open systems approach is discussed throughout the book. The industry now recognizes that vendor-dependent (i.e., proprietary) systems reduce the ability of enterprises to react to new market demands. Open systems offer flexibility and stability. However, the nature of open systems is becoming very complex, confusing customers and vendors as to what open really is. The challenge is to secure the elusive benefits of open systems amid an industry struggling with many turbulent technologies.

This book also raises concerns about trends towards the disintegration of enterprise systems and fragmentation of enterprise databases. Global competition is driving enterprises to make intelligent use of information technology. Unfortunately, our current technology is accelerating these trends in the short term. With the mainframe platform declining and exciting things happening on the desktop, our enterprise systems and data will gravitate towards smaller and more autonomous units.

The good news is that this new world of computing will foster creativity and responsiveness—qualities that have been sorely lacking. The bad news is that we lack the knowledge and skills for managing this new world of computing in the large. Small-scale systems are and will be extraordinary successes, while large-scale attempts will be striking disasters. Our current technology does not scale gracefully to the enterprise level. And, the experiences accumulated over the years concerning large systems development and administration is not as applicable as we would like. This dilemma suggests that enterprises will be forced to limit the unit size of their operations because of the limits inherent in current information technology.

This situation leaves the MIS professional of the future ill prepared to cope with the demands of this new world of computing. This book is directed to those professionals. I hope that they will find new insights, renewed motivation, and even a few practical solutions. In particular, the audience for this book is system designers, information architects, data administrators, database administrators, LAN administrators, and desktop software developers.

The chapters flow from the general through fundamentals to architectures and products and back to the general. The first chapter sets the stage with challenges, shifts in paradigms, open systems, and an introduction to enterprise database connectivity. The second and third chapters describe the fundamentals of databases, SQL, front-end tools, transactions, concurrency, and security. The fourth and fifth chapters talk about architectures, first in terms of centralized systems and then distributed systems. Client-server computing is discussed extensively here. The sixth chapter presents the problems of proprietary systems and offers in solution several approaches—*common interface, common gateway,* and *common protocol.* The next three chapters expand on connectivity architectures in terms of the functions—*access management, copy man-*

agement, and *warehouse management*. The last chapter returns to the issues raised in the first, tying together previous concepts and suggesting practical actions.

Writing a substantive book is not done in isolation. Many people have contributed, directly and indirectly, to the thoughts contained herein. I can only acknowledge a few of those people. First, I thank the great folks at Micro Decisionware (especially Rick Patch) for their understanding and encouragement. Many of the insights of this book were derived at MDI from solving practical problems and developing real products. Second, I thank DataBase Associates (especially Colin White) for giving me a platform to test my articles and seminars. Third, there are many companies that allowed me to roam their halls, stealing ideas for this book—Microsoft, Baxter-Healthcare, Shell Oil, 3M, Sybase, IBM—to name just a few. Fourth, I thank the people who attended my seminars over the years and patiently taught me how these systems really worked. Those seminars allowed me to crystalize many of the thoughts contained in this book. Special thanks to the attendees of the first DEAD seminar over the snowy Halloween of '91. Fifth, my thinking has been molded from many personal relationships forged over the years. In particular, I am indebted to:

- Herb Edelstein who always points me in right direction
- Kyle Geiger who knows more about EDC than I will ever know
- Rob Goldring who cheerfully challenges my half-baked ideas
- Mike Purcell who quietly reveals the practical solutions
- Dwayne Walker who shares his intuitions on market dynamics

Finally, I thank my wife, Linda Hackathorn, who marked mistakes with a loving check. My appreciation to Diane Cerra of John Wiley & Sons, and Rebecca Herr and Alan Bernhard of Argent Associates for their invaluable assistance in publishing this book.

Boulder, Colorado
February, 1993

1

INTRODUCTION

This book is an in-depth appraisal of the latest concepts and technologies for interconnecting heterogeneous databases across an enterprise from mainframe systems to the workstation desktop. A special emphasis is placed on the problems and solutions for *deploying enterprise applications to the desktop*, particularly since a critical issue is how enterprise data is shared to and from the desktop. To handle this challenge, we are witnessing the true merging of database management with data communications. Once considered distinct, these technologies are merging into a new hybrid field called *Enterprise Database Connectivity*, or simply EDC.

With recent product announcements by major vendors, the EDC field is particularly fast-moving. Fundamental architectural decisions are now being made by many large companies for the basic components for their information systems through the 1990s. Enterprise database connectivity is key to these decisions, especially as it integrates the desktop with local area networks and mainframes.

The basic theme of this book is that the *sharing of information* is the critical constraint for building information systems for our enterprises in the 1990s. The technologies available to us in the 1990s have given us great freedom in designing and operating our enterprise systems. The limitations inherent in the economy of scale with larger systems no longer force us to centralize. Distributed systems with distributed data are now a reality.

The objective of this book is to assist you in understanding these architectural issues and in positioning your company to best utilize the advances in enterprise database connectivity.

▼ 1.1 CHALLENGES OF THE 1990S

This decade has brought a complete rethinking of the fundamentals of information systems in enterprises. The cost effectiveness and flexibility of traditional centralized systems operated on mainframe platforms are in question. LAN-based systems supporting workgroups are undergoing a difficult transition from casual printer spooling to critical data sharing. The new generation of graphical software on powerful workstations has tremendous potential for enabling sophisticated applications, but this new software lacks adequate development methodologies.

Dramatic leaps in applying information technology (IT) in a large enterprise seem so close, yet continue to be elusive. Why doesn't this technology all work together? We will examine this dilemma in terms of the challenges faced by enterprises and their information systems in the 1990s.

1.1.1 World Turned Upside Down

In the writings of Tom Peters (especially *Thriving on Chaos*, 1987), the notion that the world is turned upside down on us is vividly described. No longer can businesses plan five years (or even a couple of years) ahead. No longer can companies assume that basic markets will continue to exist. No longer can businesses identify clear competitors. It is a new ballgame with new rules, and even the bases have been rearranged.

Fundamental changes are occurring in businesses. Global competition is driving enterprises toward increased responsiveness to customers, near-perfect quality in products, outrageous customer service, and minimal cost of production. Successful enterprises will be focused on ever-changing niche markets, will be managed by smaller and flatter organization, and will revere flexibility and innovation.

As argued by Davis and Davidson in their book *2020 Vision* (1991), a company should not be in the same business in five years. If it is, the company is probably in the process of going out of business soon. This bold prediction is based on the fact that all marketplaces are changing rapidly. Being responsive to the marketplace implies that the basic business of the company must also be changing dramatically.

Davis and Davidson further indicate that all businesses will be *informationalized*, meaning that the basic business will decline in importance as the information by-products of that business increase in importance. As an example, the airline industry has found more profit in reservations systems than in transporting passengers.

The organization for the new enterprise is greatly flattened. Middle management is a declining profession. The emphasis is on empowering the knowledge workers at all levels, giving them greater autonomy and better productivity tools. The empowering mechanism is the workgroup—a group of persons who interact intensely to perform their job functions.

As we apply new IT to our enterprises, the focus should be on building the infrastructure for that IT. This infrastructure is much more than simply acquiring the technology; it involves basic culture changes for understanding and accepting that technology by the people involved.

1.1.2 Decline of IS Corporate Function

As we consider these changes in business and in IT, we must also question the real value of the information systems (IS) function in the enterprise. In an enterprise where everyone is computer literate to a high degree, of what value is the IS department? We often see a young employee in finance or marketing with a greater understanding of current IT (particularly on the desktop) than the twenty-year IS professional! Outsourcing (i.e., giving the entire IS function to an outside vendor) has become fashionable. Also, the decentralization of the IS responsibilities and budget to user departments has become common.

Consider the following Rich Tennant editorial cartoon in *Computerworld*. The Chief Information Officer (CIO), who is responsible for centralized corporate computing, finds himself driving a stagecoach without horses. Each of his clients has decided that taking his or her own horse to ride off in another direction is preferable to riding in the comfort of the stagecoach. Has the stagecoach line become an obsolete service to these clients? Apparently so.

The implication is that centralized corporate computing has become an obsolete service to our enterprises. What responsibilities of the IS function should remain centralized in the enterprise? Are we moving

4 ▼ Introduction

Figure 1.1. The Bewildered CIO. Courtesy Rich Tennant/Computerworld.

toward some form of organized anarchy, in which everyone rides their own horses in different directions?

1.1.3 Disintegration of Enterprise Systems

The control and organization of the IS function in the enterprise will continue to be debated through this decade. But, the more important issue is the control and organization of enterprise systems (i.e., information systems that span the enterprise crossing numerous organizational boundaries and supporting various organizational functions).

In many ways, we are witnessing the general disintegration of enterprise systems in many large corporations worldwide. This disintegration is most prevalent in the new applications that appear almost daily on desktop workstations in the form of personal spreadsheets and databases. Desktop tools have become very effective ways for end users to implement these personal applications. The disintegration comes when these personal applications start to be used as workgroup or even enterprise applications without anyone realizing this fact. Hence, the proper management of these new applications is ignored.

What is the role of enterprise systems in the 1990s? What are the requirements for control across organizational boundaries, via information systems? What are the requirements for coordination across organizational functions, via information systems?

The assumption of this book is that enterprise systems continue to be an important requirement regardless of whether or not corporate computing is centralized.

1.1.4 Fragmentation of Enterprise Data

The main casualty of this disintegration of enterprise systems is the fragmentation of enterprise data. It does not matter how a specific business function is supported by the information system. It is, for instance, a simple cost/performance decision to determine what platform should perform a specific function. On the other hand, it does matter greatly how the data of that function is shared within the workgroup and across the enterprise.

With the new generation of desktop applications, the real database is often perceived to be a personal database that extracts its necessary contents from a myriad of data resources. This trend is causing the fragmentation of enterprise data into numerous isolated presentation-centered islands.

Enterprise data is to be shared, not carved into little copies and extracted into the wind. To share data implies that the logical representations and values of that data appear the same to all consumers. Any single change is applied to a single logical data element, and any concurrent changes to that data element are resolved; hence, consistency and integrity of the data are maintained.

The recurring theme of this book is that the critical challenge of this decade is the exploitation of information technology to enable the *sharing of information across the enterprise*. Without this essential capability, we cannot build effective enterprise systems. And without effective enterprise systems, the enterprise cannot realize the strategic advantage of utilizing available information about its customers, suppliers, and so on, to operate its core business.

6 ▼ Introduction

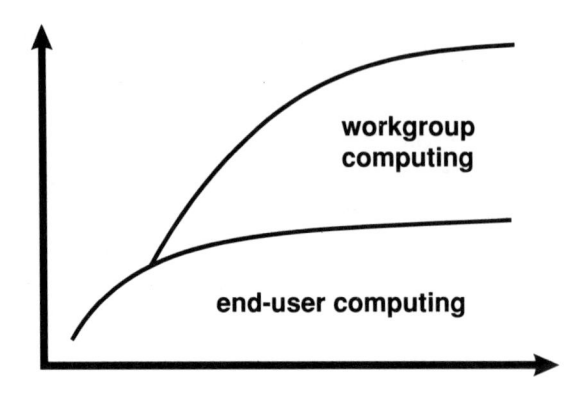

Figure 1.2. *End-user computing and workgroup computing.*

▼ 1.2 SHIFTS IN FUNDAMENTAL PARADIGMS

To deal with these challenges, we need to understand that several paradigms fundamental to information technology are shifting dramatically. In particular, these paradigms are:

- The workgroup is the architecture!
- The network is the system!
- The desktop is the application!
- Process and data are the same!

1.2.1 The Workgroup Is the Architecture

Over the last several decades, the focus of information systems has shifted. In the early days, the focus of information systems was on the entire enterprise driven by production applications on mainframe platforms and then on minicomputer platforms. In the 1980s, the focus was on the individual aided by personal computers. Thus, this decade matured the role of *end-user computing* with its objective of personal productivity.

In the 1990s, the focus has shifted to *workgroups* based on local area networks. This decade is now evolving *workgroup computing* that supports the information processing of the workgroup.

What is a workgroup? It is a small number of persons who work together closely to perform an interrelated set of business functions. The activities of a workgroup are tightly linked, so that one function depends on the nature and timing of other functions. Thus, workgroup activities have high levels of interaction and high degrees of resource sharing.

Workgroup computing augments end-user computing, rather than replacing it. End-user computing will continue to grow in enterprises through this decade, but at a reduced rate. Workgroup computing will build upon end-user computing and have a greater rate of growth.

1.2.2 The Network Is the System

The interconnection of the information system has become more important than the nodes of that system. The *glass house* (i.e., jargon for the machine room of a mainframe system) was the impression that most people had of the information system. No longer! Today processing is performed on a variety of platforms.

Down-sizing is the term applied to porting applications from larger platforms (especially IBM mainframes) to smaller platforms (especially powerful workstations). The motivation is typically for significant cost reductions and for greater flexibility, at the risk of greater instability. Down-sizing is now being redefined in terms of *right-sizing* or the placement of applications on the proper platform whether it is large or small.

Another aspect is the blurring of the local area network (LAN) with the wide area network (WAN). With the greater capacities of telecommunications lines for ISDN, T1, and fiber optics, the usual distinctions between LAN and WAN are disappearing. One firm has invested extensively in fiber optics among their major data centers. They are now able to locate their LAN servers in the machine rooms of their data centers, rather than placing them physically close to the users of those servers.

1.2.3 The Desktop is the Application

Today the image of IT to most people is the desktop, not the glass house. When was the last time that someone asked to have a tour of the mainframe machine room? Typical users now think of an application in terms of *graphical user interface* (GUI) screens. Character-oriented screens (like those of a 3270 or VT100 terminal) may display the same raw amount of data; however, the mode of interaction with the GUI screens is fundamentally different.

With the character-oriented screens, the interaction with the user can be characterized as *procedure driven interaction* (PDI). Interaction with the user is active only in specific contexts. When the application requires input or choices from the user, the application drives that interaction in a stimulus-response mode. At any point in the interaction, the user has a limited set of responses to invoke. The transition to subsequent states is determined by the application logic with little influence by the user. The best flexibility offered by PDI is an *escape* operation that backs up to a previous context.

With PDI, the feeling for the user is like that of riding a bus. If the bus is going where you want it to go, the rider is happy; however, if the bus deviates from the rider's desired route, the rider can be very frustrated.

Over the last ten years, the industry has witnessed the emergence of high-resolution color monitors and mouse devices. We have entered the *point-and-click* generation of GUI applications based on widely accepted windowing packages, such as Microsoft Windows. This new style of user interaction has been called *direct object manipulation*, or DOM (Shneiderman, 1983). The DOM type of interaction with the user is always active with a virtually unlimited set of responses available to the user. The data objects should be continuously displayed with a variety of viewing perspectives and should continually be synchronized with the underlying data. Application programs will therefore be drastically restructured into numerous program fragments driven by complex patterns of events. The roles of stimulus-response are completely reversed from the PDI style to the DOM style. In other words, the user is driving his/her own automobile with DOM.

The issue is that the critical data for tomorrow's business is being generated at the desktop. Further, the critical applications to run tomorrow's business are emerging from spreadsheets developed on the desktop. To what extent will this critical data and these critical applications evolve into the enterprise systems to run tomorrow's business?

1.2.4 Process and Data Are the Same

The literature in our industry has traditionally emphasized either process or data as two independent and sometimes competing aspects. Whether in systems design or distributed networks, the emphasize is either one of a data-orientation or of a process-orientation. In academia, computer scientists have separated based on whether the focus is on programming theory or database theory. Likewise in the industry, designers of distributed systems have divided themselves into separate

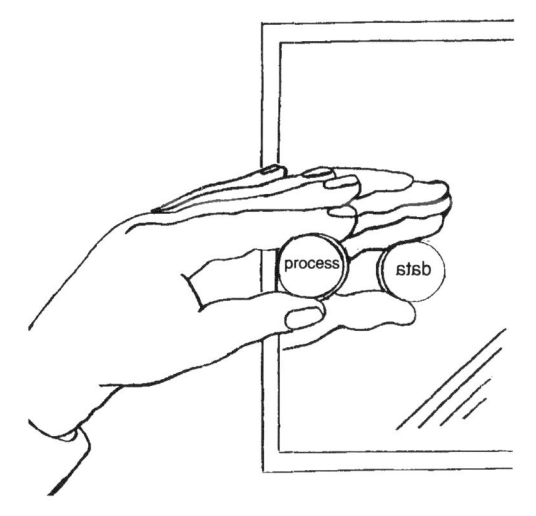

Figure 1.3. *Process and data as opposite sides of a coin.*

groups depending on whether they view their task as distributing data versus distributing process.

This traditional notion of separating process and data is too narrow to deal with the critical issues of database connectivity across the enterprise. We must deal with databases in a broader sense—not only as data in its static nature, but also data in its dynamic nature. In other words, a database must deal with a collection of processes in the same manner that it deals with a collection of data. A true melding of process and data is required.

Let's consider briefly the history of process and then of data. The process aspects (as embodied in application programs) have been the primary focus of computer systems from the 1960s and into the 1970s. Efficiency considerations ruled these times. There was even vigorous debates as to whether assembly language or the new higher-level languages (i.e., COBOL and FORTRAN) should used for programming applications. In the 1970s, the large mainframe systems were forced to make room for the minicomputer systems. Departmental computing was in vogue; let the departments run their own data processing shop. The 1980s brought the personal computer and its revolution of a reversed economy of scale. The cry was "computer power to the people," and a PC on every desktop became a reality.

In contrast, the data aspects were embodied in indexed sequential file and field formats of records through the early decades of the industry. Spin the tapes; do the daily sort-merge; keep the grandfather master tape in the offsite vault. In the mid-1970s people realized that this program-centered approach fragmented important data across an increasingly complex array of application programs. The cry of users became "free that critical data from programs" (so that users can produce critical ad hoc reports). Thus, data independence became a blessed term, and DBMS vendors flourished. Hence, the trend to integrate data has been from fragmented ISAM files to the centralized enterprise databases of today.

As we moved through the 1980s and into the 1990s, we moved through simpler data models (e.g., hierarchical) into the relational data model, and we are now pondering various object-oriented data models. It is important to note that this evolution of data models is also an evolution of integrating the concepts of static data with dynamic process. Views on relational tables and encapsulation of data objects are examples.

To extend the concept of database as consisting of both process and data, the key is to realize that process and data are really the same thing. They are simply different perspectives on the same underlying object.

The concept of duality from physics is appropriate. Duality is defined as two concepts which are perceived to be dissimilar but in fact are different perspectives on the same concept. A good analogy is the two sides of a coin: the sides can be very distinct, but to focus on these distinctions loses sight of the underlying concept of a coin. Duality has played a key role is our understanding of the physics of light. A controversy raged for several centuries on whether light was composed of waves or of particles. Some experiments supported one view, while other experiments support the other view. In 1900, Max Planck proposed that light was electromagnetic waves that radiated in little packets of energy, called photons. He showed that light was both waves and particles, depending upon your perspective. In other words, both views were right, and to some extent both views were wrong! The important point was that to focus on the distinctions between waves and particles loses sight (pardon the pun) of the real concept of light.

As we consider database connectivity in the coming chapters, we will blend process and data together. We will discuss data management in parallel with process management. We will consider client-server architecture in two ways: as separating data functions; and as separating process functions.

▼ 1.3 DEPLOYING ENTERPRISE APPLICATIONS TO THE DESKTOP

We have considered the challenges of the 1990s and the shifts in fundamental paradigms. But what should be our priorities?

Over the next three to five years, the primary priority is *deploying enterprise applications to the desktop*. With the shift away from traditional large systems to the desktop, the only integrating factor is the extent to which the desktop can be intimately incorporated into systems that span the enterprise.

If this integration does not occur, then the enterprise will face a division of its information system into centralized (and decaying) enterprise systems and into distributed (but isolated) desktop systems—both of which are in competition to dominate workgroup systems. This is not a desirable situation!

1.3.1 Some Definitions

To explore the issues with deploying enterprise applications to the desktop, we first must sharpen our definitions of key terms.

1.3.1.1 *What is an enterprise?*

An *enterprise* is a group of persons that are motivated by a common objective and utilize common resources to accomplish that objective.

An *organization* is the policies and procedures by which persons interact. An organization can be explicitly defined (e.g., as in a typical corporation) or informally defined (e.g., a neighborhood action group). Its structure can be perceived to be static or dynamic. Every enterprise has some type of organization, or it could not support a common objective with common resources. However, every organization is not necessarily an enterprise.

1.3.1.2 *What is an enterprise application?*

In general, an *application* is a set of software programs that support a specific business function by a user in a specific job position. In other words, the designer of an application needs to know *what* and *who*. The degree to which a business function or job position is (or can be) specified determines how narrow or broad an application is specified.

One can discuss applications as being vertical or horizontal depending on whether they deal with the details for a single business function or the coordination among several business functions. A *vertical application* is one that deals with multiple levels of a single business function; hence, a vertical application is likely to be used within a specific organizational unit. For example, a human resource application may deal with many aspects of personnel management and is used only within the personnel department. On the other hand, a *horizontal application* is one that deals with the coordination among different business functions; hence, a horizontal application is likely to be used by many organizational units within the enterprise. For example, a budgeting application that assists in tracking and planning departmental budgets could be used by every department in the enterprise.

An *enterprise application* is an application whose business function or job position spans the enterprise, either in a vertical or horizontal sense. For enterprise applications, the business function is one that many organizational units perform, or the job position is one that many organizational units possess.

An alternative to a single enterprise application is to have each organizational unit do their own application. If development costs were low enough, why not? Each application would be customized to its environment. And in fact, this situation is close to what exists in many corporations today for some newer application areas. Obviously an application for payroll or accounts receivable should be an enterprise application for any large corporation. But what about career planning and tracking? Is this important function supported by an enterprise application accessible to employees?

The main advantages of an enterprise application are consistency and uniformity. The consistency is focused on institutionalizing formal policies concerning the major subjects and activities of the enterprise. For example, an enterprise application in order entry would embody, along with other things, the enterprise's policies towards customers. How are credit ratings determined and implemented? How responsive is the order entry process to the customer's needs?

The uniformity is focused on efficiency and effectiveness in performing the particular business function. If an enterprise application is uniform, the economics of scale can drive the enterprise application toward higher levels of efficiency. If it was designed correctly, the enterprise application should attain greater effectiveness in performing the business function.

Although enterprise applications are desirable for the purposes of consistency and uniformity, there must also be a balance with non-enterprise applications, those whose scope is unique to an individual, or a single workgroup, or a specialized business function. If all applications were enterprise applications, the information system for the enterprise would be too rigid. We would lose the flexibility to react quickly to new business challenges.

The challenge is to maintain a proper balance. Blindly defending traditional enterprise applications on a centralized mainframe can be as devastating to the enterprise as carelessly fostering an incoherent mass of personal spreadsheets and databases.

1.3.1.3 What is an enterprise database?

The concept of an enterprise database can be complex. There are at least two definitions in the context of this book, a broad definition and a narrow definition.

The broad definition: An *enterprise database* is the collection of any data that can affect decisions or can be affected by decisions within the enterprise. In effect, the enterprise database is the reflection (or model) of reality that the enterprise perceives. This data can be in many forms. It can be formal (e.g., residing in a relational database on the mainframe) or informal (e.g., prior experiences of a manager). It can be structured (e.g., in a tabular form) or unstructured (e.g., in letters and memorandums). To leverage the investment in information technology, we must convert the relevant data to a formal and structured form.

The narrow definition: An enterprise database is the formal data that resides in a database management system on some platform within the information system. The database could be designed using either the relational or object-oriented data models, as long as there is some level of database connectivity within the enterprise system. In other words, the database must be able to be shared across the enterprise.

Using these definitions, let's explore three issues in deploying enterprise applications to the desktop:

- Development: traditional activities of analysis, design, and implementation.

- Deployment: new activities such as installation, support, and maintenance.
- The mechanism for sharing data between the desktop and the enterprise.

1.3.2 Development as Analyzing, Designing, and Implementing

The first issue is how to appropriately develop applications that will reside on the desktop. The traditional system life cycle has been the approach for developing enterprise applications since the early days of data processing. Many other texts have covered this subject in detail (e.g., Couger, Colter, and Knapp, 1982). In recent years, system development methodologies have emphasized computer-assisted systems engineering (CASE) tools as the means for employing these methodologies.

As we consider the desktop, current CASE technology does not handle GUI applications adequately. Most tools focus on the 3270-screen era with centralized mainframe applications. The event-driven nature of direct object manipulation is difficult to handle through the design process. In fact, rapid prototyping with GUI front-end development tools is eliminating many traditional steps in the system life cycle.

We need a new generation of CASE tools—ones that design to the GUI desktop, support distributed (usually client-server) architectures, and incorporate the concepts of object-oriented databases.

1.3.3 Deployment as Installing, Supporting, and Maintaining

The second issue with deploying enterprise applications to the desktop is the activity of deploying those applications. In the past, an enterprise application resided on a centralized system so that deploying the application implied that the application was made available for execution. In the typical IBM mainframe site, the debugged version of the application was moved from the CICS test region to the library of the CICS production region. This was a simple operation that could be quickly reversed if there were problems with the new version.

The current context for enterprise applications is a diverse array of 20,000 or more intelligent workstations connected to hundreds of local area networks. Since the enterprise application may operate on each of those workstations, you may have 20,000 copies of the application to distribute, support, and maintain. This is what is meant by deploying!

This current context is qualitatively different than the previous centralized enterprise application. As an industry, we do not have the policies or tools to properly deploy an enterprise application to 20,000 workstations or even to several hundred LAN servers.

1.3.4 Sharing Data Across the Enterprise

The third issue is how do we share data across the enterprise and, especially, to the desktop. At the heart of these questions is the critical function of sharing of data across the enterprise. What does this mean? The purpose of a database management system (DBMS) is to manage the data as a database, such as designing schemas, allocating physical storage, inserting and updating data, and retrieving the desired data.

As we share the data in a database, the value to the corporation increases dramatically; it can be applied in many other business processes and decisions. And as we share this data, several other functions must be supported, such as:

- integrity
- security
- concurrency
- availability
- recoverability
- manageability

First, the DBMS must insure the data integrity so that changes by one person are consistent with other data. In particular, transactional integrity implies that a series of changes must be applied as a *unit of work* (UOW), i.e., all or nothing. Second, the DBMS must insure the data security at several levels to permit access and updates by only proper persons for legitimate actions. Third, the DBMS must insure the data concurrency so that access and updates to data are made easily and efficiently by many persons without tripping over each other. Fourth, the DBMS must be available whenever needed. Fifth, the DBMS must recover the data through backup and restore facilities in the event of hardware and software failures. And finally, the DBMS must be manageable across the enterprise, possibly at hundreds of sites.

In summary, to obtain the value from our database, we must share the data freely. To share the data, we must insure the integrity, security, etc. of the data. These functions above have been the basic *motherhoods* of database systems for twenty years. What is new is that the data sharing must be performed enterprise-wide. Or, in other words, the data from a variety of databases must be distributed and managed over many database platforms, most of which are quite different from one another. This brings us to the topics of distributed and federated databases.

1.3.5 Implications of Federated Databases

For many years the extension of database technology to handle databases distributed across multiple platforms has been heralded. The concept of *distributed databases* (DDB) is quite simple. A DDB is a database that is logically a single database but in fact is physically distributed among multiple sites—and the user does not know the difference! However, the DDB practice (i.e., building reliable and efficient DDB products) is quite complex. The basic issues, such as location transparency and site autonomy, have been fully discussed by others (Date, 1987).

Let's assume that the nasty practical problems of DDB are solved and that we have stable and efficient DDB products available. There are several additional barriers to DDB, which are revealed when we examine the following hidden assumptions.

First, a DDB assumes a top-down logical design from the perspective of a centralized database that is divided into separate physical databases. The result of this design process is a single global schema. Second, a DDB assumes that the database platforms are homogeneous; all use the same DBMS engine to insure proper coordination. Third, a DDB assumes that the same data model (e.g., relational) is used by all nodes. And finally, a DDB assumes that there is central ownership of the data so that the prior assumptions can be insured.

The problem is that, even with proper DDB products, typical enterprise information systems have not had the luxury of adhering to a top-down design and have not been constructed upon homogeneous database platforms. The true story is that most corporations have legacy systems with a twenty-year history that is both a heritage and burden. Retrofitting those legacy systems into the DDB framework may be an impossible task.

We need to redefine the objective of data sharing across the enterprise, not as a distributed database, but as a *federated database* (FDB). A federated database is defined as a bottom-up, post-design exercise to provide interoperability among autonomous and heterogeneous database platforms. The coupling among databases is not a tight coupling (as in DDB), but a loose coupling that allows data to be distributed among these platforms while insuring the motherhood of integrity, security, concurrency, and maintenance (Sheth and Larson, 1990). In our enterprises today, we really are dealing with federated databases, rather than distributed databases. With these federated databases, we have two

```
Distributed                    Federated
Database                       Database

top-down                       bottom-up
pre-design                     post-design
homogeneous                    heterogeneous
single data model              multiple data models
central ownership              autonomous ownership
```

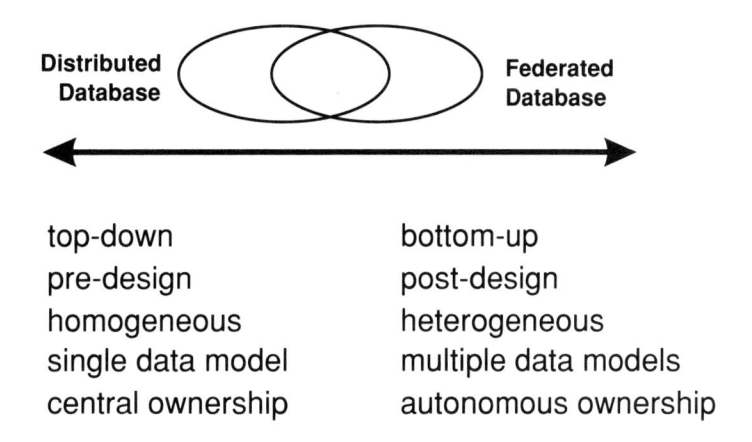

Figure 1.4. Federated databases versus distributed databases.

types of distribution problems: enterprise-to-workgroup and workgroup-to-enterprise.

1.3.5.1 Enterprise-to-workgroup distribution

In this case, data has been maintained centrally on mainframe database systems, such as IBM's DB2. Through a complex of production applications, a centralized database is fed with new data, which in turn generates various reports. The problem is that there is now an important, and increasingly vocal, class of users who reside within workgroups and feel disassociated with their data contained in the enterprise databases. The

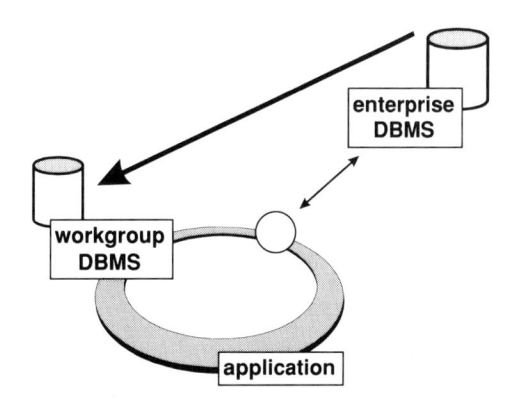

Figure 1.5. Enterprise-to-workgroup distribution.

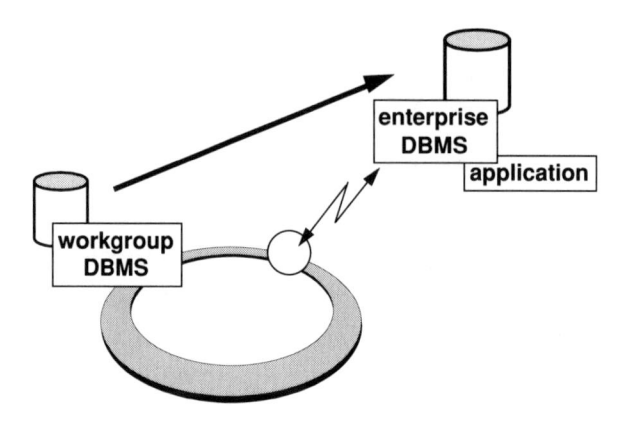

Figure 1.6. *Workgroup-to-enterprise distribution.*

challenge is to achieve a practical enterprise-to-workgroup data distribution, while:

- performing such distribution in an efficient manner
- maintaining proper security and controls
- assuring data integrity at all stages

1.3.5.2 *Workgroup-to-enterprise distribution*

The converse case is also very prevalent in most corporations, although it is often not recognized as a problem. Ad hoc database systems have evolved on stand-alone workstations using spreadsheet or simple data management tools, such as dBase. The informal application programs for maintaining this data often become critical to managing the workgroup. As stand-alone workstations evolve into LAN-based systems, these applications are enhanced with a new generation of technology, such as LAN-based relational DBMS. However, these workgroup databases do not coordinate with existing production applications operating on mainframe systems; hence, there is fragmentation of critical data across the enterprise. The challenge is to achieve a practical workgroup-to-enterprise data distribution, while:

- retaining local autonomy and control of data
- integrating with existing enterprise systems
- maintaining security, control, and integrity

▼ 1.4 PURSUIT OF OPEN SYSTEMS

How do we deploy enterprise applications to the desktop, while dealing with the implications of federated databases?

The solution is *not* more technology! We have an overabundance of technology, and we are buried in its quantity and complexity. New products are announced and new market niches emerge now as a daily occurrence. IT managers of the future may have to live in real-time control rooms, continually monitoring these product announcements, much like brokers in the international monetary market.

The situation reminds one of another editorial cartoon by Rich Tennant in *Computerworld* (December 16, 1992). To hit the bull's eye of greater productivity, businesses want more arrows of information technology, while the quiver is already overflowing with IT arrows. The solution is to learn to aim our existing arrows better.

Likewise, a key problem is that our current technologies do not work together! The individual components of our systems do their jobs, but the connectivity among components is weak. In the industry today, lev-

Figure 1.7. Need more IT arrows? Courtesy Rich Tennant/Computerworld.

els of Fear-Uncertainty-and-Doubt (FUD) are often too high for rational decision-making. Because IT components are too diffuse through the enterprise, IT decisions are now spread across all areas of the enterprise. IT products are very tempting to purchase, resulting in a patchwork quilt of technologies.

The best approach seems to be to choose the appropriate IT architecture for the enterprise based on a set of the proper open standards. We will call this approach the open systems approach.

1.4.1 The Open Systems Approach

First of all, an *open system* is a system that is implemented with components adhering to specific standards. The implication is that these components can be purchased from many independent suppliers, thus reducing dependence on any particular vendor. Likewise, the assumption is that customers support these standards by requiring them as part of their IT purchases. Thus, the market dynamics should mold the industry into a direction that tracks the good standards.

Standards can be of two types: de jure and de facto. A *de jure* standard is one that has been published by a recognized governmental standards body, such as the American National Standards Institute (ANSI) or the International Standards Organization (ISO). Each country has a national standards body, such as ANSI for the United States. Each of these national standards bodies are then represented in the ISO, which sets standards worldwide. A *de facto* standard is one published by a major industry vendor to which customers and vendors adhere. In the past, IBM has been responsible for many de facto standards, some of which evolved into de jure standards. In today's industry, no single vendor is able to establish any significant standard based primarily on their market presence. Industry consortiums of vendors or customers have assumed a role in developing de facto standards of various kinds.

Are de jure and de facto standards open? This is an interesting question! Does being a standard immediately imply that it is open? What does being open imply?

An open standard is one upon which all vendors have equal opportunity to develop and market products. Unfortunately the industry is not (and will not be) a level playing field. Even with de jure standards, vendors who actively contribute to the standardization process will have an advantage over other vendors. With de facto standards, the situation is even more complex. Since the standard is developed by one or more vendors, the openness of de facto standards is highly dependent on other factors, such as adequate documentation, licensing fees, and architectural control. The other extreme from an open standard is the *proprietary standard,* upon which only one vendor is able to develop and market products. Through maintaining trade secrets, patents, and copyrights, the vendor can prevent others from competing.

The *open systems approach* is an architectural policy that maximizes the adherence of system components to specific open standards.

1.4.2 The Elusive Benefits of Open Systems

In the ideal situation, the benefits of an open system are: application portability, system interoperability, scalability, stability, and competitive pricing. Let's explore each of these benefits.

The first benefit is *application portability,* which is movement of an application from one platform to another with minimal effort. Note that application portability is an important key to right-sizing. To port an application among platforms depends on a number of factors that get rather technical quickly. Binary compatibility has the most application portability since the executable code can be directly moved. For example, a Lotus 1-2-3 application under DOS will run on hundreds of different manufacturers' products—as long as it is an Intel 80x86 machine architecture. Even with the same machine architecture, the system facilities may be supported differently. For example, a COBOL application under S/370 MVS CICS will be difficult to port to a S/370 VM CMS environment, even though it operates on the same machine architecture.

The important point to remember about application portability is that it is primarily dependent on the interface definitions. Therefore, if an application program adheres to a specific interface definition to support some function, the source code for that application can be ported to another platform.

The second benefit of open systems is *system interoperability,* which is the ability of one system to operate with other systems through sharing common data or invoking common processes. The important point to remember about system interoperability is that it is primarily dependent on the protocol definitions. In other words, defining the protocol (i.e., commands and arguments) that flows between the systems enables the systems to interoperate.

The third benefit is *scalability*, which is the ability to choose alternative components that have greater (or lesser) capacity. Ideally, an open system can be easily scaled up by selecting a platform with greater processor or storage capabilities. Scalability is a special case of portability in which the application has a specific migration path through a sequence of platforms having greater capacities.

The fourth benefit is *stability,* which enables an open system to be maintained despite the lack of viability by any one vendor. In the past, it was common to have a system that was vendor dependent, so that the whims and fortunes of that vendor had a grave impact on your ability to maintain that system. With an open system, switching to another vendor is not so traumatic, thus offering greater stability to the system.

The final benefit is *competitive pricing*. The components for an open system should tend towards commodity items, subject to competitive bidding by a number of vendors.

1.4.3 Standards, Standards, Standards . . .

These benefits of the Open Systems approach have been elusive, however. There are several difficulties. The first is that there are overlapping standards from many differing standards groups. In the EDC area, the following governmental bodies affect de jure standards (Stallings, 1985):

- **Organization of International Standards** (ISO). A voluntary organization of standard bodies from participating countries, the ISO deals with a wide range of standards. One of the ISO technical committees, TC97, deals with standards concerning information systems. This committee developed the OSI reference model and protocols for various layers of that model.
- **American National Standards Institute** (ANSI). A nonprofit corporation composed of manufacturers, users, and other interested parties, ANSI serves as the national clearinghouse for voluntary standards for the United States and is its designated voting member to ISO.
- **National Institute of Science and Technology** (NIST). Part of the U.S. Department of Commerce, NIST issues the U.S. Federal Information Processing Standards (FIPS) for equipment purchased by the U.S. government.

In addition, there are several important industry consortium groups: (King, 1992)

- **Advanced Computing Environment** (ACE). Founded in April 1991 by Acer Group, Compaq, DEC, Microsoft, MIPS Computer, and SCO, this group now has over 200 members who are hardware and software vendors. The objective is to establish a binary standard based on the MIPS R4000 processor. With the departure of Compaq and a shift in DEC's interest, ACE is fading.
- **Corporation for Open Systems.** Founded in January 1986 by Control Data, DEC, HP, IBM, Prime, Wang, and Xerox, this group now has 51 members who are system vendors and U.S. government agencies. The objective is to establish the MAP/TOP specifications based on OSI, ISDN, etc., primarily in manufacturing environments.
- **Object Management Group.** This group was founded in April 1989 by 3Com, Canon, Data General, Gold Hill, HP, Objectivity, Philips, Prime, and Unisys. It now has over 150 members who are primarily vendors of object-oriented software. The objective is to promote standards for object-oriented models, such as the Object Request Broker.
- **Open Software Foundation** (OSF). Founded in May 1988 by Apollo, Bull, DEC, HP, IBM, Nixdorf, and Siemens, OSF now has over 300 members who are systems and software vendors. Its objective is to supply portable systems software based on the OSF/1 UNIX version and extended with the Distributed Computing Environment (DCE) and the Distributed Management Environment (DME).
- **SQL Access Group** (SAG). Founded in September 1989 by DEC, HP, Informix, Ingres, Oracle, Sun, Tandem, Teradata, and Unify; now has over 45 members who are mostly DBMS vendors. The objective is to promote database interoperability by assisting ISO and ANSI SQL standards. Technical specifications on SQL APIs and OSI Remote Database Access are published through X/Open.
- **UNIX International.** This group was founded in December 1988 by Amdahl, Control Data, Data General, Fujitsu, ICL, Informix, Intel, Motorola, NCR, Olivetti, TI, and Unisys, and now has over 240 members who are software and chip vendors. The objective is to ensure UNIX-based open systems via documents such as the UI-Atlas road-map requirements.
- **X/Open.** Founded in 1984 as the Open UNIX Group by Bull, ICL, Nixdorf, Nokia, Philips, and Siemens. X/Open now has over 80 members. Its objective is to promote open, multivendor common ap-

plication environments through publishing portability guides and branding products that conform.

A second difficulty is that the standards set by the above groups are often immature or nonexistent in critical areas. Technology is evolving rapidly in many areas, especially EDC. It takes time and quality thinking to generate adequate standards.

The final difficulty is that balancing the two types of standards (i.e., de jure and de facto) is a wicked decision for an enterprise. There are striking examples of both de jure and de facto standards that lack industry acceptance.

Understanding the issues and choosing the proper standard is often a delicate decision that should be subject to continual review. Although the open system approach is desired in EDC, its benefits are often elusive.

▼ 1.5 ENTERPRISE DATABASE CONNECTIVITY

We have discussed the challenges of the 1990s and recent shifts in paradigms, resulting in the priority for deploying enterprise applications to the desktop. Using the open systems approach, the sharing of data across the enterprise brings us to the topic of *Enterprise Database Connectivity* (EDC).

EDC is defined as the concepts and practices of interconnecting federated databases. EDC focuses on defining and managing a uniform architecture that spans the enterprise for sustaining this connectivity.

1.5.1 Functional Layers of EDC

To deal with its complexity, EDC can be considered as having three layers of increasing functionality, which consist of the following functions: access management, copy management, and warehouse management. The higher layers build upon the required functions of the lower layers. These layers constitute the range of functions necessary to support the connectivity of databases across the enterprise, both for decision support and for production purposes. Further, these layers are enabled by the facilities of data management (e.g., SQL) and process management (e.g., transactions) as described in the next two chapters.

1.5.1.1 *Access management*

Access management is managing the architecture to provide access from any client to any data resource. In particular, it focuses on the ability of

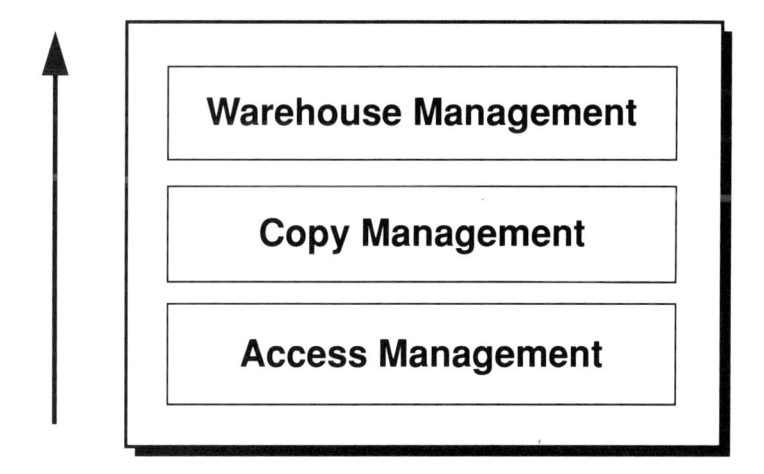

Figure 1.8. *EDC layers.*

a client application to directly access a local or remote database. Initial data access was focused on providing production applications access to the local database. Recently, data access shifted to providing decision support tools (e.g., spreadsheet) access to various remote databases using client-server architectures. In the future, data access will blend both objectives into a continuous spectrum from production to decision support. With current technology, access management deals with the problems of SQL transparency and network plumbing.

1.5.1.2 Copy management

Copy management is managing the architecture to provide coordination between any two data resources via the copying of data and processes. In particular, it focuses on the execution, scheduling, and monitoring of copies from one database to another for the purposes of data staging. With current technology, copy management deals with the distinction between extracts and replicas, refreshing volatile data, resynchronizing replicas, and copy recovery.

1.5.1.3 Warehouse management

Warehouse management is managing the architecture to transform data (and processes) as it flows among data resources and to best support its consumption by a business community. In particular, it focuses on both direct and staged access by end users based upon an enterprise information directory. Warehouse management is more than a separate rela-

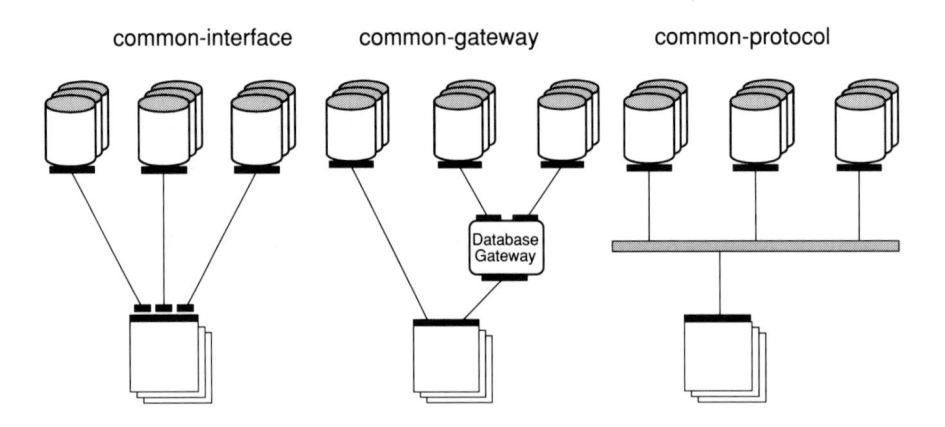

Figure 1.9. *EDC architectures.*

tional database that aggregates data from production databases. The challenge is to anticipate the usage patterns and to add value to the information through a variety of transformations.

1.5.2 Common Architectures for EDC

To support the three EDC functional layers, there can be three architectural approaches, as shown in Figure 1.9. The objective is that of database connectivity transparency—the client application should not be aware of the variations in server types, data models, SQL languages, and so on. As new data resources are introduced, there should be minimal impact on the application and the usage of the application. There are three approaches to attain this objective: common-interface, common-gateway, and common-protocol. These approaches are not exclusive. In most practical situations, there is a mixture of these approaches, as they form the common building blocks for an EDC architecture.

1.5.2.1 *Common interface*

This approach focuses on defining a single interface used by the client application to access multiple types of servers. The goal is that the program be designed and coded once and thereafter work with a variety of data resources. The common interface smoothes out the differences among database types so there is minimal impact on the application. Usually the common interface consists of a set of client drivers, each one unique to the particular server type.

1.5.2.2 *Common gateway*
This approach adds a new element—a database gateway that translates requests and results between the client and multiple types of servers. The value added for the gateway is that the client application is only aware that it is interacting with one type of server.

1.5.2.3 *Common protocol*
This approach focuses on defining the single protocol by which the client application can interact with multiple types of servers. Through the client translating requests into the common protocol and the server translating results into the same protocol, differences among server types should have minimal impact on the application.

▼ ▼ ▼ ▼ ▼ ▼

Later in the book, we will return to a detailed discussion of the EDC functional layers and architectural approaches; in the next chapters, however, we need to construct a foundation by covering the following topics: fundamentals of data management, fundamentals of process management, building centralized systems, and, building distributed systems.

▼ DISCUSSION QUESTIONS

1. From your experience, how has connecting personal computers with local area networks changed the nature of your information processing?

2. What really is important about the new graphical user interfaces and the products using these interfaces?

3. What are the similarities and differences among personal applications, workgroup applications, and enterprise applications?

4. What are the major distinctions between distributed databases and federated databases?

5. Why is it important to distribute data between workgroups and the enterprise?

6. Write down your definition of an open system. What are the objectives of your open systems? Is it based on standards? What kind? Are critical components available within a healthy marketplace?

7. What are the requirements for effective application portability? For effective system interoperability?

8. What are the three functional layers to Enterprise Database Connectivity? What are the major distinctions among them?

2

FUNDAMENTALS OF DATA MANAGEMENT

This chapter covers the management of databases within our enterprises in a broader sense. It focuses on the concepts and practices important to connectivity among federated databases of the enterprise. We need to deal with data that may not be managed by a conventional database management system, and with data not usually identified as databases, such as sequential files on magnetic tape, indexed sequential files of dBase programs, electronic mail messages, or word processing libraries. Further, there is a symmetry between this chapter and the next chapter on Process Management. If there is a duality of data and process, these two chapters describe what we know about the two sides of the coin.

This chapter does not attempt to summarize the entire database management field, since various other texts (e.g., Date, 1990; Martin, 1977) have adequately covered this established field. Further, there are several excellent texts dealing with aspects of distributed databases (e.g., Özsu and Valduriez, 1991; Gray and Reuter, 1992). In particular, this chapter emphasizes:

- relational versus object-oriented data models
- SQL as a connectivity language
- database programming interfaces
- database front-end tools

▼ 2.1 DATABASE MANAGEMENT SYSTEMS

A *database management system* (DBMS) is a collection of programs and utilities for organizing, storing, updating, and retrieving data. The main objective of a DBMS is to capture data so that it adequately models the real world. That is, the DBMS must model the important entities (both internal and external to the organization) that relate to the business of the enterprise.

Within a DBMS, data has both content and structure. Often the structuring among data elements may be more important than the content of the data elements. For instance, it may be more important to know the various characteristics that are available for customers (e.g., credit rating) than the actual customer address for a customer.

The value of a database increases significantly when that data is shared. A personal database may be important to an individual, but the value of that database increases when shared among a workgroup. To share data properly, a DBMS must also support security, integrity, and concurrency controls for that data. These three aspects will be discussed in detail in the next chapter.

The basic functions of a DBMS are threefold:

- **Data Manipulation:** organizing data content by inserting, updating, deleting, and retrieving data.
- **Data Definition:** structuring data elements into logical and physical schemas.
- **Integrity Constraints:** insuring data security, integrity, and concurrency

More specifically, a DBMS usually offers the following set of functions or facilities:

- data manipulation language
- data definition language
- data loading facility
- database backup and recovery facility
- database programming interface
- application development tools
- query and reporting tools

The components for a DBMS can be illustrated in a few blocks, as

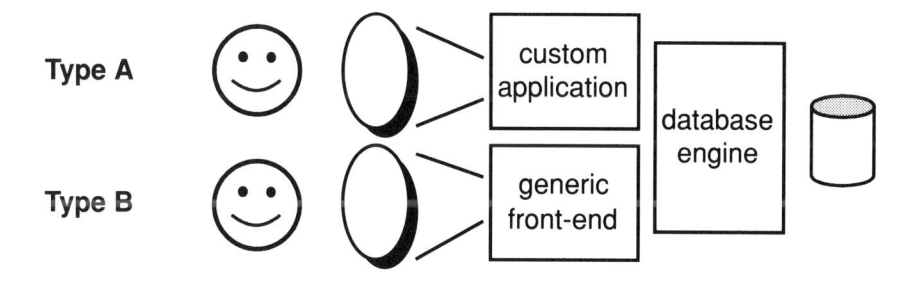

Figure 2.1. What is a DBMS?

shown in Figure 2.1. First, the DBMS consists of a database engine that performs the low-level operations required to support the above functions. Second, the DBMS consists of a custom application, designed and implemented by the user to perform some specific business function. In the 1970s, the early days of DBMS, custom applications written in 3GL language (COBOL) were the primary emphasis of a DBMS. Third, the DBMS consists of a generic front-end tool, which also permits a user to design and implement a specific business function.

2.1.1 Production versus Decision Support

For many years, a continuing controversy in the DBMS field has been over the distinction between production applications and decision support applications. Figure 2.1 illustrates this distinction with two categories of users (i.e., people denoted by smiling faces). The production user (Type A) typically utilizes the custom application, while the decision support user (Type B) utilizes the generic front-end application. Further distinctions are shown in the table below. First, production applications are designed and implemented for efficiency. The perspective

	Production	**Decision Support**
Focus	efficiency	flexibility
Interface	static	evolving
Function	narrow	broad
Availability	high	low (tolerance for)

32 ▼ Fundamentals of Data Management

is that of "heads-down" clerical personnel whose full-time job responsibility is to perform certain applications repeatedly. On the other hand, decision support applications require flexibility since the business function is ill-defined or continually changing. Second, production applications are static in terms of their interface to users. Since the application supports many people, changes to the user interface (i.e., appearance and behavior of the application) can result in significant user retraining and support requirements. On the other hand, decision support applications are usually developed in close association with the user(s) and are continually evolving. Third, production applications target a narrow business function, performing that function in-depth. On the other hand, decision support applications must span broad business functions. Finally, a production application needs high availability since an outage may cause a significant loss of business revenue (such as, in an airline reservation system). On the other hand, decision support applications have loose deadlines and are usually supplemental, being less critical to the business.

One must realize that the distinctions between production and decision support are merely extremes on a complex dimension. All variations along this dimension are possible, and the variations are significant. For instance, consider Figure 2.2, in which an efficiency axis is contrasted with a flexibility axis. The above discussion would indicate that all applications should be in the upper-right (i.e., production with

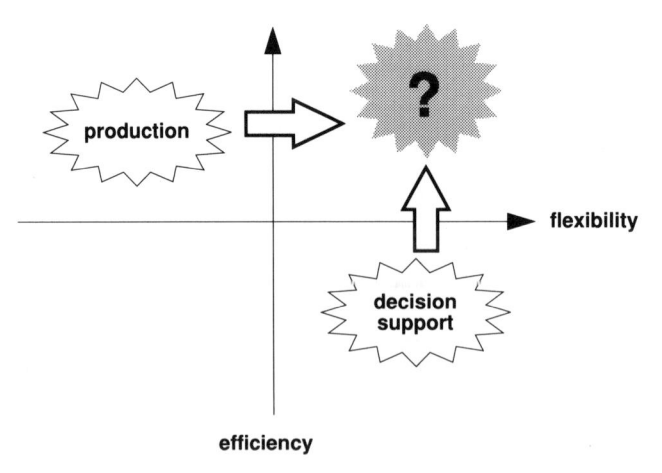

Figure 2.2. *Efficiency versus flexibility.*

high efficiency and low flexibility) or in the lower-left (i.e., decision support with high flexibility and low efficiency).

But can we design and implement applications that are both efficient and flexible? We certainly can do the opposite! This figure challenges our normal wisdom of production versus decision support. Is it possible to have an application serve both interests? If so, why are these distinctions between them important?

After twenty years, the controversy continues, but with a different exterior. The controversy has shifted from a concern of *machine* efficiency and availability to a concern of *user* efficiency and availability. Even with contemporary technologies, there continue to be significant trade-offs in resources between implementing applications at the two extremes.

The key questions strike at the heart of the application development methodologies and of the client-server architectures. Do the new technologies for distributed systems give us greater freedom in methodologies and architectures? In future systems, will we be able to blur this hard distinction between production and decision support? Or more importantly, as business conditions change, will we be able to move applications from a decision support mode to a production mode, or vice versa? In other words, can production applications be designed to be extendible by their users? Critical decision support applications that have matured may be easily incorporated into a formal re-engineering methodology, resulting in a rigorously designed production application (with documentation, of course).

These questions add a zest to our exploration of the deployment of enterprise applications to the desktop. If we properly design the mechanisms for sharing data (i.e., among desktops, desktop-to-workgroup, workgroup-to-enterprise, etc.), can we have greater freedom in designing applications for the desktop? I believe so.

▼ 2.2 DATA MODELS

As mentioned earlier, the main objective of a DBMS is to model accurately the real world. The way that the database is structured determines the adequacy of this modeling.

A data model is the basic framework for performing this modeling. An analogy is the toolbox for a carpenter. One toolbox could contain a hammer and nails, while another toolbox could contain a screwdriver and screws. The carpenter could build most items with either toolbox. However, building a house with screws would be difficult, and building a fine cabinet with nails would be an act of violence.

The adequacy of a data model depends, therefore, upon the reality that it is attempting to model. There is no ultimate data model, just like there is no ultimate toolbox for all carpenters.

One aspect about modeling reality—data versus process—is important. Earlier we discussed the duality of data and process—the idea that they are merely different perspectives on a single underlying concept, which we call an object. We will continue to refer to data and process as opposite sides of a coin, sometimes referring to the whole coin as an object. This aspect of data/process duality is crucial to the distinction between the relational data model and the object-oriented data model.

2.2.1 Historical Perspective

The evolution of data models is instructive. It is always wise to maintain a good historical perspective, to avoid repeating the mistakes of the past.

The initial data models within computer systems were *file access methods* that allow the program to interact with files. The dominant model was the sequential file, which was a file name referring to a set of records of fixed or varying length. The important aspect was that the programs using that file contained the information about its structure.

The next step in data models occurred in the late 1960s when commercial DBMS products appeared supporting the hierarchical data model. This model incorporated the structure of the data with the contents and, hence, can be called the first true database. The hierarchical data model supported the basic one-to-many (parent-to-children) logical relationship. For example, an employee could be assigned to one department, and a department could have many employees assigned to it. A critical restriction of the hierarchical data model was that an entity could have only one parent. In our example, an employee could only have a department as a parent.

The third step was the network data model, in which this restriction of only one parent was eliminated. The network data model followed the CODASYL (Conference on Data System Language) specification, which explicitly represented many-to-many relationships.

The fourth step was the relational data model that concentrated on the logical structure of data and attempted to eliminate aspects dealing with the physical storage of data. Once commercially viable products based on the relational data model appeared, this data model dominated our thinking about databases through most of the 1980s. The advantages of the relational data model were that it could handle any situation of hierarchies or networks and do so with greater flexibility. New objects in the database could be created dynamically, rather than incurring a separate data structuring phase. Today, the relational data model has matured and many products support it.

Newer and more complex data models have been proposed for twenty years. Entity-relationship, semantic nets, and other models have all contributed to our knowledge of how information can be structured, but have not had a great commercial impact. Recently there has been a convergence on the object-oriented data model, which subsumes many of the important aspects of these complex data models. In the next sections, we will examine the relational and object-oriented data models in greater detail.

2.2.2 Relational Data Model

In the relational data model (RDM), the world looks deceivingly simple. Everything is a simple table, in which columns describe some attribute or characteristic and rows indicate an actual person or thing.

In the evolution of the RDM, several objectives motivated developers (Codd, 1971; Date, 1990):

- flexibility in data structuring (without predefining structures explicitly)
- simplifying the view of data by the user
- operations at the level of set of rows
- criteria for designing databases
- integration of the data dictionary with the database
- more recently, the basis for building distributed systems

Let's examine these objectives in more detail. The first objective was to avoid the difficult process of defining the database structure prior to its usage. This requirement often required elaborate unloading and loading of the database for any changes to its structure. The second objective of the RDM was to simplify the view of data for the user. This objective was accomplished mainly by separating the logical view of data from the physical view, implying a degree of independence of data from the programs that utilize it. The third objective was to construct operations on data that spanned sets of data rather than single rows. Previous data models provided a way of navigating through data one row at a time; RDM defined a way of processing many rows at a time. The fourth objective was to define a procedure for properly designing databases. Previously database design was an art reserved for a few specialists. The concept of normalization in database design opened this mystical process to everyone (including software vendors). The fifth objective was to incorporate an integrated data dictionary into the database, so that a user could query the database and ask what tables were available. With this objective came the realization that a database was a general information resource, used for purposes that its designers could never have conceived. Finally, the RDM is now being used as the basis for building many kinds of distributed systems. Because of its commonality among many products, the RDM provides a relatively open mechanism of sharing data. We will investigate this objective in more detail in the discussion of SQL later.

Given these objectives, the RDM is actually quite complex, despite its simple appearance. Other texts (Date, 1990) have adequately described these important aspects, such as primary and foreign keys; domain definitions; projection, restriction, and join; and normalization.

The requirements for a product supporting the RDM are threefold:

1. **Relational data structure** by which all data is maintained within the database. Each item is a single value; all values in a column are of the same type; columns are named but without ordering; and each row is unique with no implicit ordering.

2. **Relational data language** through which all database operations are performed. Although there are alternatives, we will focus on SQL, as does the industry.

3. **Relational integrity rules** to insure that data remains valid.

2.2.3 Object-Oriented Data Model

The *object-oriented data model* (OODM) is a higher-level data model as compared to RDM because OODM can express constructs that are difficult in RDM, such as type hierarchy. Other texts and articles cover the subject of OODM in greater detail (Khoshafian and Abnous, 1990; Goodman, 1991).

The reason that OODM is important for database connectivity is that OODM provides a framework for blending data and process into a more generic object. For example, the birth date of an employee is usually contained in the column for that row in the relational table EMPLOYEE. However, the age of an employee is a calculation, obtained by subtracting the birth date from today's date. The age attribute would not appear in an RDM table but be left to the application logic to calculate. In the OODM, the two attributes could appear similar to an external user of the EMPLOYEE object but be implemented internally (within the database) quite differently.

Let's explore the relationship of OODM to database connectivity by examining some OODM concepts and terminology. To start with the basics, everything is an *object*. An object *instance* is a specific object that is usually reflected in some tangible "thing" in the real world. For example, we could have the object instance for customer #1234. An object *class* (or object type) is the definition for object instances that are all similar to each other. We would then have a customer object class where customer #1234 is one instance of that class. Since everything is an object, quite complex structures of objects can be constructed with no distinction between what is system defined and what is user defined.

Every object has a unique system-assigned object *identifier*. The object identifier is the "pointer" by which different objects refer to one another. An identifier is similar to a primary key in RDM and is guaranteed to be unique and not NULL. An object identifier may be redundant when a good primary key does exist (such as customer number), but an object identifier is always present in the OODM.

A class is defined in two ways, one external and the other internal. First, its *specification* refers to the characteristics of the object class that are visible (external). Specification can be described as *behavior* (i.e., what the object can do) or *method* (i.e., procedures or programs that can operate upon the object). For example, the customer class can be specified as a behavior of what it does when sent an invoice or as a method called sent-invoice-for-shipped-product with specific arguments.

Second, the *representation* of a class refers to its hidden, or internal, characteristics. In the object representation, data and process can be integrated without such complexity being visible to the user of that object. The concept is object *encapsulation*, in which the distinction is clearly made between the specification (external) and the representation (internal) for an object class.

We can then classify or group object classes into an *IS-A hierarchy* where one object *is a* type of another object. One class can be a *generalization* of another; conversely, one class can be a *specialization* of another. For example, the person class could be a generalization of the customer class; likewise, the big-customer is a specialization of the customer class. The important aspect of the IS-A hierarchy is that a subclass *inherits* its base specifications from its parent class. Thus, any code used to implement a class can be immediately used for any specialization of that class. For example, we do not have to start from scratch to implement the behavior of a big-customer since most of its behavior is already specified in the customer class.

The next OODM concept is *overloading*, which means that the same method can be applied to different classes, resulting in different behaviors. For example, the enter-order method can be applied to a random customer. The OODM system determines what type of customer (e.g., big or small) and applies the appropriate method. Overloading encourages the definition of common or generic methods that operate over a wide range of classes, in much the same way that class inheritance encourages common behaviors for classes.

The preceding OODM concepts allow us to consider databases in a more general manner than just relational databases. Further, these concepts allow us to consider client-server architectures from the perspective of both database servers and application servers.

▼ 2.3 SQL AS A CONNECTIVITY LANGUAGE

In this section we will examine SQL as a database connectivity language, with emphasis on the relational data model. Various extensions to SQL are emerging, however, that support aspects of the object-oriented data model, such as stored procedures. These extensions are becoming increasingly important to database connectivity.

SQL stands for Structured Query Language and is pronounced either as "S-Q-L" or as "see-quel." In fact, it was originally called SEQUEL as part of the IBM San Jose research project on System R (Astrahan et al., 1976) in the mid-1970s. It was first commercialized by Oracle Corporation in the late 1970s. IBM offered SQL products in the early 1980s with

SQL/DS under the VM/370 operating system and then DB2 under the MVS/370 operating system. The mid 1980s saw a stampede of vendors offering SQL database systems. SQL products then dominated the database market.

In the early 1980s, ANSI and ISO initiated efforts to standardize the language, resulting in the 1986 and 1989 SQL standards. During 1992 a more comprehensive standard (previously called SQL-2 and now SQL-92) has emerged. Other texts have described the history and standards of SQL (Date, 1987); our purpose here is to examine the features pertaining to connectivity among databases.

2.3.1 Features for Connectivity

SQL was initially conceived as a query language for databases. The aim of most database administrators was to instruct the corporate masses in the SQL language and to give them SQL query tools, thereby offloading the burden of end-user database access. This aim was never realized because SQL proved to be too difficult a language for end-users. Beyond simple selections and projections on a single table or view, most users were not able to use SQL.

Next, SQL was perceived as a programming language. Although it lacked the normal control features, SQL was thought to provide all the required processing against corporate data. It certainly was an advance over its predecessors, but to be useful, SQL had to be embedded in another language or significantly extended.

SQL is now being viewed more as a connectivity language, rather than a query or programming language. SQL is now being advocated as the universal mechanism to access and manipulating all enterprise data in whatever form. For example, the IBM Information Warehouse framework adopts SQL as the connection mechanism for both relational and nonrelational data.

Some important SQL features for connectivity are connection, data types, and system tables. The CONNECT statement in SQL is relatively new. For example, its appearance in the IBM SAA Common Programming Interface Level 2 occurred in April 1991. This statement allows the application logic to switch database connections, rather than fixing the connection definition during program development.

The data type definitions in the current SQL standard (i.e., ANSI-89)

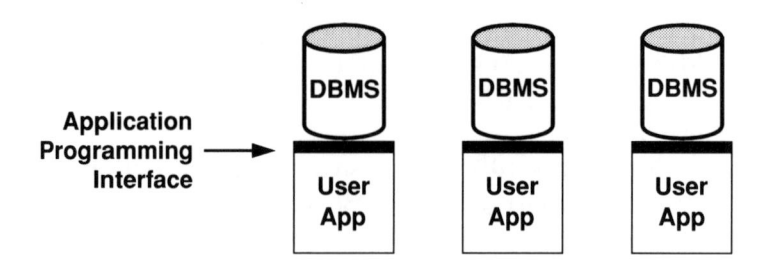

Figure 2.3. Traditional database interfaces.

provide a basic set (e.g., INTEGER, SMALLINT, CHAR, VARCHAR). Further refinements are needed with:

- date and time
- character set and conversions
- encoding of float, decimal, etc.
- multimedia data, such as sound and video

The standard definition of system tables is also weak, implying that query tools must have special SQL generation for system tables depending on the SQL engine.

▼ 2.4 DATABASE PROGRAMMING INTERFACES

At the heart of any database application is its *application programming interface* (or API) to the database. This API may be hidden from the user, as in interactive tools, but the aspects of that interface still influence its performance and functionality. In this section we will explore programming interfaces for databases, especially embedded versus call-level interfaces.

We can think of a traditional API as a layer that "glues" together the user application to the DBMS (see Figure 2.3). This is a traditional version in the sense that the application and the DBMS reside on the same platform. In Chapter 5, Building Distributed Systems, we will consider situations where the application and database reside on different platforms.

2.4.1 Basic Distinctions

There are basically two approaches to providing database interfaces: embedded and call-level.

2.4.1.1 Embedded API

The embedded API implies that the SQL statement is "embedded" into a traditional third-generation language, such as COBOL, FORTRAN, PL/1, C, or ADA. COBOL is by far the most popular language for using embedded SQL.

Consider a simple example of embedded SQL in COBOL, as shown in Figure 2.4. Note that there are the usual COBOL code sections with some "EXEC SQL ... END-EXEC" sections interspersed. When the COBOL application is processed, a precompilation step is performed on the program, in which the SQL sections are stripped out and processed separately from the COBOL program. This is illustrated in Figure 2.5. On the left side is the normal compilation and linking of a COBOL (or any other 3GL language). On the right side is the new stuff—the binding of the SQL to an access plan within the database. Note that both are necessary for the application to executed.

In other words, database interaction is required not only when the user executes the application, but also when the programmer develops the application. This is often referred to as program preparation.

```
DCL  xcnum    char(5);
DCL  xname    char(20);
DCL  xcity    char(15);

ask user for value of current city

EXEC SQL INCLUDE SQLCA;
EXEC SQL DECLARE customer TABLE
    (c#      char(5),
     name    char(25),
     city    char(15));
EXEC SQL DECLARE X CURSOR FOR
    SELECT c#, name, city
    FROM customer
    WHERE city = :xcity;

EXEC SQL OPEN X;
    IF SQLCODE <> 0
        THEN do some exception processing;
    DO WHILE SQLCODE = 0;
        EXEC SQL FETCH X INTO :xcnum, :xname; :xcity;
        do something interesting;
    IF SQLCODE <> 0 THEN do some exception processing;
    END;

EXEC SQL CLOSE X;
```

Figure 2.4. *Example of embedded SQL in COBOL.*

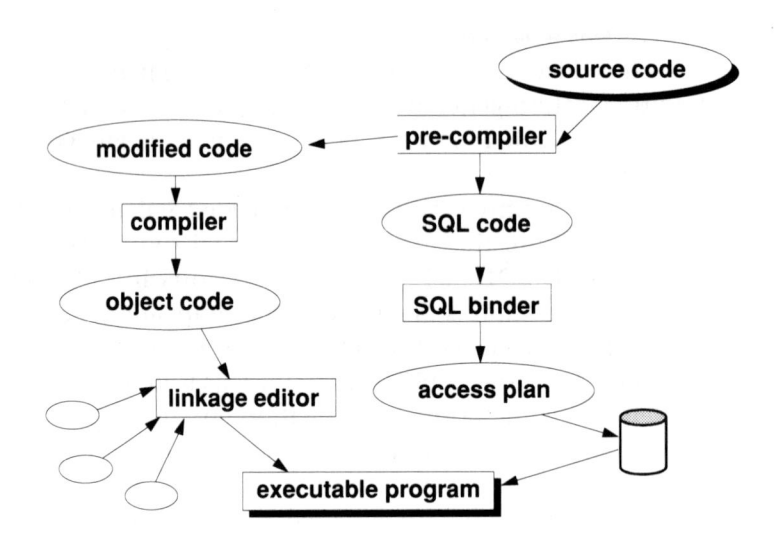

Figure 2.5. Processing embedded API.

Finally, embedded API is the more traditional approach to database applications and is the focus of most standardization efforts. The embedded API is usually preferred by large corporation development groups because it is similar to other forms of application development procedures (especially in COBOL).

2.4.1.2 Call-Level API

The call-level API is conceptually simpler than the embedded API. It is simply a call to procedures or functions to invoke the proper operations at various points in the application. The typical sequence is:

- establish connection to database
- prepare a buffer containing SQL statements
- process the request buffer
- process status and results

Figure 2.6 gives an example of using the call-level interface of Sybase/Microsoft SQL Server API (called DB-library). At point A, the application opens its connection to the database, passing information on the user identification. At point B, an SQL statement is processed to retrieve customers for a certain city. The rows are then processed one at a time. Finally, at point C, the connection with the database is closed.

```
                #include <header files...>
                int message_handlers();

                main()
                {   char cnum[5], name[20], city[15];
                    setup message handlers
                    login = dblogin();
                    DBSETLUSER(login, "user-id");
                    DBSETLPWD (login, "password");
A →                 dbproc = dbopen(login, "server-name");
                         ask user for value of current city;
                    dbcmd(dbproc, "SELECT c#, name, city FROM customer");
                    dbfcmd(dbproc, "WHERE city = %s", city);

B →                 if (dbsqlexec(dbproc) == FAIL)
                    {    do some exception processing    }
                    else
                    { while (dbresults(dbproc) != NO_MORE_RESULTS)
                        { dbbind(dbproc),1,CHARBIND,sizeof(c#),c#);
                          dbbind(dbproc),1,CHARBIND,sizeof(name),name);
                          dbbind(dbproc),1,CHARBIND,sizeof(city),city);

                          while (dbnextrow(dbproc) != NO_MORE_ROWS)
                              {         do something interesting;
                              }}}
C →                 dbclose(dbproc);
                }
```

Figure 2.6. *Example of call-level program in C.*

Several points can be made concerning the comparison with the embedded SQL example. First, the connection is implicit with the embedded example. Through some mechanism other than application code, the connection is established with the database. Second, the concept of a cursor is not present in the call-level example, since each row is retrieved explicitly into a buffer area.

The call-level API is often preferred by software vendors because it is easier to develop and distribute high-volume "shrink-wrapped" products. Because the target database is not available or even known during program preparation, applications written to an embedded API require a more difficult installation procedure. The application installation with a call-level API is "load and go," since the initialization processing is done during the program execution.

2.4.1.3 SQL binding time

Although the easier installation with a call-level API is desired, what are the disadvantages of this API? This question brings us to the topic of SQL binding time (sometimes called compile time). In the previous section, we stated that an embedded API required bind processing during

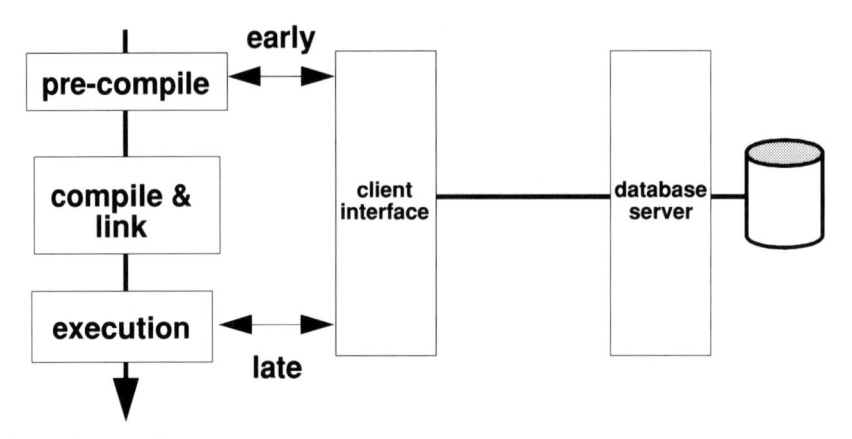

Figure 2.7. *Binding times.*

program preparation. This is usually the case, but it is not always. Let's examine this issue in greater detail.

With either the embedded API or the call-level API, the processing of the SQL statements can be handled as either static SQL, processed during program preparation, or dynamic SQL, processed during program execution. What is required to process an SQL statement? SQL processing implies that SQL text is converted to an internal form that can be executed efficiently by the database engine. This processing, called SQL binding, involves the following steps:

- parse the text of the SQL request into tokens
- validate identifiers for tables, columns, and creators
- check authorizations of user submitting request
- optimize database access
- generate machine code for optimized access path
- bind the access path to the database

The processing could be a considerable effort, especially in the access optimization. The result is an *access path*, which hopefully is an efficient procedure to retrieve or update the data for the application.

The issue is *when* is this processing performed? It must be performed sometime. Static SQL implies that SQL binding is performed early during program preparation; dynamic SQL implies that SQL binding is performed late during program execution. Figure 2.7 illustrates this distinction between early and late binding, which has the classical tradeoffs between efficiency and flexibility. The actual situation is usually much more complex, involving various combinations of early and late binding. Any sophisticated database tool requires both binding types. Many production applications prepare a dynamic SQL statement once and execute it many times during a single execution of the application. Smarter database engines retain the binding process for dynamic SQL in a cache with the expectation that the same SQL will be executed more efficiently subsequently. And then, some database engines reserve the final stages of checking and optimization to execution in any case, so the pure advantages of static SQL are negated.

Static SQL is more efficient but less flexible; dynamic SQL is less efficient but more flexible. If an application binds a specific SQL statement once and executes it many times, then static is obviously preferred. If an application binds and executes a specific SQL statement once (such as with an ad hoc query), then dynamic SQL is preferred. However, the situation is complex so that only careful benchmarking of realistic applications will yield an estimate of the performance advantages of static SQL.

We are now back to the previous question: Is embedded better than call-level API?

2.4.1.4 Embedded versus call-level APIs

With most contemporary database products, the implementations of embedded API and of call-level API are functionally similar. In other words, the same application can be programmed in either API with equivalent function and with equivalent performance. Why?

This situation is summarized in Figure 2.8 as a two-by-two table of the API types contrasted with static/dynamic binding. Note that all combinations are possible. The assumed mode for embedded API is sta-

	Static	Dynamic
Embedded	assumed mode	yes, with effort
Call-Level	yes, with PSO	assumed mode

Figure 2.8. Embedded versus call-level.

tic SQL, and the assumed mode for call-level API is dynamic SQL. If one requires dynamic SQL with an embedded API, program preparation requires more effort, doubling the lines of code and expertise needed to generate that code. More steps are required, along with a new data structure called the SQL Data Area, which indicates the nature of the result set. Software vendors of generic utilities do not like using an embedded API for their database tools for this reason.

The final combination (using call-level API for static SQL) presents a new and interesting concept linked to our previous discussions of the relational data model and the object-oriented data model. This concept is called persistent SQL object.

2.4.1.5 Persistent SQL objects

What is a *persistent SQL object* (PSO)? It is similar to an access plan as generated during binding, but it is not quite the same.

An SQL object consists, in part, of one or more SQL statements that have been bound to a database. Since an SQL object performs a certain function against certain database tables, one could refer to an SQL object using the object-oriented data model as a method for manipulating the underlying database object.

A persistent SQL object is an object that has the following three properties: it is persistent, it is shared, and it is named. The term persistent means that the object persists beyond the execution of the application. In other words, the object has an existence independent of the application that uses the object. It does not disappear when the application terminates, as with dynamic SQL.

Second, a PSO can be shared. Applications using embedded API with static SQL create SQL objects all the time! However, the existence of these objects is known only to that specific application. An SQL object created by one application cannot be shared with other applications. For general SQL objects, the implication is that these objects can be shared with other applications; hence, a shared PSO reenforces the similarity to methods in the OODM.

Finally, a PSO must be named. To be shared, an application needs to reference the PSO via an established and unique name. It is often difficult to determine the proper naming scheme in a large complex programming environment. Moreover, once the naming of PSOs is determined, these objects must be maintained through some mechanism for creating, deleting, and updating.

```
CREATE PROCEDURE cust_list @cust_city char(15) = null
  as
  if @cust_no is null
     print "Please give a customer city" 624
  else
     select cno, name, city
       from customer
       where city = @city
```

Figure 2.9. *Example of a stored procedure.*

The best example of a PSO implementation is a *stored procedure,* which was introduced by Sybase Corporation around 1985. The stored procedure satisfies the characteristics of a PSO: it is persistent, shared, and named. In addition, a stored procedure contains program logic with the SQL statements. These features allow significant portions of the application logic to be encapsulated in the stored procedure, rather than in the application. Figure 2.9 shows an example of an SQL Server stored procedure that retrieves all the customers for a certain city. The application would invoke this stored procedure with the following statement:

```
execute cust_city Denver
```

The stored procedure would insert the parameter for the city and execute the proper SQL. Note that the application does not know (or care) about the customer table.

▼ 2.5 DATABASE FRONT-END TOOLS

Since the early days of DBMS products, vendors have provided query and reporting tools with their database products. Recently, the front-end tool area has exploded with a variety of exciting products, stimulated by two factors:

- Client-server architecture has "opened" the playing field so that the field is not limited to just vendors of DBMS products.
- Graphical user interface (GUI) environments have increased the design alternatives for interacting with users.

With the variety of front-end tools increasing weekly, the emphasis for developing enterprise applications on the desktop has shifted dramatically to these new tools. To understand this trend, we must examine the interaction between the development power and technical skill requirements.

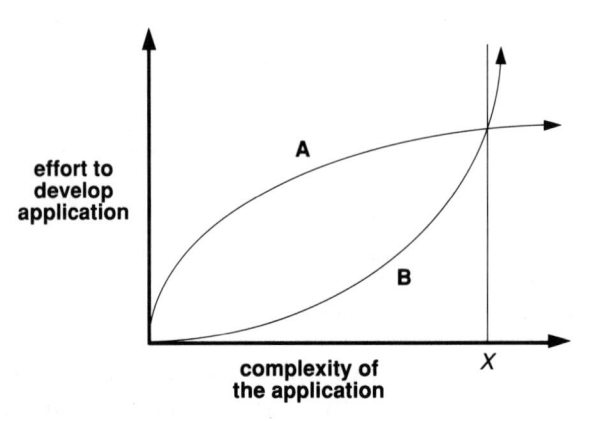

Figure 2.10. Effort versus complexity.

The first aspect of front-end tools is the quest for dazzling improvements in programming productivity. It is very difficult to implement innovative GUI applications in traditional 3GL languages, such as COBOL. The event-driven and message-passing structure of GUI applications exceeds the capabilities of most traditional languages. Even the C language requires copious amounts of code for the simplest GUI application. The days of custom GUI applications written in traditional languages are numbered.

The industry desperately needs tools with better development power. This development power must range from simple to complex. It must allow for the quick and easy development of simple applications as well as accommodating the depth and maintainability of complex applications.

This two-edged requirement is illustrated in Figure 2.10. The horizontal axis is the complexity of the application to be developed, while the vertical axis is the effort required to develop that application. We would hope that there is a roughly linear relationship between the two axes, or in other words, that a unit of effort will result in a unit of better application, without any surprises!

Curve A represents the traditional programming languages, such as COBOL. Initially, there is a steep section implying that simple applications require a lot of effort; but more complex applications require less marginal effort. On the other hand, curve B represents fourth generation languages (4GL). Simple applications require very little effort; however, but complex applications "hit the wall." This is an "I gotcha" phenomenon in which a development group is seduced into using a simple 4GL tool, resulting in early successes. They are then trapped with a dependence on the tool even after application requirements increase.

There is some point where the two curves intersect. To the right of point X in the figure, it is better to adopt curve B tools; to the left, it is better to adopt curve A tools. The challenge is to recognize when a situation is to the left or right of point X and to ease the transition (in either direction) between the two types of tools.

The GUI environments have enhanced the differences between curves A and B. The goal for a front-end tool vendor is to offer products that will extend point X as far right as possible and that will enable easy transition to traditional languages. For example, the Borland Paradox product has a simple keystroke macro facility that is appropriate for simple applications, but the product can also embed those macros into their full Paradox Application Language for more complex applications.

The second aspect of front-end tools is the quest to enable end users to code their own applications. Traditionally, all application implementation was performed by MIS development group. The advent of end-user computing in the 1980s marked an abrupt change in direction: "If an application cannot be developed in my spreadsheet utility, then it is not worth doing."

In the 1990s two modes are emerging for application development in large enterprises. The first mode is a reincarnation of the traditional development mode with a formal system life cycle by an MIS development group but with the twist that the mainframe platform is one of several alternatives. The second mode is a "do-it-yourself" approach with the twist that a "good" end-user application must be formally promoted to the status of an enterprise application. We are now evolving towards two development modes, one top-down and the other bottom-up. Both modes must complement the other. The challenge is therefore to design enterprise applications so that they are extensible by users and to utilize the proper front-end tools so end users can easily promote their applications to the status of enterprise applications.

Figure 2.11 illustrates the relationship that is evolving between the development power of the tool versus the skills required to use the tool. This is a special case of the previous figure showing effort versus complexity. Again, there should be a linear relationship so that additional skills allow more powerful tools to be utilized. The four quadrants indi-

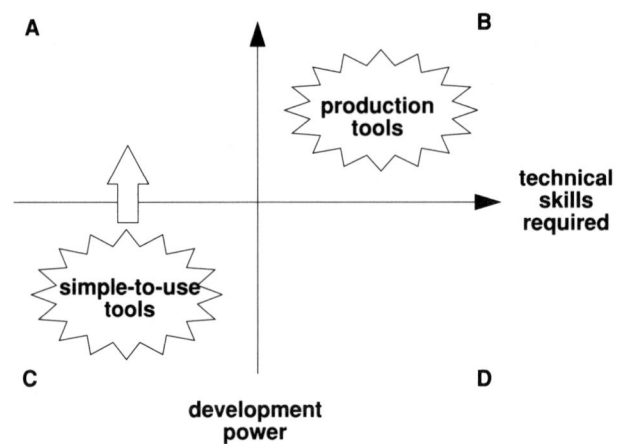

Figure 2.11. Power versus skill.

cate the four extremes; quadrant C tools are simple tools for simple applications, while quadrant B tools are complex tools for complex applications. Using GUI techniques in these tools, an interesting trend is apparent: the entire axis is shifting upwards. This implies that simple tools are able to develop complex applications. Nonprogrammers can now develop complex applications that previously required extensive COBOL programming experience. We have certainly witnessed this development with spreadsheet utilities, and the trend is now spreading to traditional database applications.

2.5.1 Categories

The front-end tools can be roughly divided into five categories:
- Simple query and reporting
- Complex analysis
- Application development environment
- Application code generators
- Database administration tools

The first category involves tools that specify a relational result set and format it into a presentable form. Few calculations, outside of totals and counts, are performed on the result set.

The second category involves tools that perform extensive manipulations and/or calculations on the result set. Trend analysis and charting are examples of these features.

The third category involves tools that emphasize application development (i.e., implementing an application for use by others). This category supplies the complete environment for this development, implying that the deployed application must be executed within this environment. The challenge for application development tools is to support the large team development projects that are common in large data processing groups. So far, tools in this category have focused on support for one or two developers.

The fourth category involves tools that also emphasize application development but result in the generation of 3GL code. The advantage is that this code can be understood, modified, and processed in traditional ways; however, it can be overly complex.

The final category involves tools that assist in the administration and maintenance of databases. Whereas with conventional mainframe databases, the database administrator (DBA) had to worry about one or two database systems; the DBA for distributed systems may have to cope with hundreds of database servers, each with the complexity of the former mainframe databases. We do not yet understand and certainly do not have tools for this situation.

2.5.2 API of Front-End Tools

Another confusing aspect of front-end tools is that many of them provide an API layer in addition to the GUI tools. Typically a C programmer can utilize this API to achieve a higher level of functionality than is normally provided by the usual database API. For example, Pioneer Software has a front-end tool called Q+E to query and update relational tables interactively. They also have a QELIB product with an API that allows database access from C.

In any high-end front-end tool, an API is becoming a requirement to complement the GUI tool. As the complexity of the application increases, there will always be a point where it is desirable to switch to a normal programming language (as described in Figure 2.10). Such an API does provide the escape mechanism to revert back to normal programming when needed.

2.5.3 Desktop Integration Mechanisms

Just as important as the API of the front-end tool is the integration mechanisms supported by that tool. The integration mechanism allows one application to share data with another application on that desktop. An example would be a custom application built with PowerSoft PowerBuilder interacting with a spreadsheet built with Microsoft Excel.

There are several levels of integration mechanisms: file import/export, spreadsheet links, copy/cut/paste to clipboard, Dynamic Data Exchange (DDE), and Object Linking and Embedding (OLE). First, file import/export has been supported by most GUI tools for many years; however, it is highly dependent on the context of the tools and standards established for that context. For instance, graphical tools (such as CorelDraw, Aldus Freehand, and Adobe Illustrator) can exchange graphic files in a variety of formats, each having subtle advantages and disadvantages.

Second, spreadsheet utilities for many years have had to support interaction among detail and consolidate spreadsheets. Usually, this interaction was performed in a manner unique to the spreadsheet product.

Third, the clipboard provides a mechanism to universally move objects (text, graphics, and the like) among applications. The actions are implemented as cut (copy to clipboard and delete original), copy (duplicate original to clipboard), and paste (obtain contexts of clipboard).

Fourth, Microsoft specified the mechanism for DDE as an initial attempt to have concurrently executing applications interact. For instance, a database utility could be retrieving live data that is continuously varying, while at the same time pass that data to another program (such as Microsoft Excel) that charts the data in real time. DDE is particularly effective at highly interactive but low volume situations and has recently been extended to operate across desktop with the Microsoft Windows for Workgroups product.

Finally, the Microsoft Object Linking and Embedding (OLE) allows a complex object (such as an Excel spreadsheet) from one application to be linked to or embedded in another application. Linking implies that the original object is not copied but only a link to the object is copied. The object remains active within the initial application, so that any changes in that object are reflected in subsequent usage by the second application. On the other hand, embedded implies that the original object is copied into the second application so that changes to the object occur independently in each application. The definition of an OLE object is quite flexible, allowing for its evolution to arbitrary multimedia contexts (such as full motion video).

These integration mechanisms will be increasingly important to building enterprise applications on the desktop because of the ease of assembling complex applications from individual components and the flexibility to add new functions to meet future requirements.

▼ 2.6 PROBLEMS WITH DATA TRANSPARENCY

At this point you are probably wondering why there are any problems with using SQL as a connectivity language. If all vendors are compliant to the SQL standards, then an SQL statement that operates correctly against one SQL database should operate correctly against another. Right?

This question certainly strikes at the heart of why the industry wants to use SQL as a connectivity language among heterogeneous database systems. The variations by the vendors in interpreting the SQL standard and the extensions to the SQL standard cause significant and subtle problems. We will refer to these as *SQL transparency* problems.

Let's examine these problems in detail by contrasting two SQL database systems: IBM OS/2 Extended Services Database Management (DBM) with its SAA SQL, and Microsoft/Sybase SQL Server under OS/2 with its TRANSACT-SQL.

2.6.1 Database Interface

The first problem area is simply the mechanism by which an application or user directly submits the SQL statements to the database system. Usually we refer to this mechanism as the Application Programming Interface or simply API. One can consider an API in a broad context to include both traditional programming interfaces (e.g., C procedure calls) or interactive interfaces (e.g., enter raw SQL). In either case, each vendor usually supplies several APIs unique to its product. At the very least, an application would have to be relinked with another API library to utilize another vendor's database system.

A simple example of problems with an interactive API was that of the SQL Server utility called ISQL, a simple utility that allows a user to enter ad hoc SQL statements and receive the results as a simple formatted data stream. This is a utility that every vendor has in some form. A person using the ISQL utility was having difficulty: ISQL would not execute any SQL statements. After checking all the obvious solutions, the problem was found to be simply the unique manner in which ISQL terminates a statement: the user must enter the command "go" followed by a carriage return to execute the previously entered SQL statements.

This simple problem illustrates that minor variations in the database interface can cause major problems. The absence of a simple "go" terminator can cause a big difference to the user. Note that, if one has a complex stream of SQL statements to apply in batch to a SQL Server database, one would be required to insert "go" statements after each SQL statement.

2.6.2 Database Connection

A second problem area is the manner in which a connection is established to a specific database. Assume that the previous problem is resolved; with the same application we can interface to different types of database systems. Each vendor has a different way of connecting to a specific database since such connections are not part of any SQL standards.

Continuing the previous example, the ISQL utility requires that the server name is specified on the command line when the utility is invoked and that a database name is specified in a DBUSE statement. A similar mechanism is used at the programming interface for any SQL Server application. Through the combination of server/database, SQL statements will be applied to the correct target.

In contrast, the IBM Extended Services Database Manager has a CONNECT statement to specify the server name, which is then mapped via a local directory to a remote SAA database.

The problem is that an application must be programmed differently depending on whether it is connecting to SQL Server or to Database Manager. This is a *wicked problem* (see definition in glossary) in the sense that the semantics of what you are connecting to are subtly different.

2.6.3 SQL Syntax and Semantics

The third problem area is the variation in SQL syntax and semantics. The current SQL standards have given the industry some degree of compatibility with the four DML statements: SELECT, INSERT, UPDATE, and DELETE. However, other SQL statements for data definition, transaction management, and security administration vary widely.

Even with the DML statements, there are significant differences in the vendors' interpretation of the SQL standard. For instance, SQL

Server assumes that certain keywords are optional, such as the INTO keyword in the INSERT statement; on the other hand, DBM assumes that such keywords are required. Thus, a shortened INSERT statement will execute correctly by SQL Server but give a syntax error by DBM.

Who is at fault? SQL Server for allowing optional keywords, which is not specified in the SQL standard, or DBM for requiring optional keywords, which is not specified in the SQL standard? Or the user for taking advantage of a SQL extension offered by a vendor? The answer is not obvious, but the result—lack of SQL transparency—is obvious.

These variations in SQL implementations can cause more subtle problems in the semantics. For instance, a user can specify in a CREATE TABLE statement whether a column allows NULL values or not. With DBM, the default (if not specified) is to allow NULL values for that column; with SQL Server, the default is the opposite. This implies that the same CREATE statement will generate a table with different semantics in the two database systems. In particular, the assumed integrity constraints for NULL values in primary keys may be negated. This is another wicked problem.

2.6.4 System Catalog Tables

Traditional database applications usually assume specific tables and columns; hence, these applications have no need to refer to the system catalog, which contains information on tables, columns, authorizations, etc. However, the need to refer to the system catalog increases when the application has a more decision-support orientation and spans several remote databases. Even in the case where an application can assume specific tables and columns, the SQL generation may depend on other factors, such as whether a column is indexed.

We therefore have a situation in which an increasing percentage of database applications need to utilize system catalogs, while system catalogs are one of the weakest areas in the SQL standards. Each SQL implementation has taken a different approach to the structure and content of its system catalog.

Perhaps the greatest variation in system catalogs is between the two databases previously mentioned, DBM and SQL Server. In this case, the basic interpretation of the primary key to table and column information is fundamentally different. DBM takes a more traditional approach, emphasizing the importance of tables and columns by using a concatenated character key of creator and table. SQL Server adopts a more innovative approach, emphasizing the universality of all database objects and using a simple (but arbitrary) binary integer to identify a table or column. Thus, the logic that processes information from these system catalogs must be fundamentally different.

Solutions to the catalog problem are emerging. In the SQL2 standard, generic system catalog tables are defined, requiring the vendor to implement these tables with the proper information. In newer versions of SQL Server, a set of stored procedures that return detailed catalog information are supported.

2.6.5 Data Types and Encodings

Although every database system supports the simple data types for integer and character, there are numerous transparency problems with most other data types, such as varying character strings, decimal, date/time, and binary data. For example, DBM supports date/time with two data types, a DATE data type and a TIME data type. SQL Server also supports date/time but with one data type, DATETIME. Therefore, if one is moving DATETIME column on SQL Server to DATE column on DBM, information on TIME is lost. In the converse situation, superfluous information on TIME is assumed. You lose either way!

In addition, the data encoding for similar data types may be incompatible. The typical API returns a data value in the binary encoding for that value. For instance, an integer value is typically returned as a two-complement binary of specific length (16-bit, 32-bit, etc.), rather than the character representation for that integer. Because they share the same Intel 80x86 machine architecture, SQL Server and DBM will generate compatible binary encodings for integers. DBM and its larger brother, DB2, are not able to directly exchange integers in their native binary encoding, however, since the Intel architecture exchanges the higher and lower bytes of a two-byte integer and the 370 architecture does not. Likewise, DBM uses ASCII for its normal character encoding, while DB2 uses EBCDIC. And, the mapping of ASCII to and from EBCDIC is nontrivial, especially with international character sets.

2.6.6 Status Codes and Messages

Every database system must return a status code upon the completion of each SQL operation. Even successful operations may indicate some unusual situations. In addition, the status code can usually be supplemented with one or more textual messages. In every application, the application logic depends on these status codes. Highly unusual conditions may be displayed to the user for interpretation and corrective action.

At the programming level, DBM returns this status code as binary value in a field called SQLCODE in the SQL Communication Area (SQLCA). SQL Server handles error conditions through two call-back procedures that receive an integer identifying an error condition. Not only are the status codes for errors incompatible, but the frameworks for handling errors are basically different. In addition, some error conditions in DBM do not exist in SQL Server, and vice versa. Therefore, an application written to solve all the other SQL transparency problems will not function properly because of incompatible error conditions.

2.6.7 Collating Sequences

When a SELECT statement with an ORDER-BY clause is issued, the data is sorted in the collating sequence defined by the database engine, usually determined by the underlying hardware architecture (e.g., the machine instruction for comparing characters). Usually, the database administrator, application programmer, or casual user has no control over this collating sequence. Therefore, identical data on two different database systems may be presented to the application as a different sequence. If a user is browsing through data, this different sequence may not be noticed, but basic sort/merge operations will not work properly.

2.6.8 Data Semantics

The last transparency problem is the hardest of all to resolve. In fact, this problem is independent of the database vendor or even the hardware architecture; it simply depends on how the database is designed and used. Consider two databases, from any vendor on any platform, dealing with some aspects of shipping and distribution of the company's product. Both databases contain various columns labelled as "shipping date" in various ways. But what does shipping date mean in each of those columns? Is it the date that the customer's order was ready for shipping? Was scheduled to be shipped? Was actually shipped? Or, some combination of the above? In particular, would the results of a join between "shipping date" columns be valid?

Note that this data semantics problem can exist within a single database, regardless of how carefully it is designed initially. This problem is substantially increased, however, when data from multiple databases are combined.

▼ DISCUSSION QUESTIONS

1. What effect do applications for production vs. decision support have on the design and operation of a database management system?

2. Distinguish the relational data model from the object-oriented data model.

3. What are the three ways in which SQL has been used? Which one is more important today?

4. Contrast embedded versus call-level programming interfaces for database applications. Which is better?

5. What is a persistent SQL object? How is it related to stored procedures?

6. What is your (or your company's) favorite development tool for database applications? Why?

7. List some characteristics of a good GUI development tool that distinguishes it from third generation tools.

8. What are some problems with using SQL of one DBMS vendor against the database of another DBMS vendor?

9. What determines the collating sequence of rows sorted by an ORDER BY clause in an SQL SELECT statement?

3

FUNDAMENTALS OF PROCESS MANAGEMENT

The previous chapter on data management focused on the static nature of data—APIs, data models, database tools, and SQL transparency. This chapter focuses on the dynamic nature of data—transactions, properties, concurrency, and security. We examine ways of performing complex changes to our data while maintaining its integrity. The key to this chapter is the concept of a *transaction*, an indivisible unit of work for which all changes to data are performed or no changes are performed.

▼ 3.1 TRANSACTION CONTROL

In this section, the definition, properties, and control of transactions are explained. Let's begin with the assumption that only one application is active against our database; subsequent sections will deal with the problems of handling multiple transactions concurrently. We will consider both the relational data model and the object-oriented data model, implying parallels between process management and data management. The technology of these two areas may eventually blend together.

3.1.1 What Is a Transaction? And Why Is it Important?

A transaction, often called a unit of work, is fundamental to insuring the integrity of our databases. The usual day-to-day transaction in the typical enterprise involves a complex sequence of actions. In this environment, the ability of a DBMS product to support proper transaction management is a critical feature of that product.

The sequence is highly dependent on other data and on the mind set of the person using the application. It is often the case that a person proceeds part way through a transaction and discovers a "show-stopper," a situation that rules this transaction invalid. For instance, transferring funds between accounts is valid only if there are sufficient funds in the original account. Several changes could have been made to the database prior to this point. Those changes must be negated or aborted, or the database is a mess!

The principle is that the application moves the database from one point of consistency to another. When viewed at one of these points, the database will appear to be consistent—customers will have the proper invoices to existing products. Beneath the surface, however, the database is a sea of chaos with continual changes flowing from multiple concurrent transactions.

It is important to note that the concept of a transaction is not limited to relational databases. In fact, a transaction takes on greater importance as we consider the object-oriented data model. A method, or procedure, of a database object can perform many complex changes, and an application can invoke many methods.

So, what is a transaction? In the context of this book, a transaction is one or more database actions (e.g., SQL statements) that are treated as a single unit of work. Either all actions of that transaction are performed, or none of the actions are performed. If the transaction is successful, the transaction is said to be *committed*. If the transaction is not successful, the transaction is said to be *rolled back* or *aborted*.

3.1.2 ACID Properties

To better understand what a transaction is, let's examine a set of four properties often called the ACID properties: Atomicity, Consistency, Isolation, and Durability.

Atomicity is the requirement for an indivisible unit of work. Transactions are all-or-nothing propositions. We'll examine the issue of when transactions should start and end in detail in the next two sections.

Consistency is the requirement that the application move the database from one state of consistency to another state of consistency. In other words, when a transaction is committed, the application must ensure that all the data affected is now in a consistent state. There can be disagreements about the requirements for a consistent state, but the important point is to avoid the obviously inconsistent states.

Isolation is the requirement that the behavior of a transaction not be affected by other transactions. A transaction executes in isolation from other transactions, and once a transaction is initiated, its effects should be the same regardless of any other actions to that database. This isolation property is usually interpreted as a requirement to serialize transactions. In other words, concurrent transactions behave as if they were executed serially, without overlap. This serializability is usually determined at the start of the transaction.

Durability is the requirement that, once a transaction is committed, its effects on the database are durable or permanent. No subsequent actions or failures to that database can cause the changes affected by a committed transaction to be lost. This is a tricky requirement for a DBMS product, which is usually addressed by the basic physics of magnetic recording on disk storage units.

3.1.3 COMMIT and ROLLBACK

The mechanism for transaction control is well defined for the relational data model. The SQL language defines statements for COMMIT and ROLLBACK that allow the application to specify the termination of a transaction. Relational DBMS products now have more than ten years of history in providing the proper facilities to support transaction control.

Let's examine the aspects of transaction control as defined in the RDM. First, transactions are assumed to be chained. From the moment an application establishes a connection to a particular database, it has automatically initiated a transaction. The execution of the application stays within some transaction boundary until it terminates its database connection. Therefore, a transaction is immediately chained to another transaction during the database connection. This chaining is performed automatically by the DBMS.

The application determines when and if the current transaction in this chain is committed or aborted. By issuing either a COMMIT or ROLLBACK statement at the proper point in the application logic, the application terminates (successfully or unsuccessfully) the current transaction, thus implicitly initiating a new transaction. To examine these transaction boundaries, we'll use diagrams with these conventions:

- A single database action (usually, an SQL statement) is represented by a vertical bar.
- Depending on the database API, an application can group a sequence of these actions into a single request, represented by a rectangle. It is important to note that within a request the application has given up control to the DBMS; the application is waiting for a response from the database.
- The transaction boundary is represented by a shaded area. All actions within this shaded area are to be committed or aborted together as a unit of work. Note that an entire request by definition must be in the same unit of work.
- Two important database actions are the COMMIT and ROLLBACK statements. They will be represented by a vertical line with an opened circle and a vertical line with a slashed circle, respectively.

In the classic database application, the application resides close to the DBMS on the same platform. Usually, each database action is a separate request; in other words, the application regains control after each SQL statement. Distributed systems have the advantage of batching several database actions in a single request.

The unit of work continues until one of the following conditions occurs: COMMIT, ROLLBACK, or application termination. In the next section, we will consider short transactions in which the DBMS can be an auto-commit at the end of each request. For now, the application should explicitly specify the commit/abort actions.

In Figure 3.1, we have two transactions: A and B. Transaction A was completed successfully, while transaction B was aborted. Note the shading that defines the transaction boundaries for A and B.

3.1.4 Short versus Long Transactions

In the context of database connectivity, one of the key characteristics of transactions is whether a person is allowed to make decisions about its outcome within the boundaries of the transaction. For example, a teller at a bank modifies a complex loan account. Does the teller interact or converse with the application logic during the transaction? Data on the account is presented; the application solicits a decision from the teller based on this data. Or, does the teller submit the transaction which is immediately executed without any further interaction with the teller?

In other words, is the duration of the transaction dependent on a per-

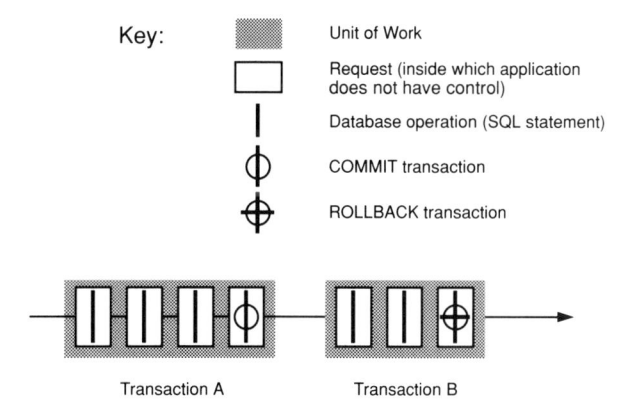

Figure 3.1. Transaction boundaries: classical case.

son analyzing information and making a decision based on this information? If so, this transaction is called a long (or sometimes conversational or interactive) transaction; if not, then this transaction is called a short (or sometimes batch) transaction. To examine this distinction between long and short transactions, let's continue with our diagrams of transaction boundaries, with the following addition: A circle with a question mark represents think time, or decision time, on the part of the application user. The application has given up control to the user, and is waiting for a response from the user.

Let's consider the case of short transactions. In Figure 3.2, we have two requests, followed by think time, and finally a third request. This figure represents a short transaction since the think time is not within any shaded area and since consecutive requests are not part of the same transaction. In this case, the DBMS is only aware of three separate (inde-

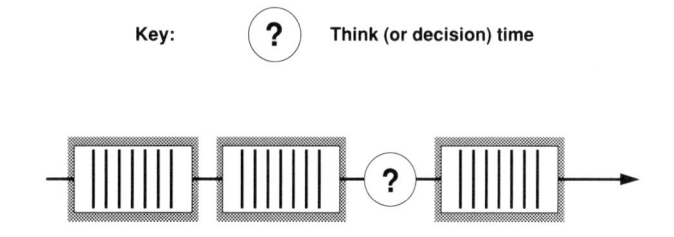

Figure 3.2. Transaction boundaries: short transaction.

Transaction A (weak)

Transaction B (strong)

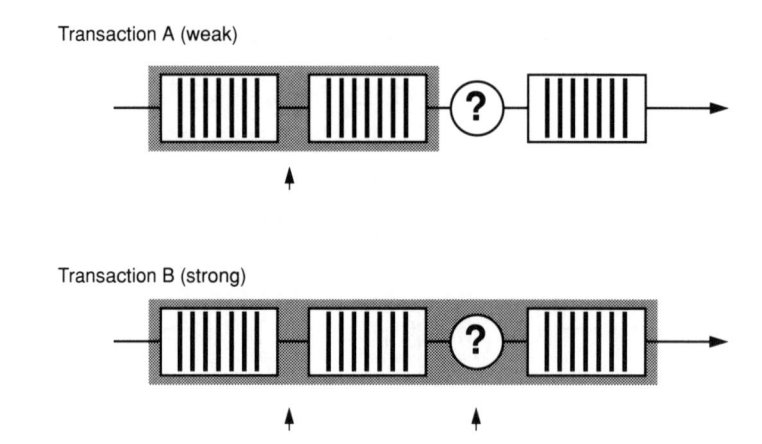

Figure 3.3. *Transaction boundaries: long transaction.*

pendent) transactions that could have been initiated by three separate applications. And, the DBMS treats these transactions as being independent of each other. The failure of one request does not necessarily affect another request, but the application can detect failures and, based on its logic, respond differently to these failures. In effect for short transactions, each request ends with a COMMIT statement, either explicitly requested by the application or implicitly enforced by the DBMS.

Now, consider the case of long transactions. In Figure 3.3, we see that there are two types of long transactions: a weak type in which an application only has control during a transaction and a strong type in which the person has control during a transaction. In both types of long transactions, the DBMS is not in control of the transaction boundaries. Therefore, database resources that are being consumed by the transaction are indeterminate as far as the DBMS is concerned.

In the weak type of long transaction (i.e., transaction A of Figure 3.3), the transaction spans the first two requests. During the interval between requests, the application has control and, based on its logic, is determining the next action. The DBMS is not in control and does not know when the transaction will end. If the application is on the same platform as the DBMS, this interval could be a reliable fraction of a second.

For example, a CICS transaction program (TP) using DB2 usually operates as a long transaction of a mild nature. System designers are not concerned about allowing the CICS TP control within a transaction since CICS and DB2 are closely and reliably coupled. However, a CICS TP sometimes hangs in the middle of a transaction, causing problems for the DB2 DBMS, which recovers by aborting that transaction. The client-server architecture thus implies that a weak long transaction also has to deal with communication problems between the client and server platforms.

In the strong type of long transaction (i.e., transaction B of Figure 3.3), we see that the transaction spans think time. During the intervals between requests, the user (not the DBMS or application) has control and is determining what to do next. The simplest situation would be for the user to determine whether to commit or abort the previous database actions. This is a simple final confirmation that these actions are OK. The other extreme that often occurs in GUI applications is an ongoing think time between all requests during which the user can point-and-click at a myriad of actions.

What is the trade-off between the various types of short and long transactions? It is the classical trade-off between efficiency and flexibility. Short transactions are more efficient but limit the flexibility of the user or application; long transactions are more flexible but could place serious efficiency constraints on the DBMS. As we will see, this trade-off is intensified when we consider distributed systems. Design alternatives for distributed systems often involve the proper definition of transaction boundaries. The designer often struggles with the implications of choosing between one big (long) transaction or several smaller (short) transactions.

3.1.5 What Really Is a Transaction?

An increasingly important issue is that the basic notion of a transaction is becoming less clear. In classical data processing, a transaction was well defined, and the application was designed around one or more transactions. With GUI applications, the determination of when a transaction starts and when it ends is not so obvious. Many GUI applications today are designed to consider each database action as an atomic transaction, oblivious to such problems as dirty reads. Later, application logic and user intervention is added to compensate for any concurrency problems.

For example, a customer ordering system may report the availability of a certain product, without reserving the product. When the customer

Figure 3.4. Splintered transaction.

Figure 3.5. Ultralong transaction.

actually orders the product a few minutes later, that product may be sold out. This is often the case with seating availability on airline flights.

In some ways, this is not a bad approach! It certainly minimizes the database resources. But where has our notion of a transaction gone? We call this type of transaction a splintered transaction.

In classical data processing, a transaction was considered to have a long duration if it executes for more than a few seconds. Today, we have important applications desiring transactions spanning days or weeks. For instance, CAD/CAM systems might desire to check out engineering drawings from the database for several days while the designer makes some modifications. How does a database handle this ultralong transaction?

Both the splintered and ultralong transactions place significant demands on the database. In the next section, we will investigate these demands in terms of concurrency controls.

▼ 3.2 CONCURRENCY CONTROL

In the previous section we assumed that one transaction at a time would execute against the database. In this section, we will consider the case in which many transactions are concurrently executing against the database.

As a side note, there is a subtle distinction between the terms concurrent and simultaneous. *Concurrent* means that several activities are happening in the same unit of time, but not necessary at exactly the same time. *Simultaneous* means that several activities are happening at exactly the same instant of time. Operating on a single processor platform, a database engine can only process a single transaction at any instant in time; however, the effect over several seconds is that many transactions are being executed concurrently—apparently at the same time, but not exactly. On multiprocessor platforms, a database engine can process multiple transactions simultaneously.

It is not as important whether transactions are processed concurrently or simultaneously, but whether they are overlapping. That is, can a second transaction start before the first one finishes? If the answer is NO, then we have a very poorly performing database. In this case, all transactions line up in a single queue; they are processed one at a time. Fortunately, there is typically a lot of wait time within each transaction as data is read or written to disk. In every commercial DBMS product, transactions are processed concurrently (and maybe simultaneously with multiple processors), and they overlap.

3.2.1 Concurrency Problems

So, what are the problems with concurrent transactions? Simply put, they may trip over each other! One transaction may interfere with the proper execution of another transaction, and the effects of the transaction may be dependent on other transactions that are executing concurrently. This is *not* a desirable situation. The execution of concurrent transactions should be independent of one another.

Let's assume that our database is a "free-for-all" database (i.e., no constraints on concurrent transactions). The potential problems with concurrent transactions can be roughly divided into four categories: dirty read, nonrepeatable read, phantom rows, and lost update.

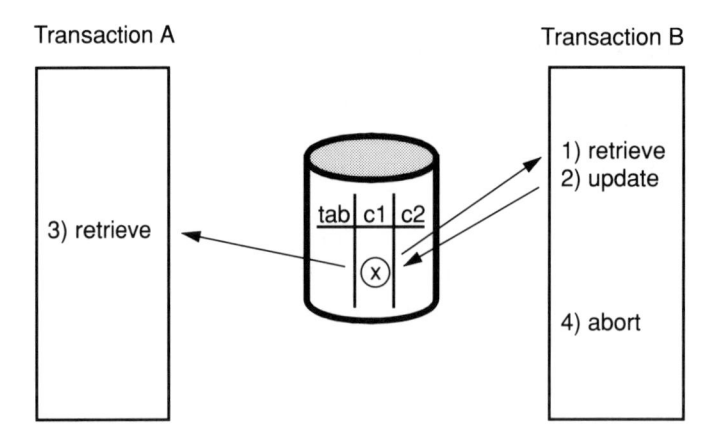

Figure 3.6. Concurrency problem: dirty read.

3.2.1.1 *Dirty read*

Figure 3.6 shows the sequence of database actions that result in the *dirty read* problem. Transaction B starts by doing an update action to a certain database object. Later, transaction A retrieves that object and uses its values in some processing. Finally, transaction B decides to abort the transaction, returning the object to its original values.

For example, assume that a customer credit rating is being changed to a lower value by transaction B. Another transaction A tries to place an order but exceeds the credit rating, thereby rejecting the order. Transaction B discovers some error condition and aborts the transaction causing the credit rating to regain its original value. The problem is that transaction A has proceeded based on faulty data. It was dirty data, data that was not validated by a commit by the first transaction.

3.2.1.2 *Non-repeatable read*

Figure 3.7 shows the sequence of database actions that result in the *non-repeatable read* problem. In this case, transaction A starts by retrieving the database object. Then, transaction B updates the object. And finally, transaction A repeats the initial retrieval and finds that the data has changed.

This problem of nonrepeatable read often occurs in transactions processing involving large amounts of data used for summary (e.g., totals) or grouping (e.g., reports with control breaks). It is a nonrepeatable read because the data changes every time the transaction retrieves it.

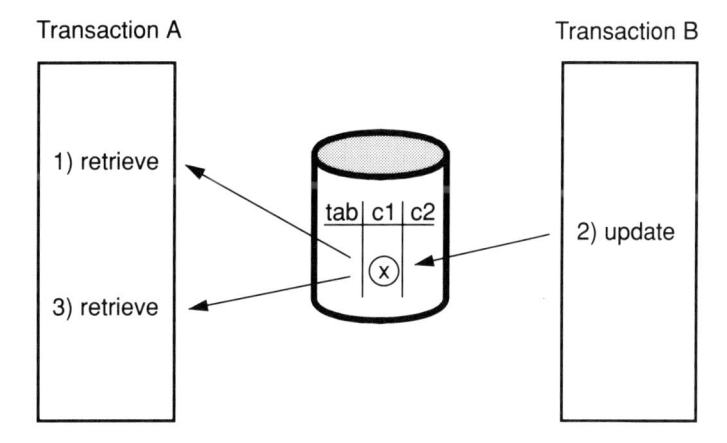

Figure 3.7. Concurrency problem: nonrepeatable read.

3.2.1.3 Phantom rows

Figure 3.8 shows the sequence of database actions that result in the *phantom row* problem, which is a special case of the previous non-repeatable read. In this case, transaction A starts again by retrieving the database object consisting of several rows. Then, transaction B inserts or deletes rows of that object. And finally, transaction A repeats the initial retrieval and finds that some of the initial rows are absent or that new rows have mysteriously appeared.

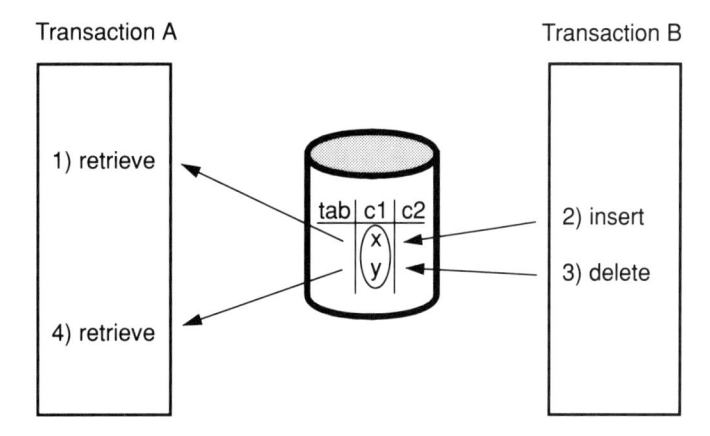

Figure 3.8. Concurrency problem: phantom rows.

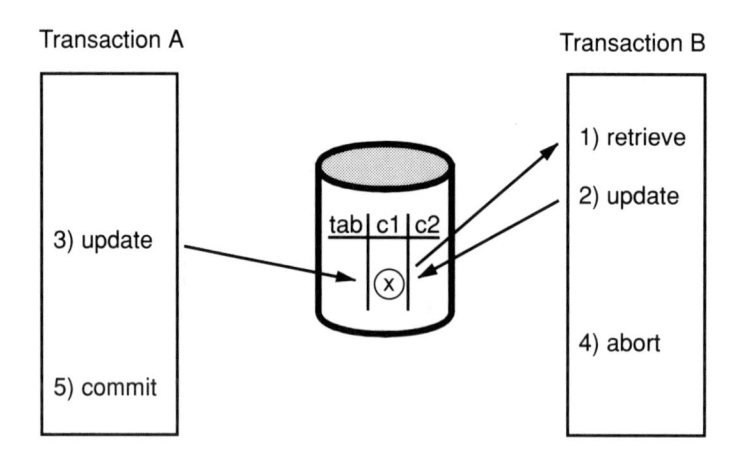

Figure 3.9. *Concurrency problem: lost update.*

This problem of phantom rows often occurs in transaction processing involving large amounts of data. For instance, a report that lists all customers in Colorado by company name may then list the same customers by zip code. The problem is that the two lists are not the same. Between the generation of the two customer lists, another transaction has deleted some old customers and inserted some new ones.

3.2.1.4 Lost update

Figure 3.9 shows the sequence of database actions that result in the *lost update* problem. In this case, transaction B starts by updating some database object. Then, transaction A also updates the same object. And finally, transaction B decides to abort its transaction.

The problem of lost update is that the changes of transaction A are lost when transaction B is aborted. And, transaction A does not realize this problem.

For example, one transaction may update a customer credit rating, followed shortly by another transaction doing the same. The first transaction aborts, causing the changes of the second transaction to disappear.

3.2.2 Pessimistic Concurrency Control

Solutions to the above concurrency problems have classically taken a pessimistic approach that locks the database object, thus preventing other transactions from using that object. The assumption is that another transaction will probably interfere with the proper execution of the current transaction. To prevent this interference, the data is locked prior to its use. For this reason, classic locking schemes are considered pessimistic.

First, let's consider what happens in a simple locking scheme. If a transaction refers (i.e., retrieves, updates, inserts, or deletes) to an object, a lock is placed on that object. Whenever another transaction refers to that object, the transaction is blocked until the specific lock is released by the first transaction. This simple lock scheme does solve most of the four concurrency problems:

- No more dirty reads: any attempt to retrieve an object that has been updated prior to commit is blocked.
- No more nonrepeatable reads: any attempt to update an object that has been retrieved is blocked.
- No more phantom rows. Well, almost. Any attempt to delete an object that has been retrieved is blocked, but any attempt to insert an object that might have been retrieved is difficult to recognize. A simple lock mechanism does not solve the problem of inserting new rows, which might cause new rows to mysteriously appear on subsequent retrievals of an earlier transaction. Various solutions have been proposed, using index locking on primary key values.
- No more lost updates: any attempt to update an object that has been updated prior to commit is blocked.

Although this simple locking scheme is effective, it does place a heavy penalty on database performance and causes another problem to occur—deadlocks. Along with the deadlock problem, let's consider several popular refinements to this simple locking scheme:

- locking types
- locking granularity
- isolation levels
- locking duration
- deadlock detection and resolution

3.2.2.1 Locking types

One rather obvious way that our simple locking scheme is wasteful is that there is only one locking type. For instance, a transaction that is only retrieving (and not updating) a database object will block another transaction that is retrieving the same object. Two or more transactions that are only retrieving data will not interfere with each other; hence, no locking is required.

The solution is to create different types of locks. For instance, consider a locking scheme in which there are shared locks and exclusive locks. If a transaction is retrieval only, it requests a shared lock. If a transaction will update, it requests an exclusive lock. Share locks are compatible; that is, a transaction requesting a share lock on an object which already has a share lock will not be blocked. Both transactions will execute concurrently without interfering with each other.

Every DBMS vendor has taken different and elaborate approaches to lock types. Other database texts describe such details (e.g., McGoveran, 1992 for Sybase SQL Server).

3.2.2.2 Locking granularity

Another refinement of the classical locking scheme is locking granularity. In the above discussion, the scope of locking was the database object, which is defined in this discussion as any data the transaction utilizes. In the simplest case, an object could be a couple of column values from a single row in a relational table, in a complex case, an object could be an entire result table materialized from joining several other tables and views. Therefore, whenever a lock of any type is placed on a database object, its scope can be narrow or broad in a very complex fashion.

In all DBMS products, the scope of locking is not mapped precisely to the database object. Instead, the scope is an approximation usually based on one of the following granularity levels:

- row (within a table)
- page (several rows within a table bounded by physical storage)
- table (all the rows within a table)

A lock manager based on these granularity levels can be implemented in an efficient manner, while a lock manager based on the precise scope of a variety of database objects would be difficult to implement and inefficient to operate.

What are the trade-offs among these granularity levels? It seems that locking should always be at the lowest level to minimize the impact on other concurrent transactions. In other words, always lock at the row level. The problem with this strategy is again one of efficiency. If there are many transactions referring to many large tables, the lock manager has a lot of locks to maintain and check. The performance degradation from lock maintenance may be greater than blocking the transaction unnecessarily with coarser granularity level. For the database administrator, the decisions related to granularity levels and current transaction mixes is time-consuming and ever changing.

3.2.2.3 Isolation levels

The third refinement to the classic locking scheme is the *isolation level*, which involves varying the locking scope during the transaction execution. There are typically two kinds of isolation levels, full isolation (also called repeatable read), and partial isolation (also called cursor stability).

In the full isolation case, the locks (of any type and granularity) are maintained for the duration of the transaction execution; in other words, any reads are repeatable. In the partial isolation case, the locks are maintained only around the area of the cursor; in other words, the data is stable only around the cursor. Only the page upon which the cursor currently resides is locked in the partial isolation case, along with any pages with updates.

The trade-off between full and partial isolation is dependent on what the transaction is doing. If the transaction updates one simple database object at a time, then partial isolation is sufficient. If the transaction scans and updates large amounts of data, then full isolation is required.

3.2.2.4 Locking duration

The fourth and final refinement to the classic locking scheme is *locking duration*, based on when locks are acquired and released from the lock manager. Normally the locks are acquired when the database object is referenced and released when the transaction is committed or aborted. There are variations, however.

First, it may be more efficient to acquire all locks when the application is initiated. If an application knows which database objects will be referenced, then it is necessary to acquire the locks all at once. The application will run at full efficiency since other transactions cannot block its execution.

Second, it may be more efficient to release all locks when the application terminates. If an application knows that database objects will be needed within several different transactions within its execution, then it

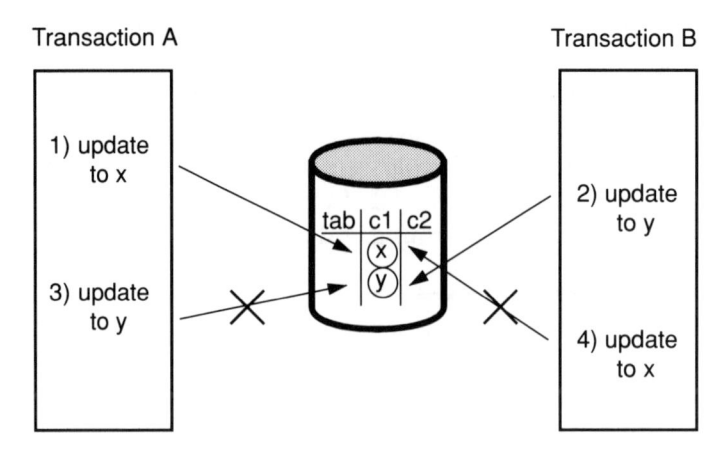

Figure 3.10. Concurrent transaction in deadlock.

is necessary to release the locks all at once at the end of the application. The application will avoid the overhead of re-acquiring those locks for each of its transactions.

3.2.2.5 Deadlock detection and resolution

We have discussed various refinements to concurrency control via classical locking. This section discusses a unique problem that occurs with any locking mechanisms: *deadlock* or the deadly embrace. When two or more transactions require access to the same set of database objects, those transactions may be blocked waiting for certain objects; the result is that all transactions are waiting indefinitely. As a simple example of a deadlock, consider Figure 3.10, in which transaction A updates object X, followed by transaction B updating object Y. The problem occurs when transaction A then attempts to update object Y, which is already locked by transaction B. Transaction A is blocked waiting for transaction B to release its locks on object Y. The deadlock is cinched when transaction B attempts to update object X. It is then blocked, resulting in both transactions waiting indefinitely on the other to release locks.

The combination of transactions and database objects causing a deadlock may be quite complex. The above illustration is the simplest case with two transactions and two objects, but a deadlock may involve any number of each.

Since the transactions are not able to prevent or resolve deadlock situations by themselves, the DBMS must be able to handle these situations. Usually there are three ways of handling deadlocks: prevention, detection, and resolution.

Deadlock prevention is very difficult to do properly; hence, few DBMS products try to prevent deadlocks. The simplest way to prevent deadlocks is to single-thread all transactions whenever they require the same set of database objects. This single thread then becomes a performance bottleneck. Another way to prevent deadlocks is to design all transactions so that they refer to database objects in a defined order. This ordering of objects is difficult to define in general, and to enforce this ordering over all transactions may be even more difficult.

Deadlock detection is absolutely necessary for the proper operation of any DBMS engine. At regular intervals (e.g., one minute), the DBMS engine should check all block transactions and their set of active locks. The engine detects a situation in which one transaction is blocked because the required object is locked by another transaction that is also blocked. By determining the sequence of blocked transactions, the DBMS engine can determine whether this sequence chains back on itself. If so, then all transactions in this sequence are in deadlock. If not, then these transactions are simply waiting for active transactions to complete.

Deadlock resolution is required once the deadlocks are detected. If the DBMS engine has determined that a certain set of transactions are in deadlock, they will wait indefinitely until the situation is resolved. Further, any other transactions that require any of the database objects locked by the deadlock transaction will also become deadlocked. This is not a desirable situation. The simplest way to resolve a deadlock is to abort one of the transactions in the deadlock. This abort will free locks for other transactions to proceed, and the aborted transaction will have to recover and be executed again. The question is which transaction to abort. There are many schemes to determine which transaction. Usually, the trick is to identify the transaction that has consumed the least amount of resources, such as locks, CPU seconds, or memory buffers.

Deadlocks are not a major problem in most systems, but they do occur on an hourly basis in active databases. Mechanisms to detect and resolve deadlocks are definitely required in any critical database. Deadlocks are quirky in their behavior. In smooth operations, they are rare. However, when the enterprise or workgroup focus its attention on spe-

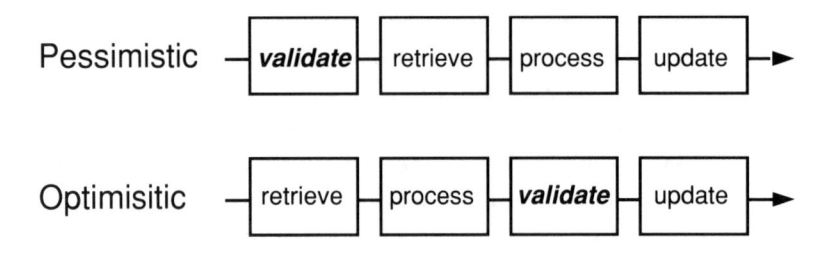

Figure 3.11. *Pessimistic versus optimistic controls.*

cific database objects (because of an emergency or exception processing), deadlocks start occurring, especially from many retrieval-only transactions blocking a few update transactions.

3.2.3 Optimistic Concurrency Control

The previous section discussed the classical (pessimistic) locking, where database objects were locked prior to usage, assuming that other transactions would probably interfere with those objects. Let's take a different approach where the assumption is optimistic (i.e., other transactions will NOT interfere). In Figure 3.11 (adapted from Özsu and Valduriez, 1991:307), the major difference between pessimistic and optimistic controls is when the data is validated by the application. With pessimistic controls, validation is performed prior to its usage, usually via a locking mechanism. The application can then perform any sequence of operations because the relevant database objects have been locked. With optimistic controls, validation is performed just prior to updating the data, usually by one of three mechanisms: value checking, timestamp ordering, and multiversioning.

Value checking is the simplest case. Just prior to updating an object, the application retrieves the object once again, checks the data values for inconsistency, and quickly updates the object. This approach is effective if considerable processing is performed prior to a decision to update an object (e.g., involving think time by the application user). It does require that the transaction utilizes an exclusive (pessimistic) lock on the object during the retrieval/update sequence (which hopefully has minor impacts). Without this locking, it is possible that the data may be changed by another transaction in the small interval between retrieval and update.

Timestamp ordering requires that the DBMS engine maintain a timestamp value whenever a database object is updated. Typically a timestamp is associated with each row in a relational table. Whenever a row is changed, the timestamp for that row is also updated. The validation involves comparing the row timestamp when data is retrieved to the two timestamp when data is to be updated. This technique is used in the Sybase SQL Server.

Multiversioning is a complex case of timestamp in which a row (or an entire page) is duplicated whenever a second transaction changes data. Depending on when the transaction is actually committed, the proper version is deemed the official version for the database. This technique is used in Interbase and Oracle.

Any of the optimistic mechanisms place an additional burden on the application logic to recover whenever the validation phase indicates data inconsistency. In the simplest case, the application can just abort the transaction and start afresh, but this simple approach may be wasteful in that some of the action within the transaction can be retained.

3.2.4 Data Uncertainty

Why are concurrency controls important? When dealing with connectivity among databases, why do we need to know about lock types, isolation levels, and such? The reason is quite simple: the value of a database is largely determined by the degree to which data can be shared, and data sharing is determined by the degree of data concurrency permitted. Finally, the degree of data concurrency is determined by the degree of concurrency control that we place on our database. The more concurrency control, the less data sharing.

Likewise, data integrity is dependent upon the degree of concurrency control. The greater the concurrency control, the greater the data integrity (or at least, avoidance of conflicts among concurrent transactions). Therefore, we have an apparent paradox in which, the more that we share data, the less integrity there is in the data.

To explore this paradox between data sharing and data integrity, we will define a new term called *data uncertainty* as the probability of knowing the real value for a certain data element. This probability is determined by a number of people (i.e., application executions) who use the same data element at the same time.

Consider the credit rating of a specific customer, for example. During a typical business day, how many people will refer to that credit rating at the same time? And, what is the probability that some other person may be changing that data? If the probability is zero, then we can share that credit rating data without difficulty. However, if the probability is not quite zero, there is an uncertainty about the precise value of that data. If someone is about to change that credit rating, that change may impact the decisions of other people in the enterprise conducting business with that customer.

Regardless of the concurrency scheme of the database system, other transactions that overlap with the update transaction will have an uncertainty as to the real value of the credit rating. Moreover in any database system, there is no indication given to these transactions (and users involving these transactions) of the degree of uncertainty.

The principle is: the more that data is shared, the more the data is uncertain. This is called the *Database Uncertainty Principle,* after the analogy of the Uncertainty Principle by Werner Heisenberg in quantum mechanics.

The conclusion is that the validity of our data in highly active databases is uncertain and that better technology of any form will not alleviate this very basic problem. There are absolute limits to the degree that we can share data across the enterprise and still retain the value of our databases. As we attempt to reap greater value from our enterprise databases by making them available to a greater number of people, we will make the data itself less valuable. If I know that there is a 50 percent chance that someone else is changing the data I am now examining, what does this data mean to me? What level of trust do I place in this data? Will I become paranoid about the data, distrusting it completely? Or, will I become apathetic about the data, not caring what its real value is?

People will have to cope with live databases, both intelligently and emotionally. The world is constantly changing, and as reflections of the true nature of this world, databases will be constantly changing. The decision processes of individuals will need to compensate for this ever changing nature of data.

▼ 3.3 SECURITY CONTROL

In the previous sections, we have discussed how to define the boundaries for a transaction and how to minimize interference among overlapping transactions. This section deals with security control, or how to specify who can use the database and for what purpose.

As a database is widely shared within a workgroup, with other workgroups, and across the enterprise, a critical concern is to ensure adequate security control of that database. Some portions of a database can be relatively open, while other portions are highly sensitive. Some people, such as the database administrator, can perform any action to the database, while others are explicitly excluded from any access to the database. Some actions (such as retrieval) are permitted by anyone, while other actions (such as drop table) are reserved for a few. Therefore, security controls must be assured and flexible.

3.3.1 Database Privileges

Most security controls in relational DBMS products are based on the emerging SQL standards for database privileges and the GRANT/REVOKE statements. It is first necessary to define carefully various levels of database privileges. A higher level of privilege allows the user to perform actions that are allowed in lower levels.

What are these privileges? Typically, you will see the following in most DBMS products:

- SELECT: retrieves data from a specific table or view
- INSERT: inserts data into a specific table or view
- UPDATE: changes data in any column for a specific table or view
- UPDATE column: changes data only in a specific column for a specific table or view
- DELETE: deletes any row in a specific table or view
- INDEX: creates an index on a column for a specific table or view
- REFERENCES: changes the referential integrity constraints between tables
- CREATE: creates a new table or view, and be the owner of that table or view
- Various administration functions: perform physical design and maintenance operations on an entire database or portions thereof (e.g., create/drop database, run statistics, allocate storage)

For the typical user, the important privileges are:

1. Can I retrieve my data (i.e., SELECT)?
2. Can I change my data (i.e., INSERT, UPDATE, or DELETE)?

82 ▼ Fundamentals of Process Management

Once those privileges have been granted by the database administrator, the user often forgets about the security controls.

3.3.2 GRANT and REVOKE

To maintain these database privileges, the DBMS product processes the GRANT and REVOKE statements, whose general syntax for handling tables or views is:

```
GRANT privilege, ... ON table/view TO user, ...
REVOKE privilege, ... ON table/view FROM user, ...
```

The upper-case terms are required as is, while the lower-case terms are to be substituted with the proper values. For "privilege" field, one or more of the above privileges can be substituted. For "table/view" field, the name of a single table or view can be substituted. For "user" field, the identification of one or more users can be substituted.

There are two interesting variations on the above syntax. First, one can grant (or revoke) ALL PRIVILEGES, meaning that the user can perform any actions to that specific table or view. Second, one can grant (or revoke) privileges to PUBLIC, meaning that all users can perform certain actions (usually retrieval) to that specific table or view.

In the case of an open database, the DBA may issue the following:

```
GRANT ALL PRIVILEGES ON table1 TO PUBLIC
```

Or, being a bit more conservative, the DBA may issue:

```
GRANT SELECT ON table1 TO PUBLIC
```

Finally, there is the question of who is allowed to issue the GRANT and REVOKE statements. When dealing with a table or view, it is the owner of that table or view, defined as the user who created the table or view.

3.3.3 View Definition

Another mechanism used for security control is the view definition. It is often forgotten as a security control, but in fact it is extremely important. With a view definition, the granularity of security can be increased down to individual data elements in complex databases.

Let's explore view definitions further. The general syntax for a view definition is quite simple:

```
CREATE VIEW view-name AS select-stmt
```

To create a view, you would give a name for the view, followed by an arbitrary SELECT statement. For instance, if you wanted anyone in the company to retrieve data on employee names and department, you would create the following view and grant SELECT on it:

```
CREATE VIEW employee AS
   select emp-name, emp-dept from emp
GRANT select ON employee TO PUBLIC
```

This is called a vertical partition since it takes a vertical slice, or set of columns, of the original "emp" table and makes it available. Note that personal information (such as home address) and sensitive company information (such as salary) is not available to PUBLIC.

We can also grant privileges for horizontal partitions (i.e., set of rows) of a table. For instance, if only information on employees in manufacturing is to be available, then the following statements would work:

```
CREATE VIEW m-employee AS
   select * from emp
   where emp-dept = "manufacturing"
GRANT select ON m-employee TO PUBLIC
```

Finally, we can use a view definition to restrict actions down to a specific value in the database. For instance, Mary is responsible for determining the credit rating for a big customer. We would grant UPDATE privileges to Mary for just that value, as follows:

```
CREATE VIEW big-cus-credit AS
   select credit from customer
      where cust-name = "BIG INC"
GRANT update ON big-cus-credit TO mary
```

3.3.4 Stored Procedures

The final mechanism for security is the stored procedure. As an alternative to granting SELECT or other privileges directly against a table or view, a database administrator could grant EXECUTE privilege, instead, to a set of stored procedures. These stored procedures can then operate upon the table or view. Figure 3.12 illustrates this concept by showing applications that invoke stored procedures, which in turn operate against the actual data. If the application or user attempts to retrieve or

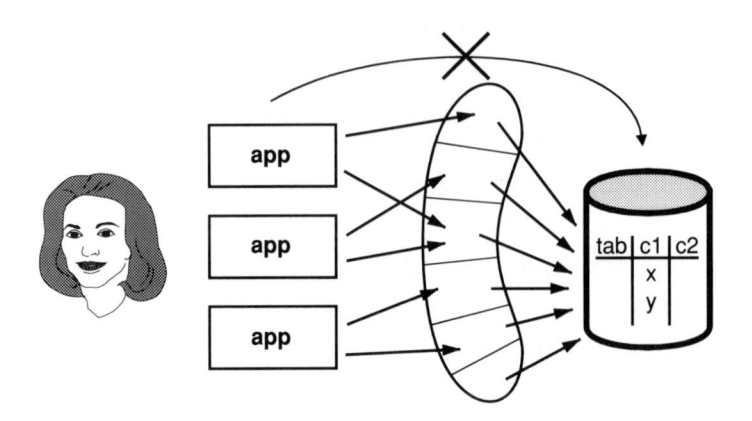

Figure 3.12. *Stored procedures as a security control.*

change the data directly, the lack of normal database privileges prevents these actions.

Within the stored procedure, the logic can check elaborate conditions to determine whether this user or application is appropriate from a security perspective. For instance, a stored procedure could check the total amount of funds transferred among bank accounts by a specific user within a 24-hour period. Limits on funds transfer could be instituted within the stored procedure as part of the bank's policies.

▼ 3.4 PROBLEMS WITH PROCESS TRANSPARENCY

The previous sections discussed various control aspects of transactions, concurrency, and security. The implicit assumption was that the application was operating against a known, predefined database. As we move into the database connectivity considerations, this assumption is no longer valid. Existing applications will have to be changed to operate against other databases, and future applications will have to be designed with the flexibility to operate against databases that are not yet conceived.

The point is that, as we consider these various control aspects, we must question the degree of transparency in changing the pairing of applications to databases. If we switch the application-database pairing, what problems may arise? In particular, what problems might occur if a different DBMS product is used?

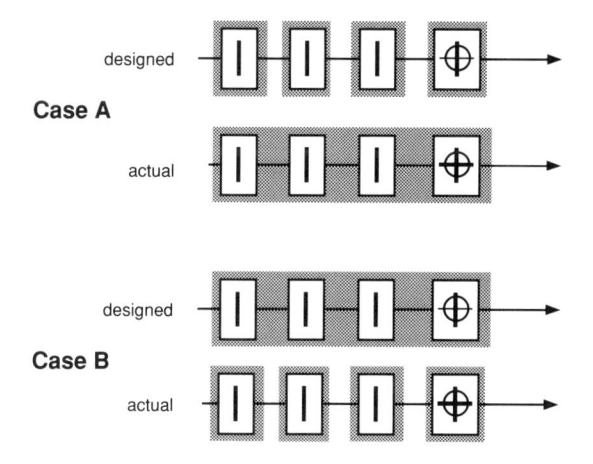

Figure 3.13. *Transaction boundaries mismatch.*

3.4.1 Transaction Boundaries Mismatch

The first problem with process transparency is a possible mismatch in transaction boundaries. If an application changes its target database, the transaction against the database may not start or end at the same points that are expected by the application.

Consider a simple example (Case A) in which the application assumes that the DBMS is automatically committing each action (request). This application may have performed correctly against a target database in which the DBMS had the autocommit mode as default. However, when the application was retargeted, the default mode was not autocommit. Note that, when an action has an error condition, an automatic rollback occurs of all actions. The application expects only the current action to be affected. But, the actual execution causes the previous actions to be also aborted, which may be a major problem for the user.

Now consider the opposite example (Case B) in which the application assumes that the DBMS only commits or aborts explicitly by a COMMIT or ROLLBACK statement from the application. However, the DBMS has a default of autocommit after each action. Now when the application issues a COMMIT or ROLLBACK, its scope is only the last statement. Therefore, it is possible that actions that were supposed to be aborted were actually not, which may also be a major problem for the user.

The mismatch of transaction boundaries may be more complex. The

Sybase SQL Server product supports nested transactions. For instance, if a program can start one transaction and then later start another transaction, normally the first transaction is automatically terminated. With nested transactions, a transaction can be started with a certain name and then selectively committed with the same name. Hence, multiple levels of transactions can exist within the same program.

If an application using nested transactions was retargeted to DB2, DB2 would return syntax errors. Further, when error conditions occur on the connection between client and server, the assumption of the DBMS is not obvious. Usually, the DBMS will perform an immediate abort, but this may not be true for all DBMS products.

3.4.2 Isolation Levels Mismatch

Another problem of process transparency involves the assumptions of isolation level by the application. Let's assume that we are dealing with only two levels: full (repeatable read) and partial (cursor stability).

Again let's consider two cases. First, the application assumes partial isolation, but the DBMS enforces full. Note that this case is OK. The application may have to perform some additional work, but the application logic will perform as expected.

Second, the application assumes full isolation, but the DBMS enforces partial. Here we have a problem. Data that were previously retrieved by the application may have been changed by another transaction. When the application decides to change that data, various concurrency problems (like lost updates) may occur.

The DBMS product should support an isolation level equal to or higher than that expected by the application. However, there is no standard way for the client to communicate that information to the database server.

3.4.3 User Identification and Privileges

The final problem with process transparency is user identification and assignment of database privileges. Each database system has an intimate linkage into its security system. As discussed in the security control section, each user who desires any kind of access to the database must first be properly identified and then assigned a set of database privileges.

First, if an application is retargeted to another database, the method for user identification may be subtly different. For example, switching an interactive DB2 user from TSO to CICS usually requires a completely different user id, even though the person is using the same database! Security parameters from terminal characteristics to database privileges must be replicated.

Second, user identification on one database system may be different on another. For instance, Jay Goode may be known as "JayG" on one database and "JGOODE" on another. Hence, the application must know which user identification is proper for which database target.

Third, the user identification may map properly among database systems, but the privilege granted to the user may vary. On one database, Jay may have retrieval and update privileges; on another, Jay has only retrieval. An application may update properly on the first database, but cause unexplained error conditions on the second database.

▼ DISCUSSION QUESTIONS

1. What is a transaction? And why is it important?

2. From memory, list the ACID properties with a one sentence definition.

3. The COMMIT and ROLLBACK statements are superfluous since a database will always commit or rollback the transaction depending on whether the application terminates normally. True or False? Why?

4. What is the major distinction between short and long transactions?

5. What are some problems that occur when two or more transactions are concurrently accessing the same data?

6. What are the differences between pessimistic and optimistic concurrency controls?

7. For pessimistic concurrency controls, what are the effects of isolation levels, locking types, locking granularity, and locking durations on performance?

8. What are the assumptions for effective SQL security controls?

9. What roles do stored procedures play with security controls?

4

BUILDING CENTRALIZED SYSTEMS

This chapter will explore the basic building blocks for centralized systems, defined as multiuser systems that are contained on one platform. The implication is that the links among components are trivial since they are on the same platform. As we distribute components on different platforms, the links among components become more complex in their nature and management.

From the perspective of centralized systems, we will concentrate in this chapter on the various layers of the application. These layers are called the Basic Application Structure and link together the presentation aspects of an application with its underlying data. We will also bring together the data aspects with the process aspects and refer to this combination as data objects.

▼ 4.1 WHY CENTRALIZED SYSTEMS?

The reader may be questioning the relevancy of a chapter on centralized systems since the book focuses on database connectivity, implying decentralized systems by its nature. The reason is quite simple: we understand centralized systems! They have served as the basis for enterprise systems for over twenty years, whether those platforms were mainframes or minicomputers. The issues of how and what to distribute across multiple platforms have become quite complex (as described in

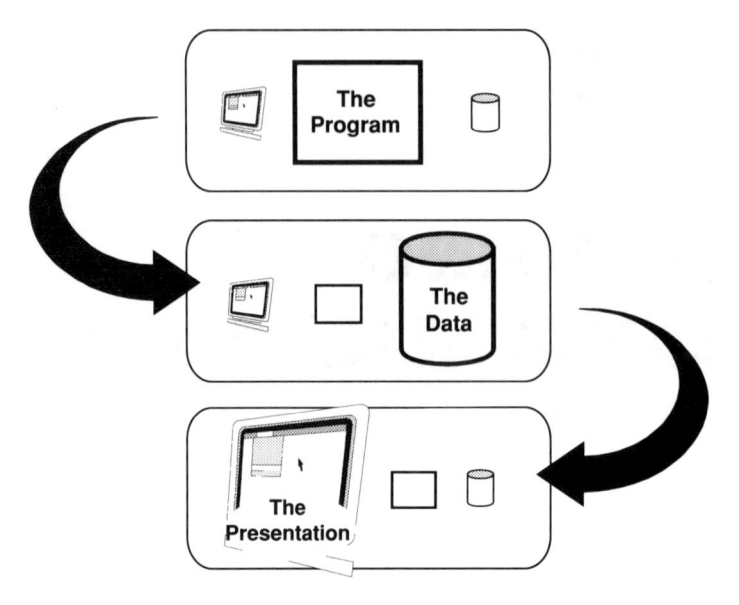

Figure 4.1. *Evolution of system architecture.*

the next chapter). This chapter concentrates on the issues that are independent of distributing components.

4.1.1 Evolution of System Architecture

Over the past twenty years, most information systems have gone through three stages of evolution, as shown in Figure 4.1. The first stage, which occurred in the 1970s, has been referred to as *program-centric* since the program was the central focus for the information system. The application program dominated the system, with the presentation and data occupying minor roles. A manager usually describes a program-centric system in terms of what applications are operational.

The second stage, which occurred during the 1980s, is referred to as *data-centric* since the database is the dominant feature. Over the past fifteen years, databases have greatly influenced application design and development. In particular, the relational data model has molded significantly our thinking about application design. Vendors of relational database management systems have flooded the industry with powerful products.

With data-centric systems, the presentation piece occupies a minor role. As described in Chapter 1, the interaction with the user can be called *procedure driven interaction* (PDI). When the application requires input from the user, the application drives that interaction according to a predefined procedure in a stimulus-response mode.

The third stage (now occurring in the 1990s) can be called presentation-centric since the manner in which data is presented to the user is the dominant feature. With high-resolution color monitors and mouse devices, we have entered the point-and-click generation of GUI applications based on widely accepted windowing environments. Also described in Chapter 1, a new style of user interaction, called *direct object manipulation* (DOM), has evolved.

Has this third stage of presentation-centric systems with direct object manipulation solved the basic problems for the industry? It certainly has solved some, but the industry is in danger of shifting too far toward presentation-centric systems, losing the benefits of prior stages. The database for a GUI application is often assumed to be a personal database that extracts from many data resources. The trend to presentation-centric systems is causing the fragmentation of enterprise information.

As stated earlier, enterprise information is to be shared, not carved into little copies and extracted into the winds. In many corporations, this results in a major problem often referred to as *extract chaos*. To share data implies that the data appears the same to all consumers. Any single change is applied to a single logical data element, and any concurrent changes to that data element are resolved; hence, consistency and integrity of data are maintained.

▼ 4.2 DATA OBJECTS AND PRESENTATION OBJECTS

To discuss the issues of sharing data in further detail, let's introduce a framework for talking about data objects and presentation objects. Figure 4.2 illustrates the concepts of data objects and presentation objects. On the right are data objects contained in the database, and on the left are presentation objects appearing on our workstation's desktop. In between, there should be some kind of linkage, which will be discussed in the next section.

First, let's refer to all accessible information resources contained in our company as *data objects* (DO), whether this information is in simple files, relational databases, object-oriented databases, or real-time data streams.

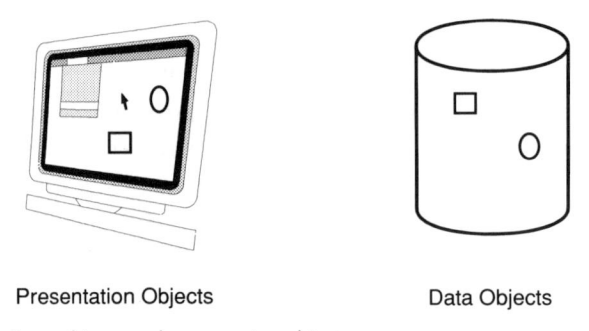

Figure 4.2. *Data objects and presentation objects.*

In an object-oriented style, we can think conceptually about these information objects as consisting of the data elements (structured in some fashion) and methods (that operated on those data elements). Using the metaphor of relational databases, we have a number of tables; each table has some columns with its typing characteristics; certain columns can uniquely identify a row in a table; and certain columns contain similar values and can be used as join paths among tables. In addition, stored procedures, triggers, and integrity constraints are the DO methods that operate on the underlying data elements.

Second, let's define another term, the *presentation object* (PO). A PO consists of its image (the way that it appears on the workstation screen) and a set of behaviors (how it responds to various user actions).

In current windowing systems (e.g., Microsoft Windows and IBM Presentation Manager), the typical components for a PO are:

- label box (displaying constant data)
- text or edit box (displaying data and allowing editing of that data)
- icons representing objects (on which actions can be performed)
- graphic or picture box (usually bit map of some image)
- frame or group box (clustering together other primitives)
- push or command button (invoking a procedure or function)
- check box or button (displaying an on/off condition)
- radio or option button (displaying a choice among several options)
- combo box (combining the list and edit boxes)
- list box (displaying several lines of data where one or more can be selected)
- scroll bars (controlling the movement through other primitives)

- sound and video players (reproducing sound and video)
- drawing primitives (such as lines, circles, etc.)

We can vary the properties of these PO primitives, such as size, positioning, coloring, active/inactive, etc. On future GUI desktops, we should be able to control multimedia, solid perspectives, 3D rotation, texturing, lighting, animation, and more. These primitives can be used to construct higher-level presentation objects by arranging the primitives into a frame or dialogue box.

Actions or events can be performed by the user to these PO primitives, such as click, double click, drag, drop, key press, key release, and so on. The PO can selectively respond to these events via a set of event-driven procedures. The events generate messages that are directed to the procedures of the underlying objects. Hence, application programs are restructured into numerous program fragments driven by complex patterns of events.

4.2.1 Sharing Data Objects

To build enterprise systems we need some mechanism to logically integrate data objects in a controlled fashion. The presentation objects are personal to the user of the workstation. If the data objects are not shared, then our information system consists of isolated islands. What are the key concepts for integrating and controlling data?

First, a DO can be shared across desktops. In the simplest case, one person should be able to share a DO with another person. Most networking systems support a simple file to be shared. But, what about sharing a relational table? Therefore, a DO on my desktop can be classified according to one of three categories:

- personal DO that is not shared
- personal DO that is shared
- shared DO from somewhere else

The mechanism for sharing should support various degrees of sharing, such read only versus update. The grant and revoke of privileges in SQL is a possible model.

Second, a shared DO can be *protected*. A protected DO implies that this information resource is shared with other users with the following characteristics:

Presentation Objects   **Data Objects**

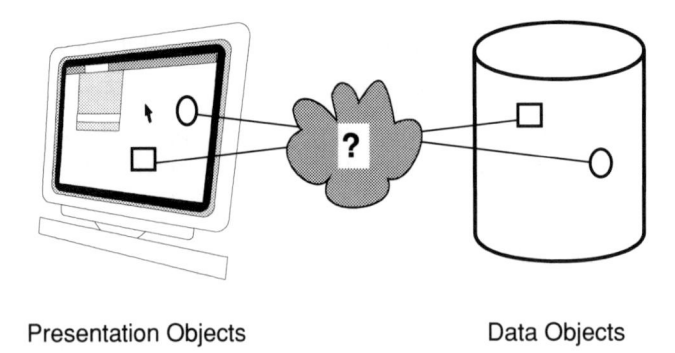

Figure 4.3. *Linking presentation objects and data objects.*

- completely secure from illegal actions
- insures integrity constraints
- maintains transaction control
- always available for access
- recoverable from disaster
- supported and maintained
- documented
- adequately managed as an organizational asset

The implication is that a protected DO is owned by a specific organizational unit within the enterprise. It is formally blessed by that organizational unit as being a valid representation of real world (at least as perceived by that unit). This unit can be a small workgroup, a department, section, division, or the entire corporation.

In summary, a data object can be shared; if shared, a data object can be protected. A protected DO is owned by an organizational unit. The sharing of data objects across the enterprise is the basis for building enterprise systems.

▼ 4.3 BASIC APPLICATION STRUCTURE

What links a presentation object to a specific data object? The collection of all presentation objects for a user is the representation in the *presentation space* (PS; i.e., desktop) for that user. Likewise, the collection of all accessible data objects for a user is the representation in the *data space* for that user. The data space reflects the important aspects of the real world for that user.

Basic Application Structure ▼ 95

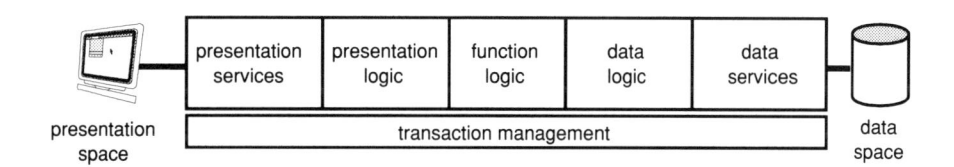

Figure 4.4. Basic application structure.

How can we maintain the PS so that it accurately reflects the real world? In general, the linkage between the presentation object and data object has the general format of a *Basic Application Structure* (BAS), consisting of a layering of functions that connect the presentation object to a data object. These layers are built upon the facilities for transaction management, which enable the application to perform a series of actions to both the presentation space and the data space as a single unit of work. To leave the database in a consistent state, all actions are performed, or none are performed.

4.3.1 Presentation Service

Presentation Service (PS) presents information to the user and receives responses from the user. The presentation services determine the image (or "look") of the desktop. In older applications, PS was a simple protocol for terminal display (e.g., VT100 or 3270). X-Windows defined a more complex display protocol for windowing. With DOM (direct object manipulation) applications, the presentation service is provided by GUI windowing products, such as Microsoft Windows and IBM Presentation Manager.

4.3.2 Presentation Logic

Presentation Logic (PL) enhances the PS and determines the behavior (or "feel") of the desktop to the user. In older applications, PL was the subroutine to accept a "yes/no" response from the user. With DOM applications, PL is typically the collection of distinct procedures invoked in response to events. For example, the action of dragging and dropping presentation objects (e.g., file icon to another directory) requires a complex logic (e.g., checking for adequate disk space).

The point is that PL maintains the integrity of the semantics of the presentation space. In other words, the look and feel of the desktop is intuitive and consistent.

4.3.3 Function Logic

Function Logic (FL) performs the business function of the specific application. FL is often called the "business rules" of the application. Unlike the other layers, FL is the only part that is unique to this specific application, independent of the presentation objects and the data objects. For example, the procedure for determining the credit rating for a new customer may involve a complex sequence of calculations, database access, and user response.

An interesting question, not yet answered, is whether FL disappears in a properly designed system. Given a well-designed set of presentation objects and data objects, is there a need for function logic? Should all function logic be incorporated on the left side (PS/PL) and/or the right side (DL/DS) of the BAS?

4.3.4 Data Logic

Data Logic (DL) determines the behavior or methods for manipulating the data objects within the data resource. In older applications, the DL was buried in the COBOL code that interpreted data record formats; it was closely intertwined with the application logic. In relational databases, relational views are a simple example of DL; views are defined in SQL logic and materialized only when requested. With more recent relational databases, DL can now be encapsulated within stored procedures that can be managed as part of the database.

4.3.5 Data Service

Data Service (DS) manages the definition of structure and manipulation of values for the underlying data objects of the data resource. In older applications, the DS was the file management of the operating systems. In relational databases, the DS is provided by a SQL interface to the relational engine.

▼ 4.4 TYPES OF LINKAGES

From a specific presentation object to its underlying data object, there are three types of linkages that filter through the various BAS layers. They are: transaction linkage, value linkage, and structure linkage.

4.4.1 Transaction Linkage

Transaction linkage is the linking of the transaction as perceived by a user manipulating presentation objects to the transaction as committed by the database system. With the older PDI applications, the transaction definition for a specific application was clearer. The application stated "Do you want to update the customer record? Y/N" With DOM applications, many data objects can be concurrently referenced and viewed as presentation objects. The issue is whether the database systems maintain concurrency controls (e.g., through exclusive locks) on the various data objects displayed. Simple concurrency controls with DOM applications can cause serious performance problems.

4.4.2 Value Linkage

Value linkage is the linkage of data values as they appear in presentation objects with the values in the data objects. A change in one should be reflected with a change in the other, realizing that the data objects are being shared with many other users. This situation becomes increasingly difficult with DOM applications. Instead of a single value being displayed for the user's consideration, massive amounts of that database can be displayed in list boxes. Should the user be permitted to change any value? If so, how do these changes flow back to the database in an efficient manner?

4.4.3 Structure Linkage

Structure linkage is the linkage of the structure of data objects (e.g., table composition, or data typing of columns) to the appropriate presentation object. For instance, one user may alter or add a column. How will that change affect the presentation objects for another user?

Structure linkage has been called impedance matching between data objects and presentation objects. This term comes from electrical engineering and describes the balancing of loads (inductive versus capacitive). If the impedance match is poor, an engineer can cause the generator to smoke!

With structure linkage, changes in the definitions of data objects must continually match the changes in the definitions of presentation objects, in either direction. If we change the structure and values of a data object, then the respective presentation object should also change. If we change the appearance and behavior of a presentation object, then the respective data object should change in its structure or values. For example, a change in the encoding of customer status may cause older applications using that data to display incorrect information about customers.

Remember that our information world is continually changing, so value or structure linkage is a critical problem. Most GUI tools and relational database systems available today are just now becoming aware of the importance of these linkages.

▼ 4.5 GENERIC LINKAGE TECHNIQUES

There are a variety of techniques for linking presentation objects to data objects. Over the years, most techniques were highly specific to the application. Since the first query tools, generic techniques have been evolving, and with the latest GUI technology on the desktop, we are witnessing an explosion of these generic techniques. There are three primary techniques used for relational databases: table viewing, row viewing, and join path viewing.

4.5.1 Table Viewing

The first conventional method for mapping a relational table DO into a GUI PO is as a list box with scroll bars. The list box displays multiple rows from the table through which one can scroll horizontally across columns or vertically across rows. This method is usually called *table viewing*. An illustration of table viewing is shown in Figure 4.5 using the sample database from Microsoft Access. The table shows the first 14 customers in order of Customer ID, along with the first four columns of the table.

This is a good generic technique if:

- the user understands the semantics of the table
- the table contains few columns (less than ten)
- the table contains few rows (a hundred or so)
- the column size is reasonable

To illustrate the problems with table viewing, consider a customer system. Assume that the critical (and largest) table is CUSTOMER, consisting of 30 million rows and over fifty columns. An analyst in the cus-

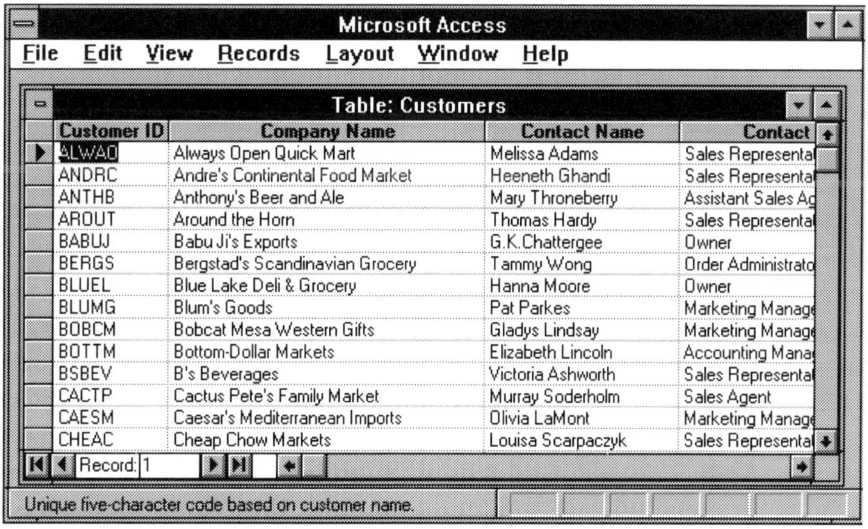

Generic Linkage Techniques ▼ 99

Figure 4.5. *Table viewing.*

tomer support group has been given the latest SQL query utility and full query privileges to the database. He eagerly does his first query:

```
SELECT * FROM CUSTOMER
```

The first 24 random customers with their first 4-5 columns were retrieved and quickly displayed on the screen. After puzzling for a few moments, he starts to scan the displayed table to the left and then down. Within seconds, he realizes that he is lost—lost in a table about the logical size of a football field while viewing the grass from a distance of 6 inches. To make things worse, the column labels are rather cryptic, with names like "CUS034_DNG".

The analyst tries another query, restricting the rows to only customers in Colorado who have submitted orders in the last two months. He unfortunately needs some technical assistance with the SQL statement since the WHERE clause requires a join with three other tables. He also selects only 12 columns which he knows contain reasonable information. After an hour of effort, the query is finally run, providing 8,534 customers, which also is not helpful.

Over these few hours, the analyst went from being excited about his discovery of this wealth of corporate information to being utterly frustrated. Although the new GUI query tool allowed him to point-and-

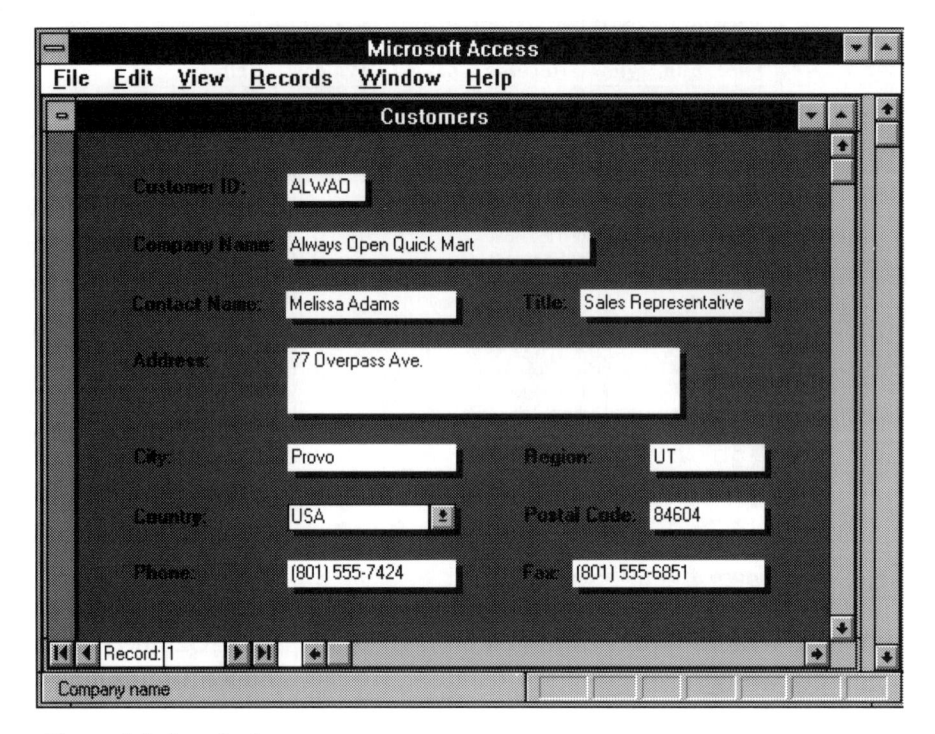

Figure 4.6. *Row viewing.*

click his way through this exploration, the basic metaphor of table viewing was inadequate.

4.5.2 Row Viewing

The second technique displays a row of data as a series of text boxes. This method is called *row viewing* since only a single row is presented at a time. An illustration of row viewing is shown in Figure 4.6, using the sample database from Microsoft Access. All the column values are displayed for a specific customer, which in this case is Always Open Quick Mart.

This method is also useful but only if:

- the user understands the semantics of the table
- the user is interested in only one row at a time
- the user is retrieving a specific row on an easy key value

- the user knows how to specify the row of interest
- the table contains few columns (less than twenty)
- the column size is reasonable

Complications arise with both of these methods when the database structure requires multiple joins across several tables to view useful information. Either views must be predefined for users or the retrieval mechanism must specify explicitly the join paths, both of which hinder generic usage of the underlying DO.

Will row viewing help our analyst? Yes, if he is interested in a specific small set of customers. For example, a certain customer can be retrieved on the customer number. Then, the values for that customer can be listed next to a column description. However, frustration for our poor analyst will come quickly when there are more than ten customers to scan. Finally, the joining of data from related tables can become more difficult.

4.5.3 Join Path Viewing

To address the complex structure problem, the third technique is viewing as a network of boxes and arrows. The boxes represent the tables, and arrows represent join paths between tables, based on the evolving concept of Bachman data structure diagrams (Bachman, 1969). This method is called *join path viewing*, since it highlights those join paths. An illustration of join path viewing is shown in Figure 4.7, using the sample database from Microsoft Access. The various tables in the database are displayed with their column names, along with lines indicating the possible join paths among the tables.

This method has the following limitations: values within tables are hidden from the user, complex join paths are confusing to the user, and values are awkward to edit in the underlying tables. It does, however, help our analyst to see where the CUSTOMER table relates to other tables. But with over 130 tables, the screen showing the possible join paths can become very confusing.

Each of the above techniques can be of value to an analyst in certain situations, but often these techniques are limited since they present all data objects in a simple generic manner. One relational table looks like another table to the user. There is little differentiation based on the underlying semantics.

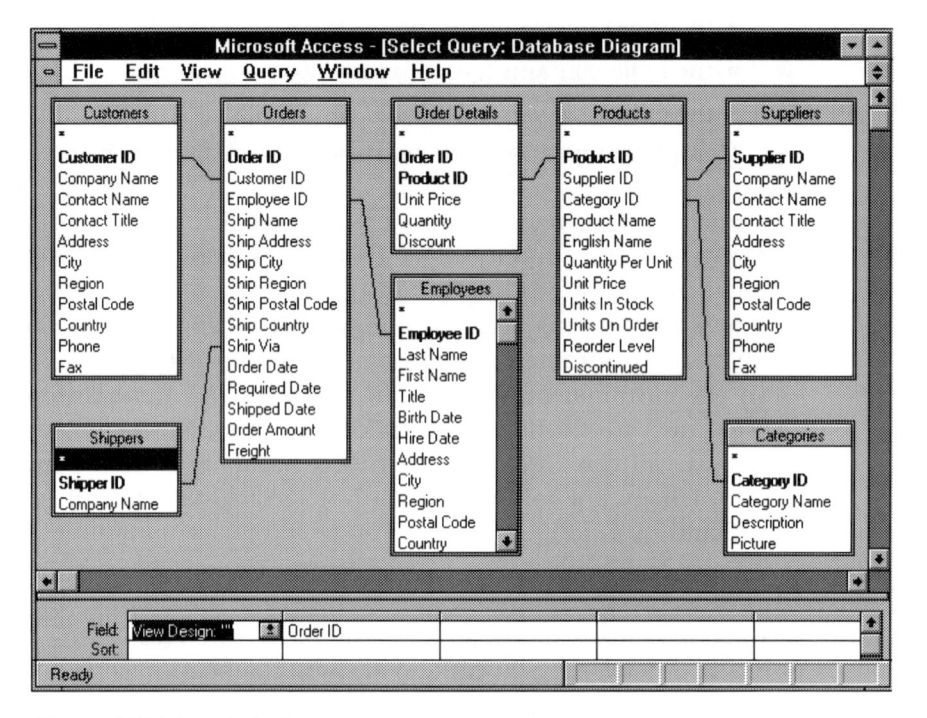

Figure 4.7. Join path viewing.

▼ 4.6 ROLES OF CLIENT AND SERVER

In the basic application structure (explained previously), who is the client and who is the server?

This question may seem to be unrelated to this chapter with its focus on centralized systems. Client and servers have to do with distributed systems, and besides, the questions seem to be trivial. The user (i.e., presentation space on left) is always the client, and the database (i.e., data space on right) is always the server. Right?

Not necessarily! The roles of client and server are very relevant to centralized systems. In fact, these roles give us clues for properly designed applications for stand-alone workstations. And, users are not always clients. In fact, the more interesting architectures are ones in which these roles are reversed.

What are the definitions of client and server? The *client* is the component that initiates action and requests services, while the *server* is the component that responds to requests and generates results. The client is the active element since only it initiates actions. On the other hand, the server is the passive element since it only responds to requests. One might even argue that the client-server roles are essentially a master-slave relationship.

It is true that normally the user (via presentation services) initiates actions. However, database systems are becoming more active (for example, with triggers) and could initiate action to which the user should respond. Further, the client-server roles can be extended to include situations in which users directly interact with other users (such as in the case of electronic mail and groupware) and in which databases directly interact with other databases (such as copy management).

So, our world continues to become more complex. In the next chapter, we will examine distributed systems including various forms of client-server architecture extending to peer-to-peer architectures.

▼ DISCUSSION QUESTIONS

1. Why build centralized systems today, when all the exciting technology deals with distributed systems?

2. Is a protected data object important? Why or why not?

3. What are the layers of the basic application structure? Do you see a clear distinction among them?

4. What are the distinctions in the roles of a client and a server? Are these roles basically a master-slave relationship? Are these distinctions relative to centralized systems?

▼ 5
BUILDING DISTRIBUTED SYSTEMS

This chapter explores the basic architectures for *distributed systems*, which are defined as multi-user systems that have components on more than one platform. In contrast to the previous chapter, the implication is that the links among components are the important aspects of distributed systems. This chapter describes the motivation for distributed systems and alternatives for distributing data and process.

▼ 5.1 WHY DISTRIBUTED SYSTEMS?

Much of the industry literature deals with some issue related to distributed systems. Our current mind-set is that centralized systems are antiquated and that distributed systems are the obvious wave of the future. The reasoning behind this mind-set tends to be muddled with visions of extraordinary feats of productivity from personal computers. We certainly do owe a lot to the emergence of personal computers in delivering on many of the old promises of information technology. However, are we really moving toward an architecture for enterprise systems that consists of a vast sea dotted with personal computer islands?

An analogy that is becoming more appropriate every day is our international telephone systems. It certainly is true that the image of the telephone system for most people is a vast sea of telephones. Thirty years ago there was one telephone per household, so that a telephone number denoted specific geographic location and, further, a specific family social unit. When the 800 prefix replaces the area code in a phone number, this geographical information is lost, and the caller does not know where the respondent is located. The 800 prefix number thus actually denotes a service of some kind. Likewise, with cellular phones, the phone number does not necessarily indicate location, since it is likely that the person is in an automobile driving somewhere. Instead, the telephone number actually denotes a person; it has become a personal identifier of sorts. Finally, with international calls, you can easily call a colleague in Europe and not realize the complexity of bridging that is required among dissimilar telephone systems.

Using the telephone analogy, should our enterprise systems evolve towards this kind of completely distributed architecture? There is a fallacy with this question: The telephone system is not basically distributed. Within a particular country, a telephone system is highly centralized in several layers of hierarchy. Each phone is connected into a central office within a metropolitan region, which can connect to other central offices and on to other areas. In fact, the telephone system is more comparable to a strict military organization. And yet, it appears distributed in scope and so responsive to our needs.

What can we learn, if anything, from this analogy? First, a centralized system can be responsive to the needs of its users. Inherent in a centralized architecture is not the image of a fortress whose walls inhibit access to its warmth and comfort. That image is more of a political artifact than a technological one. A centralized system, properly designed, can be efficient and effective in its functionality. From the Roman Empire to British seapower in the 1800s, such architectures have served us well for thousands of years in areas unrelated to information technology.

Second, the value of any system to the enterprise comes not from isolated islands of self fulfillment, but from sharing resources and coordinating activities. In fact, an extreme example of decentralized systems can appropriately be defined as anarchy or chaos. To the same extent that we all utilize public highways (i.e., sharing resources) and obey traffic signals (i.e., coordinating activities), we do give up a degree of personal freedom for a larger degree of personal benefit. On the other hand, if we all were forced to ride in buses, we might conclude that a balance involving less personal freedom was not desirable.

5.1.1 Advantages

What is the proper balance? Let's list the apparent advantages and then disadvantages to distributed systems.

5.1.1.1 *Local autonomy*

This advantage is political, not technical, in nature. Let's start by considering our ultimate IT world again. What if technology costs were zero; processing power was infinite; storage capacity was infinite; communication bandwidth was infinite; and everything worked with perfect reliability? There would then be no technical advantage to distributed systems! However, there is still a political advantage: autonomy.

A distributed system allows its subsystems to be loosely coupled. Hence, the subsystems can be relatively independent of one another. From a political perspective, the subsystems can have differing values and motivations. Subsystems can pursue their self-interests while striking a proper balance of sharing resources and coordinating activities with other subsystems.

Further, the reason that many people prefer autonomy is simply that they cannot understand the immense complexity of the greater system and therefore do not trust it. A lack of understanding implies a lack of control, which implies a lack of self-determination.

In summary, a manager seeks responsibility for a piece of the enterprise that he or she can understand, control, and trust, along with the appropriate information system for that piece. This motivation for autonomy is probably the most powerful force pushing distributed systems in our enterprises. It certainly has been the powerful force behind events in eastern Europe.

5.1.1.2 *Reliability and availability*

In our real IT world, our systems need to function properly. Reliability means that the system performs its function as designed or predicted. Availability means that the system performs its function whenever it is required. Both are necessary: a reliable system that is not often available is useless; an available system that is not adequately reliable is also useless. Distributed systems have improved reliability and availability because failure in one subsystem has limited effects on other subsystems.

5.1.1.3 *Cost reduction and avoidance*

The third advantage is cost reduction and avoidance. The old economics of scale that favored large computers in the 1960s have completely reversed. Today's guideline is that, the smaller the computer, the better cost performance. Therefore, the most cost-effective solution is to choose the smallest computer that is able to perform the task. Distributed systems allow the luxury of utilizing these smaller computers within a consistent context.

5.1.1.4 *Improved performance*

Improvements in processor power (e.g., instructions per second) are becoming more difficult. It is hard to build a 1000-MIPS machine! However, it is relatively easy to assemble one hundred 10-MIPS machines as a symmetrical multiprocessor. If one can coordinate those hundred machines, we can attain the power of a 1000-MIPS machine. Therefore, a distributed system can have greater performance than a centralized system by distributing the processing load among many processors. The critical issue is coordination among the processors.

5.1.1.5 *Flexibility and scalability*

Because of the complexity of size and heritage, centralized systems have the reputation of being inflexible. Small changes require large efforts and high costs. Distributed systems can be more flexible because changes can be made in one subsystem without impacting other subsystems. Further, the advantage of scalability is an important facet of flexibility. Distributed systems can be more scalable because additional subsystems can be added without impacting existing subsystems.

5.1.1.6 *Compatibility with desktop*

If the new paradigm is "the application is the desktop," our future systems had better be compatible with the desktop. Incorporating the desktop into our enterprise system by definition creates a distributed system. Some significant level of process and data must exist at the desktop to attain the advantages of the desktop; hence, distributed systems have a more compatible architecture for accomplishing this.

5.1.2 Disadvantages

Having considered the advantages, let's face the question of what we give up when we distribute.

5.1.2.1 Loss of reliability

The first disadvantage is a lost of reliability as compared to centralized systems, particularly mainframe platforms. This disadvantage seems to contradict the second advantage above. How can distributed systems have both improved reliability and a loss of reliability?

There are different aspects to this issue of reliability. It is certainly true that distributed systems have greater reliability because a failure in one subsystem has less impact on others. On the other hand, centralized systems have evolved greater degrees of reliability over the years by increasing reliability of individual components and by adding redundant components. Centralized systems also became more reliable by surrounding themselves with an infrastructure of policies and procedures (such as the glass house). Because it was necessary, mainframe systems pursued this greater reliability and this characteristic is one of their salient features. Therefore, when one discusses with an experienced *mainframer* the placement of an important application on many LAN-based servers, expect the natural reaction of surprise and dismay based on this perceived loss of reliability.

5.1.2.2 Loss of security

Centralized systems have an inherent security advantage because safeguards can be controlled better and placed at a smaller number of locations. It is much easier to guard a single fortress than a bunch of islands.

5.1.2.3 Increased complexity

A distributed system is more complex when viewed as a whole. The pieces are simpler, but not the whole. With distributed systems, there are more complex procedures for synchronization and coordination. Of course, this complexity is only apparent when dealing with the whole. If no one deals with the whole (that is, there is an absence of top-down design and management of the enterprise system), this complexity is not a problem. However, this situation implies that there is no enterprise system, only a federation of individual or workgroup systems.

5.1.2.4 Lack of experience

We do not understand fully distributed systems on the scale of a large corporation. Therefore, we are going to have great difficulty designing, implementing, and maintaining such systems. Even if there are a few people who can understand, there are not very many of them, and dis-

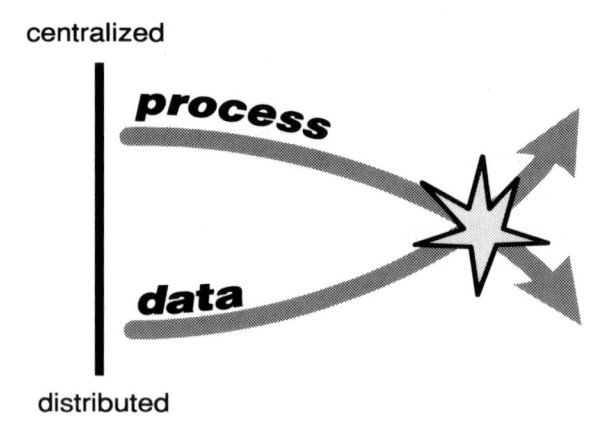

Figure 5.1. *Process and data have conflicting trends.*

tributed systems by their nature are going to require a great number of these knowledgeable people.

5.1.2.5 Difficulty with transition

In the typical large corporation, we have spent fifteen to twenty-five years evolving our current enterprise systems. These systems are called *legacy systems* and are critical to the operation of the enterprise. They cannot be replaced overnight. Even if today the technology were stable and the design were determined, the transition to a distributed system would take three to five years.

5.1.2.6 Difficulty with administration and maintenance

This is the real clunker! Assume that all previously mentioned problems are resolved, how do you administer and maintain a distributed system across a large enterprise? For instance, how do you perform a schema change to 500 LAN databases?

5.1.2.7 Natural conflicts in distributing data and process

The two trends in distributing process and integrating data are in fundamental conflict with one another! Over the past fifteen years, we have witnessed two main trends in the computer industry. One trend is to distributed process, first through minicomputers, then through personal computers, and now through workgroup servers. The second trend is to logically integrate data across the enterprise, usually through centralized databases on mainframes.

Today, every architectural decision to deploy a critical enterprise application to the desktop or to adopt a workgroup-level relational database may enhance process distribution at the expense of data integration. Hence, we often have a tense confrontation between those who want to empower users with GUI applications and those who want to empower the enterprise with quality information.

5.1.3 Summary

In summary, the advantages of distributed systems are:
- local autonomy
- improved reliability and availability
- cost reduction and avoidance
- improved performance
- improved flexibility and scalability
- compatibility with the desktop

The disadvantages of distributed systems are:
- loss of reliability
- loss of security
- increased complexity
- lack of experience
- difficulty of transition
- difficulty of administration and maintenance
- natural conflict between distributing data and process

Based on this summary, the reader is probably questioning the sanity of anyone considering distributed systems, since the disadvantages seem to outweigh the advantages. Temper this questioning, however, with the realization that essentially all existing systems are distributed to some degree. A large enterprise does not have one mainframe; it has dozens of data centers, each of which may contain several mainframes. Systems are already distributed today.

What we are exploring in this book is simply the next stage in the evolution, not revolution, of distributed systems. We have today all the advantages and disadvantages mentioned above; we are simply fine-tuning the balance between centralized and decentralized systems while accommodating new technologies that give us greater freedom of design.

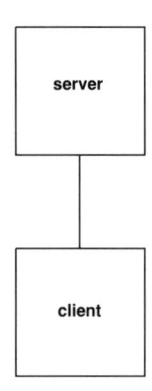

Figure 5.2. *Simple client-server architecture.*

The challenge is how to deploy enterprise applications to the desktop while allowing the sharing of data to and from that desktop. As we will see, this challenge involves greater degrees of distributing process and data to workgroups in terms of LAN database servers.

▼ 5.2 CLIENT-SERVER ARCHITECTURES

Let's consider the different types of distributed systems from the perspective of client-server architectures and the various ways in which distributed systems can be designed.

The first approach to distributed systems is the simple *client-server architecture* (CSA). Figure 5.2 shows a simple and pure version of client-server architecture. By arbitrary convention, we will show the client on the bottom and server on top. The role of the client is to initiate a request for some kind of service, while the server responds to this request, performs the service, and returns results/status to the client. The client role is active; the server role is passive. In pure CSA, the server cannot initiate anything; the client cannot respond to requests from other clients. There is a clear role differentiation; you might even state that the client is the master, and the server is the slave.

The service provided by the server can be anything. In later sections, we will emphasize database servers, where SQL requests are generated by a client, and relational result sets are returned by the server. In contrast, a print server consumes data only to spool the data to some print device.

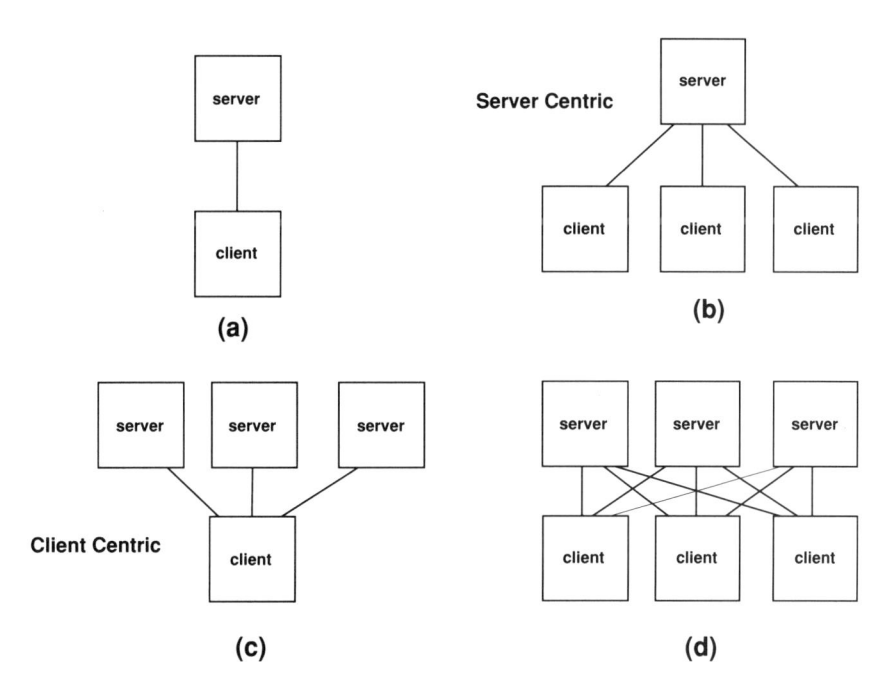

Figure 5.3. Bilevel client-server architectures.

5.2.1 Bilevel CSA

Next, let's extend simple CSA into a more general category of *bilevel CSA*. The usual CSA configuration found in most companies is shown in (b). We will refer to this configuration as *server-centric* CSA, in which many clients are serviced by a single server. On the other hand, most users think of their world as (c), or a *client-centric* CSA. Through various communication links, a user can connect to various servers, each offering a variety of services.

The more realistic configuration is shown in (d), where there is some mixture of clients and servers. In this configuration, it is useful to consider two ratios. The first ratio is the *client-to-server ratio*, which indicates the average number of clients supported by a typical server. This ratio is useful in scaling the server platform. The design of a server platform would be quite different for a ratio of 10 versus a ratio of 1000.

The second ratio is the *server-to-client ratio*, which indicates the average number of servers accessible by a typical client. If this ratio is small (i.e., 1 to 5), the client software can assume specific servers for specific

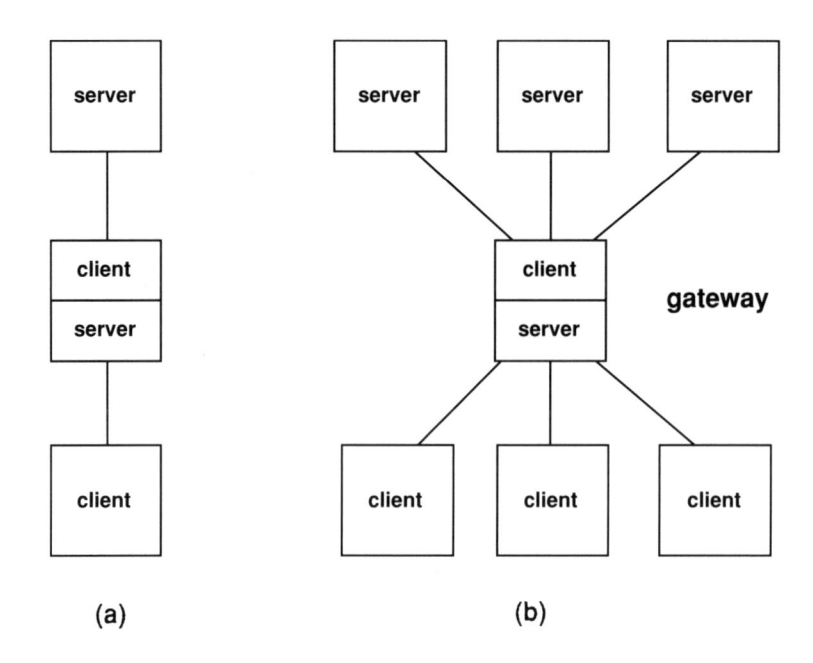

Figure 5.4. *Multilevel client-server architecture.*

functions, without involving the user. However, as this ratio grows (i.e., 10 to 100), the client software must have greater intelligence to guide the user through the server maze.

5.2.2 Multilevel CSA

Figure 5.4 extends CSA to multilevel CSA. In multilevel CSA, we allow an application to assume both the role of client and the role of server in various degrees. In other words, an application of some platform will be a server to some clients and, concurrently, a client to some servers. We refer to an application of this nature as a *gateway* since it acts as a gateway for clients to various other servers, while adding some kind of value in the process. If the gateway did not add significant value, it would be better for the client to connect directly to the proper server.

One case of multilevel CSA is shown in (b). The main objective of this gateway is one of server transparency. In other words, clients blindly connect to a specific gateway and submit their requests. The gateway interprets these requests and routes the requests to the appropriate server. We refer to this type of gateway as a *routing gateway*.

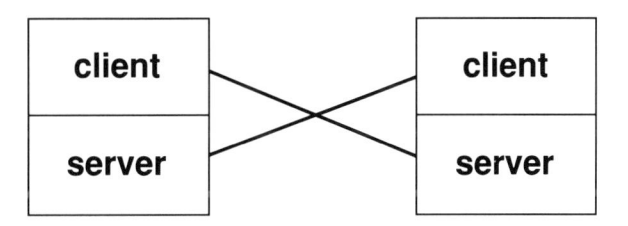

Figure 5.5. Peer-to-peer architecture.

5.2.3 Peer-to-Peer CSA

Figure 5.5 shows a further extension of CSA to a *peer-to-peer architecture* (PPA). We can consider PPA the most general case of CSA. Each of the nodes in PPA assumes roles of both client and server interchangeably. In fact, it becomes dysfunctional to dwell on who is the client or server. It is a case where processes interact with other processes on a peer basis. There is no master or slave.

5.2.4 Local and Remote Servers

We have covered three types of client-server architectures: bilevel, multilevel, and peer-to-peer. Now, let's consider a different perspective on CSA: the difference between local and remote servers. In Figure 5.6, we have a LAN with several clients and a couple of servers. Since they are

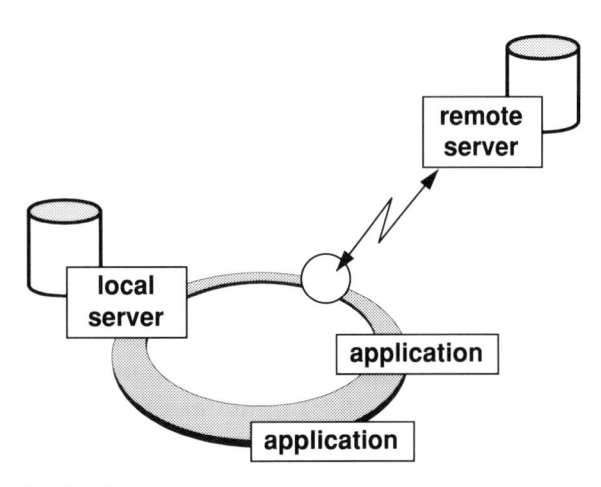

Figure 5.6. Local and remote servers.

connected via the LAN, these servers are called *local servers*.

Why are they called local servers? What is special about them? First and most obvious, the LAN provides a high bandwidth between client and server. Moving data across the LAN can be 10 to 100 times faster *and more reliable* than moving data across a Wide Area Network (WAN). Hence, the protocols and functions for connecting clients to local servers will take advantage of this speed and reliability and provide a closer logical coupling.

Second, the local server has a well-defined clientele. We can design and customize the local server to serve the clients on this specific LAN. We are not burdened with providing service to the riffraff across the enterprise; we can concentrate our resources on the requirements of our local clients.

Third and most important, the local server is often *owned* by the workgroup. This is a political distinction, not technical one. Consider the following statement: "It is *my* local server! I determine who is provided service and to what degree. I fund its acquisition and maintenance, and I am responsible for its operation (although others do the actual work). I know well the clientele for this server and can effectively design the proper applications. I am not burdened with providing services to other people. I concentrate resources on the important problems of my workgroup." Now, substitute for the pronoun "I" the manager of your favorite workgroup, department, or section. This describes the political notion of a local server.

Let's now take the next step and discuss the *remote server*. According to the figure, the remote server is remote to the LAN. There is a communication link from the local-area network to a wide-area network. Across this link, a client can connect to the remote server and be provided its specific service. This remote server could be a local server on some other LAN. Or, it could be a remote server to every client, such as with a mainframe-based server. But, we must be careful. A mainframe-based server could be attached to a single (very special) LAN and be appropriately considered a local server. Therefore, the terms local server and remote server are relative terms, depending on the factors of bandwidth and reliability, clientele commonality, and ownership.

With the advent of fiber optics as the physical interconnection for enterprise LANs, we are observing a blurring of this distinction between local and remote servers in all three categories.

First, as fiber optics are used, LAN bandwidth and reliability increase enormously, completely removing any technical motivation for close geographic placement of LAN components. As fiber optics become the basis for international networks, a "local server" to a workgroup can be placed anywhere in the world, given the same performance to that workgroup.

Second, once a server is available via a global fiber optic network, its clientele can be anywhere. Thus, the ability of a local server to focus its services and predict its demand loads diminishes.

Third, the differences in ownership and autonomy between local and remote servers also become indistinct. If the workgroup server is located a considerable distance and maintained by a separate group, the feeling of ownership and the reality of autonomy are difficult to instill.

Therefore, the advent of fiber optics can blur and even completely eliminate the distinctions between local and remote servers. To the systems designer, this can be constructive in terms of simplifying and consolidating system resources from an enterprise perspective, while delivering significant cost performance advantages. However, coherence of workgroup-centric designs will be more difficult.

It has now become necessary to refine the local-remote distinction with a workgroup-enterprise distinction. Let's define a *workgroup server* as a server owned by a workgroup and focused on supporting the information processing for that workgroup. Likewise, an *enterprise server* is a server owned by the entire enterprise (or a major portion thereof). It shares data and services across organizational boundaries and functions. It consolidates expensive resources so that they also are shared. It provides a common point of coordination so that the enterprise can move forward in a coherent direction.

What are the implications of these new definitions? There are two conclusions. First, we must evolve all servers towards local servers. WAN transports are a throw-back to days of poor communication networks. LAN transports provide better levels of service (e.g., closer coupling) for database applications. Enterprise servers especially must evolve toward being local servers so that they provide the same level of service as the local workgroup server. If not, the good aspects of being an enterprise server will die side-by-side with its poor service levels. The conclusion is that global fiber optics are necessary for building effective enterprise systems in the future.

Second, we must maintain a dynamic balance between workgroup servers and enterprise servers. We need a balance that is constantly changing as workgroup services become centralized within the enterprise servers (i.e., *up-scaling*) and enterprise services become decentralized into workgroup servers (i.e., *down-scaling*). In the chaos of current business environments, we can no longer design the system once from a top-down perspective. In conclusion, up-scaling and down-scaling are necessary for building healthy enterprise systems in the future, but we do not have the tools (or even the understanding) for accomplishing this.

5.2.5 Generic versus Custom Services

In the previous discussions, it was assumed that a client requests some service and the server responds with this service. But, what is this service?

In general, there is a great difference between generic and custom services. *Generic services* are those services that have value across a range of systems, regardless of the environment or functions of the system. *Custom services* are those services unique to a specific system, having been designed and implemented for a particular environment and function. There is obviously a wide dynamic spectrum between generic and custom services.

An example of a generic service is an SQL database server that accepts only SQL requests and returns relational result sets. On the other hand, a custom service could be built for a specific application server using a simple stored procedure or remote procedure call that invokes a remote process passing a few arguments.

A major design decision for distributed systems is where on this generic-custom spectrum we decompose our system into the client and server roles. To explore this issue further, let's revisit the Basic Application Structure from the previous chapter.

▼ 5.3 SLICING THE BASIC APPLICATION STRUCTURE

In Chapter 4, we discussed the Basic Application Structure (BAS) as the mechanism to link the presentation space with the data space. As we now consider distributed systems, the issue is where do we slice the BAS. In other words, where do we separate the client component from the server component? Note that the BAS can be separated in more than

Slicing the Basic Application Structure ▼ 119

Figure 5.7. *Slicing the BAS.*

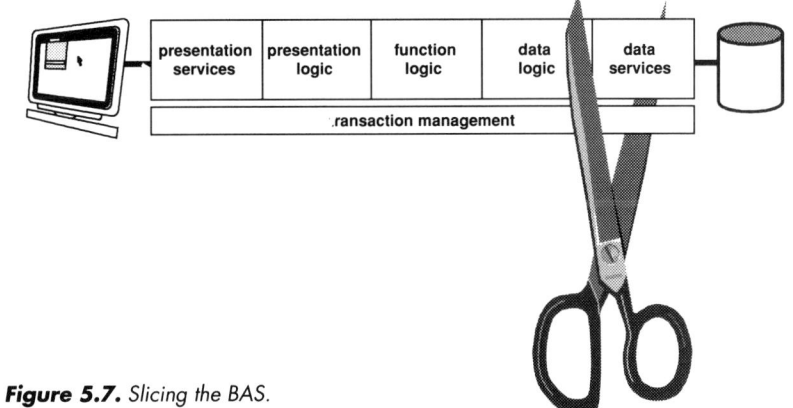

one place, thereby creating multilevel CSA as described above. Figure 5.8 shows various ways of decomposing the BAS between the client and server. In the following sections, we'll consider each of these arrangements.

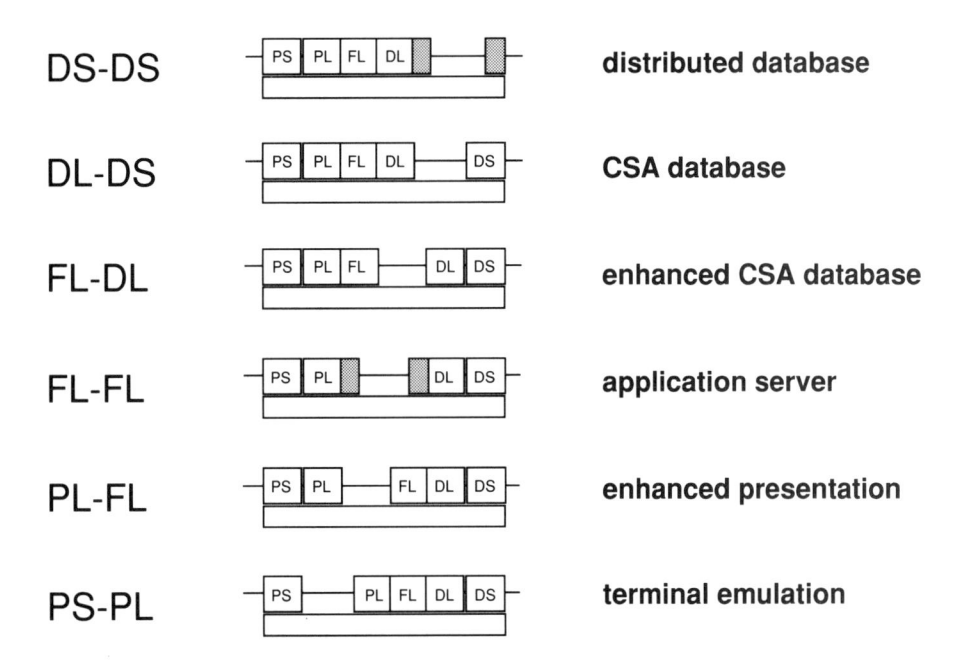

DS-DS	PS PL FL DL	**distributed database**
DL-DS	PS PL FL DL — DS	**CSA database**
FL-DL	PS PL FL — DL DS	**enhanced CSA database**
FL-FL	PS PL — DL DS	**application server**
PL-FL	PS PL — FL DL DS	**enhanced presentation**
PS-PL	PS — PL FL DL DS	**terminal emulation**

Figure 5.8. *Various BAS arrangements.*

5.3.1 Distributed Database

The first arrangement slices the BAS within the Data Services, thus allowing the database itself to be distributed. This arrangement has traditionally been called distributed database and is the topic of a following section. In this situation, the client and the database system reside on the same platform. Although some data must also reside on that platform, the implication is that the database is distributed on other platforms; hence, the database system must coordinate with other nodes to process the data requests by the client application. The important point is that the client application is not aware of the data distribution.

5.3.2 CSA Database

The second arrangement slices between the Data Services and Data Logic, indicating that data language (usually SQL) is used as the basis of the protocol. This arrangement is CSA database in a conventional sense.

For example, a COBOL application could be written on a DOS platform using the IBM SAA Common Programming Interface for SQL. Connecting via IBM LAN Server NetBios protocol on a token-ring network, the application could then process data against an IBM Database Manager on an OS-2 Extended Services/2 platform. Other examples include xBase application on a DOS Platform connected to another DOS platform with Borland dBase. The first example uses SQL as the basis for the protocol between client and server, while the second example uses the xBase language. Because SQL is higher level (i.e., less data oriented) that xBase, the first example slices the BAS more to the left than the second example.

5.3.3 Enhanced CSA Database

The third arrangement slices between the Data Logic and Function Logic, indicating that the protocol would be a method invocation against higher-level data objects. Examples include object-oriented database systems and relational database systems extended with stored procedures and the like. For example, a Windows application written in C++ on a DOS platform could connect via named pipes to Microsoft SQL Server on a Windows/NT platform. The application would only execute stored procedures without any normal SQL statements. The logic for performing those procedures would be contained entirely within the database.

5.3.4 Application Server

The fourth arrangement slices the BAS within the Function Logic, usually indicating a Remote Procedure Call (RPC) mechanism. Since part of the application logic resides on the server, the services are typically more customized, or specific to a certain application.

For example, a Motif application written in C on a Sun platform could connect via TCP/IP using the Sun RPC mechanism to other application code accessing RMS files on a VAX VMS platform. The client logic and server logic would be closely coupled.

5.3.5 Enhanced Presentation

The fifth arrangement slices between the Function Logic and Presentation Logic, implying that all of the application resides on the service with only the presentation residing on the client. Examples would be applications using X-Windows, Motif, or Open Look presentation protocols.

5.3.6 Terminal Emulation

The final arrangement slices between the Presentation Logic and Presentation Services, which is similar to Enhanced Presentation but at a lower level of presentation. The implication is that the client platform is only performing simple presentation functions (e.g., VT100 or 3270), while the server performs all other functions.

For this perspective, we have been using client-server systems for twenty years! The truth is that more end-user workstations in corporations are still used primarily for terminal emulation to mainframe systems than in a normal client-server architecture. The basic issue is the amount of logic exiting on the client platform and its contribution to the application for the user.

5.3.7 General Comparisons

This is an area of controversy caused by a clash of two cultures: database bigots and programming fanatics. Does this clash not appear like the division between data-orientation and process-orientation mentioned earlier?

From the database culture, the most effective arrangements are those that best utilize current technology, especially mature relational database systems (such as DB2, Oracle, or SQL Server) combined with widely used GUI presentation services (such as Microsoft Windows, or IBM PM).

In other words, the preferred architecture should deal with an SQL-level protocol at some level. Languages that are lower level than SQL have been shown to be relationally incomplete (i.e., you cannot do everything to the data) and insecure (i.e., you can bypass normal security). On the other hand, languages of a higher level lack industry acceptance. Nonrelational data resources can participate if they are viewed externally as relational data manipulated by a simplified SQL language.

Therefore, the database bigots would strongly argue for either a conventional CSA database or maybe an enhanced CSA database based upon SQL.

From the programming culture, the most effective arrangements are those that the programmer can design and control, especially in terms of performance and recovery. This perspective emphasizes an application server in which application logic exists on both client and server. The preferred method for interprocess communication would be some type of RPC that follows the model of procedures calling subprocedures. Therefore, the programming fanatics would strongly argue for either enhanced presentation using Motif or application servers based upon the RPC mechanism.

In conclusion, both perspectives fail to realize that their positions are quite close together. Through the wonderful dynamics of the marketplace, the substantive differences are gradually eroding as products adopt whenever features are required to stay competitive. For example, if you want an application server using RPC, use SQL Server and program the application logic into the stored procedures using the RPC format for DB-Library. If you then object to using Transact-SQL as your programming language, are you arguing on the basis of style, rather than substantive functionality?

The final point is that most actual systems are mixtures in any case. Usually there is not a clean separation into a bilevel CSA (i.e., client platform connected to a server platform). In the future, most database systems will be distributed to some degree; most SQL will be enhanced; most RPC mechanisms will return multiple result sets; most presentation systems will integrate with a local object-oriented database; most systems will be networked in confusing ways. Now, you figure out whether and how your system is doing client-server!

The real challenge will be to have the proper design and maintenance tools and methodology to evolve current systems by enhancing them with the particular technology that offers the greatest leverage.

▼ 5.4 WAYS OF DISTRIBUTING DATA

This section discusses the ways of distributing data, first by summarizing conventional notions of distributed database and then by describing partition and copy techniques.

5.4.1 What is a Distributed Database System?

For over ten years, the topic of *distributed databases* (DDB) has been discussed. (see Özsu and Valduriez, 1991). The motivation has been to provide a comprehensive solution to distributing data across the enterprise. The conventional approach has been to incorporate the entire support for DDB within a DBMS product from a single vendor. Let's explore the basic directions and assumptions of conventional DDB systems.

A DDB system consists of multiple sites connected by a network. Each site has a copy of its own DDB system. A user at any site can access any data as if the data was physically stored at the user's site. In the words of C.J. Date (1987), the basic rule is that, *to the user, a DDB looks and behaves exactly like a non-DDB*. Date offers twelve rules to evaluate a proper DDB system:

- local autonomy
- no reliance on a central site
- continuous operation
- local independence
- fragmentation independence
- replication independence
- distributed query processing
- distributed transaction processing
- hardware independence
- operating system independence
- network independence
- DBMS independence

In summary, a full DDB system implies a single, consistent logical image of the data that is physically distributed across multiple, often heterogeneous, sites. The current state of the art in DDB implementations is weak, mainly because the requirements are tough. The industry in general and DDB vendors in particular have a long road before them before achieving a practical and effective DDB implementation. Work is proceeding slowly but surely, however, as the enabling technology (such as communication networks) for supporting a practical implementation matures.

5.4.2 Techniques for Data Distribution

In this section, we want to take the concepts and techniques needed to implement full DDB systems and apply these concepts and techniques to practical systems today. More specifically, the techniques of partitioning and copying are discussed, not from the perspective of understanding internals of DDB systems, but from using these techniques to build application-specific systems today.

5.4.2.1 *Partition*

To partition data, a single database is divided, without duplication, into smaller databases on other platforms. It is important to note the phrase "without duplication."

Let's consider an example. We have a customer database that is maintained on a single mainframe, say, under DB2. If we partition that database, we must divide the customers into separate categories, without overlap. One way would be to assign the customers to branch offices closest to them. A customer would be assigned to one and only one branch office. The assumption is that most of the customer's interaction would be handled by that branch.

What if a customer wanted to conduct business at a different branch? There are several possibile options. First, the customer could be forbidden to do business at another branch. Traditional banking has had such a restriction. This restrictive approach is particularly effective for government agencies that can require, by law, customers to conduct business at certain branches. There is a side benefit of instilling a deep sense of esteem for our government agencies!

Second, the customer's assignment could be shifted to a new branch, either temporarily or permanently. Often the processing required for this change is considerable, however, requiring the old account to be closed and a new account opened.

Third, one branch could be allowed access to the database at another branch. Thus, customer data would not be duplicated, and transactions would be routed through the local database to the remote database at the other branch.

For partitioning to be a viable technique for distributing data, there must be a clear division of the data, without duplication. In the example above, partitioning probably would not be a good design because of problems in servicing customers at branches other than their assigned one.

5.4.2.1 *Copy via extract or replica*

The second technique is to copy data. Copying data is a simple and inexpensive technique—if the data never changes. Completely nonvolatile data can be copied freely for only the small cost of duplication. However, as soon as any portion of the data changes, the consistency among all copies of that data becomes a critical issue.

For example, consider historical data, say about revenues and profits for a company. As historical data, the assumption is that, once the reporting period has occurred, the data is nonvolatile. Suppose that the company generates one million CD-ROM disks containing this historical data, just because it is so proud of its financial performance. Are there any problems? Not as long as the data does not change. However, suppose that a federal agency questions the company's accounting practices and mandates changes in the reported profits for past periods. Now, what does the company do about all of that incorrect data on CD-ROM disks?

The point is that completely nonvolatile data is rare. Once data is copied, there is always a certain nonzero probability that it will change; therefore, consistency among copies is always an issue to consider.

Let's consider the opposite extreme: data that is highly volatile. Immediately after a copy is made, the data changes in some significant manner. How do we maintain consistency among copies?

First, the best way to maintain consistency is to not allow copies! If the data is highly volatile, then maintain only a single logical image of that data, through a centralized database, or through a clean partitioning of that database.

Second, copy the data with the intent that this data will not be updated. This copy is called an *extract*. The value of the extract's data is inversely proportional to its volatility over time. In other words, an extract of highly volatile data is soon worthless. It is a business judgement to appraise the value of an extract after a specific time interval. The instant that an extract is created, its value starts to decay. The decision for the user of the extract then becomes when to discard the extract or when to refresh the extract. As discussed in Chapter 8 on Copy Management, various mechanisms assist the user with this decision. Unfortunately, in most enterprises today, the practice of extracting data from centralized databases has not been managed adequately and has lead to *extract chaos*.

Third, copy the data with the intent that the data will be updated. This copy is called a *replica*. Like an extract, the value of a replica depends on the consistency among all copies; however, unlike an extract, we have the additional benefit (and burden) of directly updating the replica. As discussed in Chapter 8, there are various mechanisms for handling replica updating.

5.4.2.2 *IBM's levels of data copying*

In IBM's SAA Distributed Data Architecture (IBM Distributed Data Library, 1988), the following levels of copying data are defined:

1. **Extracted Table:** A relational result set is extracted from a remote database for read-only usage. There is no mechanism to maintain synchronization with the original database.
2. **Snapshot Table:** The same as Extracted Table, except that the copy mechanism performs a refresh of the extract periodically without user initiation.
3. **Replicated Table:** The same as Snapshot Table, except that the result set can be updated. The copy mechanism automatically propagates updates to the original database and any copies from that database.
4. **Distributed Table:** An original table is partitioned into smaller tables (either horizontally, vertically, or some combination) without duplication of data. Smaller tables are distributed to various sites.

We will not use these terms in this book, because although they are useful, there are two areas of confusion. First, these are only four cases out of a much larger set of possibilities; Chapter 8 explores other possibilities. Second, the term "snapshot" is used in this book to refer to copying data at a specific instant in time; that is, a snapshot freezes a portion of the database at a specific time, much like snapping a photograph of an athlete in midair. In contrast, the IBM usage of this term emphasizes an automatic refresh mechanism.

▼ 5.5 WAYS OF DISTRIBUTING PROCESS

This section explores the techniques for distributing process, which emphasizes how a transaction is processed against a remote database.

5.5.1 Key Aspects of Distributing Process

The key requirement for distributing process is the mechanism for coordinating two processes initiated on separate platforms. This mechanism is often called *interprocess communication* (IPC) or simply *coupling*.

This coordination can be on two levels of coupling: *execution* and *data*. First, execution coupling implies that two processes need to synchronize their executions. For example, one process may initiate another process, or one process may have to wait until another process is completed. Second, data coupling implies that two processes need to exchange data. For example, one process may retrieve data from a database, whle the other performs calculations on it.

This coordination can be either *symmetric* or *asymmetric*. If symmetric, the two processes are peers to one another, with either process able to initiate execution or data coupling with the other. If asymmetric, one process exerts control over the other, as in the client-server architecture.

This coordination can be performed by either *connections* or by *messages*. A connection mechanism requires that two processes establish, maintain, and terminate a connection (or circuit) between them. The network must allocate resources for this connection regardless of whether data is flowing. A message mechanism enables a process to send a message (also known as a packet or frame) to another process, without prior mutual establishment of a connection. Reliability of this coupling is more difficult to insure, but resources required can be less.

This coordination can be either *direct* or *indirect*. The coupling does not have to occur directly between two processes, either via connection or message. If two processes are sharing the same data object (as described in Chapter 4), these processes can coordinate their actions. If one process changes an attribute of a specific data object while another process is using that attribute, the two processes have an indirect coupling between them. In effect, an indirect coupling is like a coupling where arguments are passed by reference (to a shared data object), rather than by value.

For most of this book, we will be discussing asymmetric, direct, data coupling using connections, usually in the context of the enhanced client-server architecture. There are areas of rapidly developing technology that focus on symmetric coupling and on message-passing couplings. The maturing of remote procedure calls and distributed transaction monitors will be critical to these new areas. It will be exciting to watch the message-passing technology of electronic mail systems evolve as the basis of a new generation of client-server systems. It may be that shared data objects built upon message-passing technology will ultimately provide more effective coupling among client-server processes.

5.5.2 Levels of Distributing Database Transactions

In IBM's SAA Distributed Data Architecture (IBM Distributed Data Library, 1988), four levels of processing transactions against remote databases are defined. Figure 5.9 illustrates these four levels when an application (on the left) submits one or more requests (which can consist of

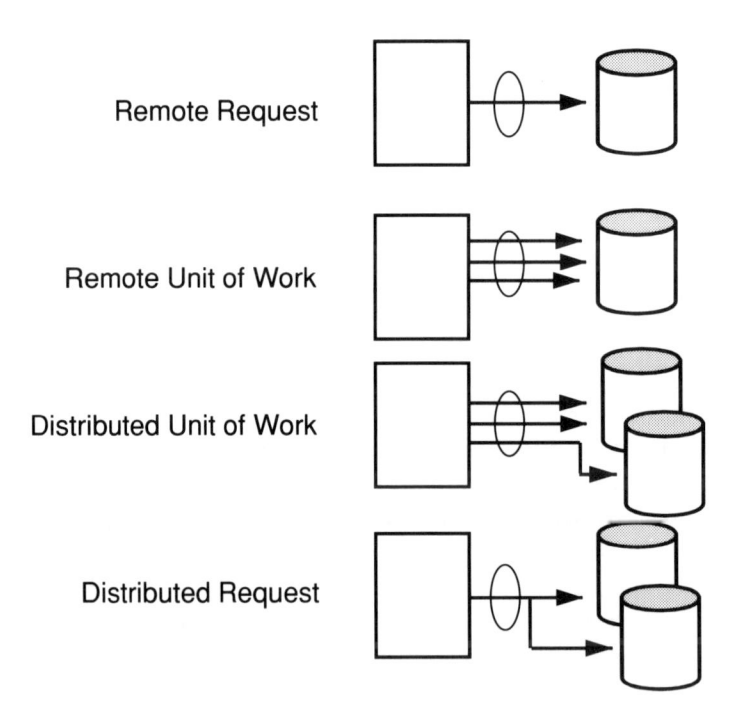

Figure 5.9. Four levels of distributing transactions.

Ways of Distributing Process ▼ 129

	Stmts per UOW	Databases per UOW	Databases per Stmts
Remote request	ONE	ONE	ONE
Remote unit of work	MANY	ONE	ONE
Distributed unit of work	MANY	MANY	ONE
Distributed request	MANY	MANY	MANY

Figure 5.10. Summary of the four levels.

one or many SQL statements, as described in Section 3.1.3) to one or more remote databases (on the right). The oval indicates which requests are contained within the same unit of work.

- **Remote Request** (RR): *One* request (as a unit of work) against *one* database.
- **Remote Unit of Work** (RUOW): *Many* requests against *one* database.
- **Distributed Unit of Work** (DUOW): *Many* requests against *many* databases, but each individual request acts against only *one* database.
- **Distributed Request** (DR): *Many* requests against *many* databases, and each request can act against *many* databases.

Figure 5.10 summarizes these four levels, showing the differences in requests per unit of work, databases per unit of work, and databases per request. The real importance of these levels lays in what additional capabilities a distributed system requires to move from one level to the next higher. These additional capabilities are:

- RR to RUOW requires a *remote commit*
- RUOW to DUOW requires a *distributed update*
- DUOW to DR requires a *distributed join*

Let's discuss each of these capabilities.

5.5.2.1 Remote commit

For an RR, the system can assume that a commit is performed after each request. As we move to a RUOW, the application must specify after several requests when a commit or abort is to be performed by the database. Therefore, a COMMIT (or ROLLBACK) statement or similar mechanism must be provided that can reliably perform the commit or abort against the remote database. Note that this capability also assumes that there is a reliable communication link between the client and server.

5.5.2.2 *Distributed update*

For an RUOW, all requests are directed to one database; hence, only the commit or abort must be performed against that one database. As we move to a DUOW, the application directs each request against possibly different databases. Now, we must coordinate the commit or abort among several databases. According to the definition of a unit of work, all the databases must commit, or all of the databases must abort. No mixtures are allowed!

A *single-site update* is a simple version of RUOW in which only one database is updated. There can be many databases from which data is retrieved, but only one database in which data is changed. Note that we can ignore the retrieval-only database, since there is nothing to commit or abort. We only have to perform a commit or abort against that one database, and this is the same requirement as in the simpler RUOW. In other words, a single-site update adds the capability of retrieving data from multiple databases, but it has the same capability as RUOW for properly updating a single database.

What about updating multiple databases within the same unit of work? We now have to coordinate that commit (or abort) across multiple databases. The mechanism often used is called a *two-phase commit*. Let's consider a simple example in which we want to do two INSERTs

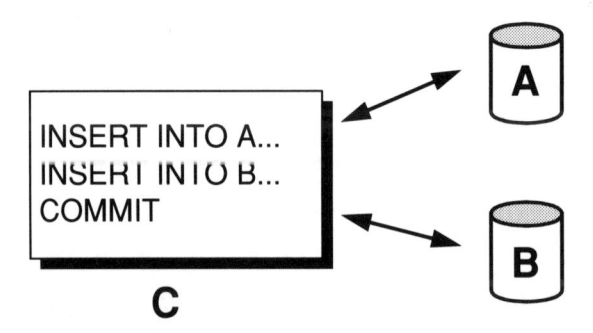

Figure 5.11. *Two-phase commit.*

against two separate databases (A and B). We do the first INSERT and then the second INSERT. We finally COMMIT those two requests. We expect that either:

- Both INSERTs are successful and committed, or
- Both INSERTs were aborted because of some error condition.

There are no other options!

But, what happens if one database cannot do the INSERT? There was a syntax error. The other database that had no problem with its INSERT will have to be forced to abort that good INSERT. How is this performed reliably, without burdening the application? Further, what happens when one of the database systems crashes in the middle of our requests? And, what happens when the communication links drop in the middle? As you can see, there are some nasty problems here.

Let's investigate the general logic behind the two-phase commit. The notion is that we will separate the request processing into two phases. First, do the work and report if it is OK. Second, wait for a coordinating signal to commit or abort. In other words, the database should not assume that successfully completing the work implies that this work should be committed.

In more detail, here are the steps:

1. The various databases process their requests.
2. The coordinator (i.e., the client interface or one of the databases) sends a "prepare to commit" signal to the databases.
3. Both databases reply either "OK" or "not OK" to the coordinator.
4. The coordinator sends a "commit" signal if all databases replied "OK" or a "rollback" signal if otherwise.
5. Both databases perform the commit (or abort) and reply with their status.
6. The coordinator completes the transaction when all databases have replied positively or attempts to fix the mess if otherwise.

Although this two-phase commit mechanism is widely cited and implemented in every system supporting distributed updates, this mechanism does not guarantee proper completion. There are still brief intervals in which certain failures are a problem. For instance, the coordinator could crash after receiving the "OK" response but before sending the "commit" signals. What do the databases do in this situation? In other words, it is very tricky to implement an effective two-

commit phase so that it performs reliably. For each possible failure, there must be an elaborate scheme to clean up this mess.

Another disadvantage of the two-phase commit is the great increase in network traffic to support the mechanism. Note the various exchanges of signals and replies. This is a big performance problem. As an implementor attempts to make the two-phase commit more efficient, its reliability is sacrificed.

5.5.2.3 *Distributed join*

For a DUOW, each request is directed to only one database. As we move to a DR, each request can act upon several databases. The prime example of a DR is a SELECT statement that joins tables contained in several databases. For example, consider the following example:

```
SELECT C1, C2, C3 FROM T1, T2 WHERE T1.C4=T2.C5
```

The tables T1 and T2 are contained in two separate databases. Data from part of T1 will be joined with part of T2. The rows will be matched properly based on a value in the C4 column of T1 being equal to a value in the C5 column of T2.

Think for a moment what the joining processing involves. We could do this join in a simple fashion by retrieving one row from T1, then retrieving all rows from T2 that match, and continuing to the next row in T1. This would be an efficient procedure if table T1 contained only a few rows. However, slightly different circumstances with tables T1 and T2 could lead to disastrous performance. If T1 contained a million rows, the performance of this row would be unacceptable.

Just like in a single database context, the critical factor is the optimizer that translates the SQL statement into an efficient procedure for accessing the data. However, with a DR, the optimizer must cover the context of several databases. This is called *global optimization*, and it is quite difficult. The global optimizer needs to know the size of affected tables, typing on joining columns, indexing on joining columns, cost of moving data across the network, and much more. Assuming all this information is available, the optimizer must make some intelligent decisions about the proper access paths.

In summary, it is easy to perform a simple distributed join. However, it is extremely difficult to do it efficiently.

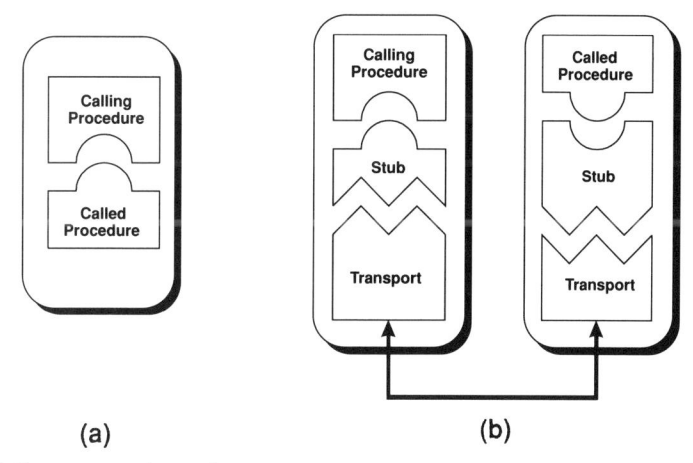

Figure 5.12. Remote procedure call.

5.5.3 Remote Procedure Call

The *remote procedure call* (RPC) mechanism is a conceptually simple way for a process on one platform to invoke a second process on another platform. Since the early days of programming, the method of having a routine in an application call a subroutine has been an enduring feature of any programming language. As shown in (a) of Figure 5.12, the *calling procedure* invokes the *called procedure*, passing a set of arguments. With RPC, this concept has been extended for distributing processes by placing a network interface between the calling and called procedures, as shown in (b). This interface usually consists of two pieces: stub and transport. The *stub* must match the procedure in terms of calling conventions (e.g., COBOL versus C) and in terms of arguments (i.e., number, ordering, type). This stub is generated uniquely for each procedure interface by using an *interface definition language* (IDL). The IDL statement is compiled and results in the code for the stub. The *transport* (also called run-time) is code that the stub utilizes to interact with the network.

For a developer to use the RPC mechanism for an application, the programmer must:

1. write the code for the calling procedure on platform A
2. write the code for the called procedure on platform B
3. define the interface using an interface definition language

4. compile the IDL statement to generate a stub on platform A

5. compile the IDL statement to generate a stub on platform B

6. link both procedures with the proper stub and transport

Note that an RSP is different than a stored procedure. A stored procedure can be invoked via an RSP mechanism, as in Sybase SQL Server Open Client. However, a stored procedure is conceptually an extension of the database and is managed as another database object. With a stored procedure, there is no analogy to an interface definition language. From the client perspective (i.e., calling procedure), RPC and stored procedures may appear similar, but they are very different when viewed from the server perspective (i.e., called procedure).

An early RPC implementation was the Apollo's Network Computing System (NCS), which was later absorbed into Hewlett-Packard. Other RPC implementations are the Sun Microsystems Transport Independent (TI) RPC and the Netwise RPC Tool. In 1990, the Open Systems Foundation chose the Hewlett-Packard NCS implementation to be part of the OSF Distributed Computing Environment (DCE).

5.5.4 Distributed Transaction Monitors

Another key technology for distributing processes is *distributed transaction monitors*. It is defined as a component of a distributed system that monitors transactions between applications and resources and insures transaction completion if successful or transaction recovery is unsuccessful. In other words, the responsibilities of a distributed transaction monitor is the same as a transaction manager within a database system, as explained in Chapter 2, but a distributed transaction monitor has been generalized to any data resource and extended across multiple platforms.

The most popular framework for a distributed transaction monitor is that of the X/Open Distributed Transaction Processing (DTP) model. As shown in Figure 5.13, the X/Open DTP model consists of three components: an application program that defines transaction and its actions, a resource manager that provides access to shared data, and a transaction manager that coordinates the transactions.

The key to this model is the interface between the application program and transaction manager. This interface is called the *TX services*. In concept, the TX services are quite simple. The application program tells the transaction manager when a global transaction (i.e., global across multiple resources) begins, using the function *tx_begin*. The application

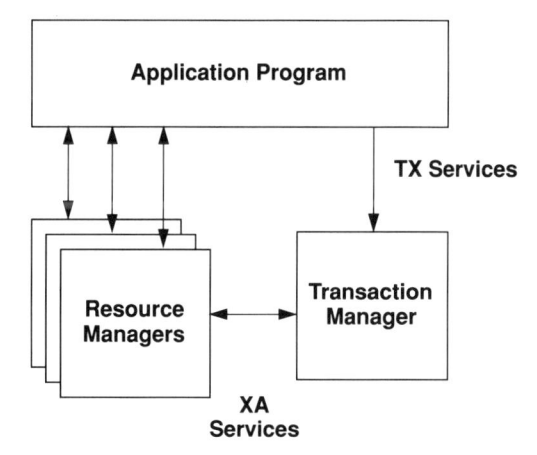

Figure 5.13. X/Open distributed transaction processing.

program proceeds to call various resource managers to utilize their resources (and changing things in the process). When the application program determines that (from its perspective) the transaction is completed, it tells the transaction manager to complete the transaction across the various resource managers. This is accomplished by the functions *tx_commit* or *tx_rollback*.

The hard work begins with the transaction manager performing a two-phase commit in coordination with the resource managers. The interface between the transaction manager and the resource managers is called the *XA services*. The critical function is the *xa_prepare* that asks each resource manager whether it can commit its portion of the transaction. It is the critical function that allows the transaction manager to use the two-phase commit mechanism. As stated, it is simple in concept.

Several companies have delivered products for distributed transaction monitors. Transarc's Encina evolved from the Camelot project at Carnegie Mellon and supports the X/Open DTP model within the OSF Distributed Computing Environment. Encina has been endorsed by IBM (to possibly build an open version of CICS), Hewlett-Packard, Sybase, Informix Software, Ingres, and others. It is important to note the DBMS vendors, since someday they may offer DBMS versions allowing transaction interoperability with other DBMS products. Other distributed transaction monitors are NCR/ATT TopEnd and Unix System Labs Tuxedo.

▼ DISCUSSION QUESTIONS

1. From your perspective, what are the pros and cons for distributed systems?

2. What is the key ingredient for evolving from client-server to peer-to-peer architectures?

3. Local versus remote servers—who cares?

4. How can the basic application structure be sliced? Do you see a clear distinction among these arrangements? What if we slice it multiple times?

5. What is the single critical characteristic of a distributed database?

6. What is the distinction between an extract and a replica? What variations in these terms have you used?

7. What would a client-server system be like if the coordination were performed by messages (via email, for example), rather than by connection? Would the user know the difference?

8. What are the three functions or capabilities needed to distribute transactions? How are these functions usually implemented within a distributed DBMS?

9. What is the difference between a distributed unit of work and a distributed request? Is this difference relevant only to a SELECT statement?

6

ARCHITECTURES FOR OPEN CONNECTIVITY

This chapter builds on the previous four chapters by examining the possible architectures for database connectivity across the enterprise. In particular, these architectures focus on interconnecting federated databases from an open systems approach. This discussion is applicable to any decomposition, or slicing, of the Basic Application Structure into presentation and data portions. For instance, these architectures can be used to architect an RPC mechanism for various application servers. For simplicity of discussion, we will concentrate on the context of a more conventional client-server system using a relational database server.

We will start by describing layered architectures and the problems of proprietary architectures for database connectivity and then suggest three basic approaches or building blocks for open architectures:

- common-interface
- common-gateway
- common-protocol

We then examine combinations of these building blocks that result in various open architectures. Criteria for evaluating architectures, such as openness or reliability, are listed and described. Finally, the relationship between the building blocks and three functional layers (access management, copy management, and warehouse management) is considered.

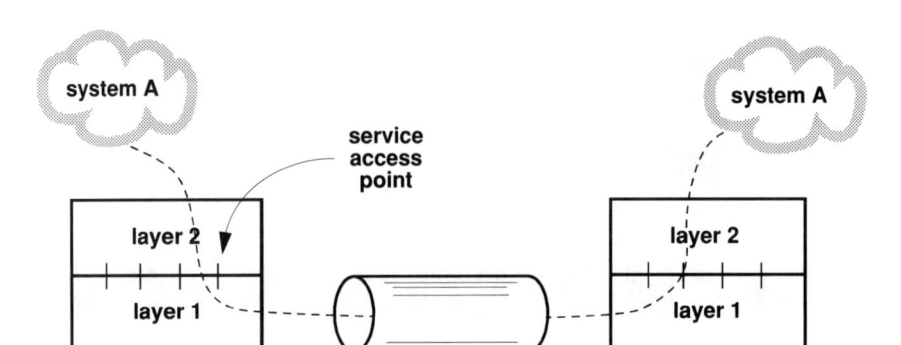

Figure 6.1. Simple two-system interconnect.

▼ 6.1 LAYERED ARCHITECTURES AND OSI

About twenty years ago, the field of data communications was in disarray. There were many competing standards for connecting communication devices. Customers typically purchased their entire systems from one vendor, and a unified (and proprietary) communication architecture was provided. As systems became more complex and global, a single-vendor solution was not adequate. Standards needed to be established so that many vendors could provide a variety of products, so the open systems approach was pursued.

One standard could not cover all the varied aspects of data communications. A framework was required to enable a number of standards to coordinate their functions. An analysis technique called *layering* was adopted. The principle is that services or functions are specified as a vertical stack of layers. Each layer performs specific services to enable interaction between two systems. A lower layer performs services that are more elementary or primitive. In Figure 6.1, two layers are shown: Layer 2 is the higher layer, while Layer 1 is the lower layer. The boundary between the two layers is referred to as the *interface*, which consists of one or more *service access points* or simply service points. If a higher layer desires a lower-level function, it would invoke the proper service point passing the proper arguments to the lower layer. The lower layer would respond by performing the desired function, and passing back updated arguments.

How can we use this layered approach for interaction between two systems? System A can interact with System B when one system invokes the services of Layer 2, which then invokes the services of Layer 1. The interesting aspect of this figure is the *pipe* between the two stacks. Across that pipe must flow some mixture of commands and data. The specification of this flow is called the *protocol*.

Let's pursue this figure with a simple example. Assume that System A desires information on a specific employee. A service point for retrieving certain employee information would be invoked. This service point may be a simple procedural call with arguments for employee last name, set of desired data, etc. In Layer 2, the appropriate SQL statement would be generated and passed to Layer 1 for processing. Layer 1 would send the statement to a remote database system.

The protocol that flows between the two systems would consist of something like:

- control information (such as user id and password)
- command to process the following SQL statement
- text of the SQL statement
- optional arguments (e.g., employee last name)

Note the close relationship between the interface and the protocol. They are different but must complement each other in a consistent manner. Much of the confusion in the EDC area stems from misunderstandings between the interface and protocol.

When two systems interact in more complex networks, there may be intermediate nodes that pass the protocol along and may even add value in the process. Consider Figure 6.2. System A sends the request for employee data. Nodes X and Y are intermediate nodes that pass on the request. They may add value, for example, by providing location transparency. System A may not know where the employee data is located, but Nodes X and Y will route the request to the proper database. Also note that the protocol between the nodes may be at different levels as it flows through the network.

The design principles behind the layered approach are quite simple:

- Create a layer where functions can be logically grouped
- Create an interface so that effects of changes are localized
- Minimize the layers and functions whenever possible

Following the layered architectural approach, a committee of the International Organization for Standards (ISO) was established in 1977. Over

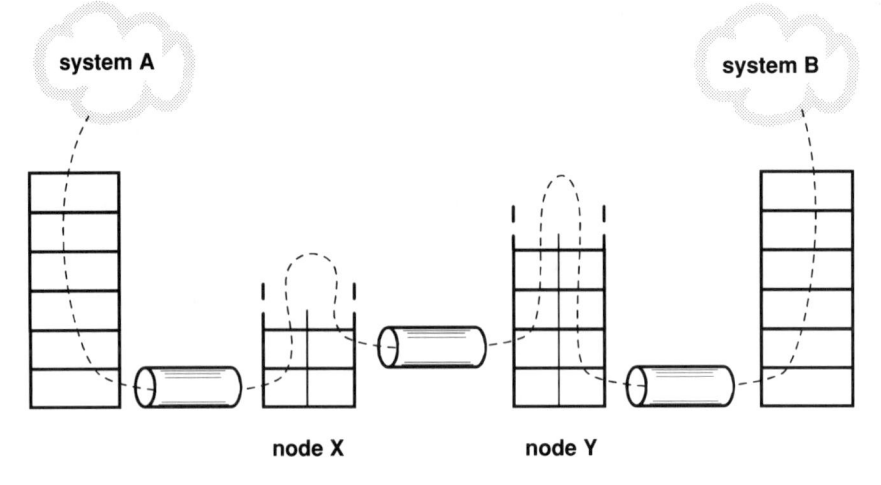

Figure 6.2. *Two systems in a network.*

the next decade, the committee generated a framework called the *Open Systems Interconnection* (OSI) reference model. The OSI reference model has been widely known in the industry since it provides the basic interconnection framework for distributed systems.

The OSI reference model consists of seven layers. These layers are discussed adequately in other texts (Martin, 1988; Stallings, 1985). Briefly, layers are described as follows:

1. **Physical**: specifies the physical medium over which a bit stream is transmitted.
2. **DataLink**: provides reliable transmission between adjacent nodes by detecting and recovering from errors.
3. **Network**: establishes, maintains, and terminates connections between nodes with possible routing among intermediate nodes.
4. **Transport**: provides end-to-end error recovery and flow control regardless of the communications facility.
5. **Session**: provides the mechanism for a session or dialogue between applications.
6. **Presentation**: resolves differences in data formats and representations between applications.
7. **Application**: provides the mechanism for applications to access the OSI services.

These layers are useful in discussing the architectural aspects of EDC.

Server
Client Interface
Client

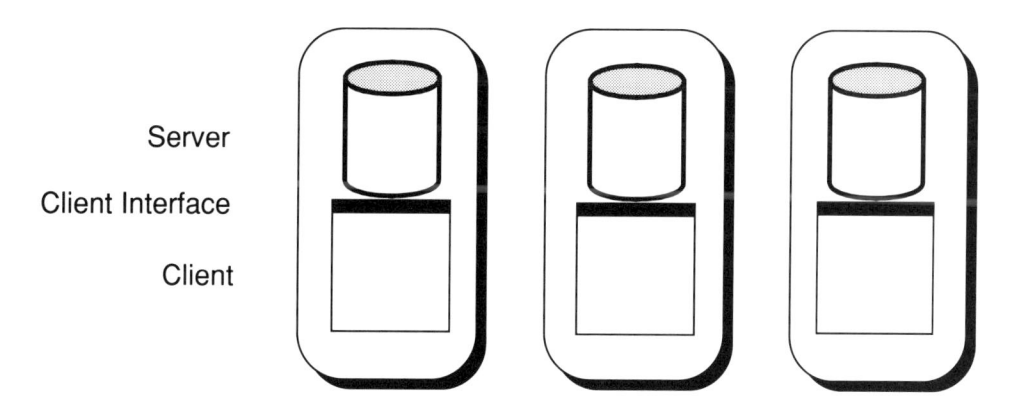

Figure 6.3. Conventional database architecture.

▼ 6.2 CLIENT-SERVER ARCHITECTURE REVISITED

In early database systems, the application was designed and implemented to perform a custom business function for the enterprise. This application was written to an interface specific to a certain database management system (DBMS) and was proprietary to the vendor of that product. When generic applications such as query tools became available for popular DBMS products from independent software vendors, they were also written using the vendor-supplied proprietary interface. As shown in Figure 6.3, both the application and database operated on the same platform, and interactions between the client and server roles were tightly coupled.

With emergence of client-server architecture, the client application and database server are on separate platforms. The interaction between client and server is usually not visible (i.e., open) to either the client application or the database server. The client-server architecture provides a structured interaction between a client and a server. There are different specific functions that the client performs (running the user's application, for example) and that the server performs (managing the database). The benefits are support for a degree of parallel processing and the clear functional differentiation between platforms. (See also the discussion in Chapter 5 on the advantages and disadvantages of distributed systems in general.)

The interactions from the client to the server are called *requests*; the interactions from the server to the client are called *results*. In the case of

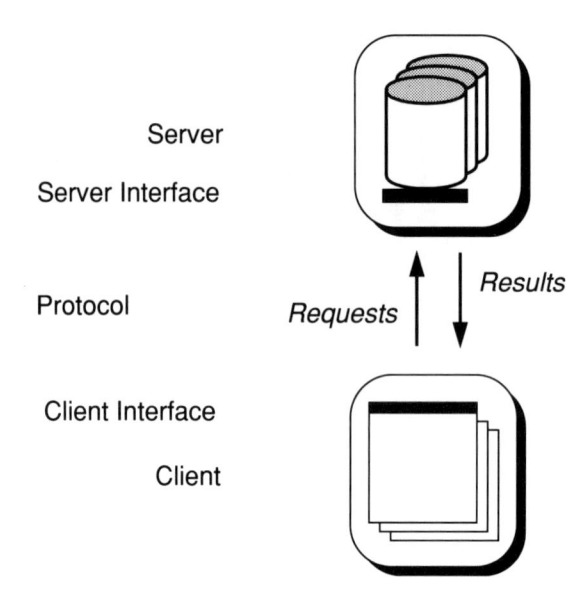

Figure 6.4. *Client-server architecture.*

SQL database servers, the requests consist of the text of SQL statements or references to previously bound SQL statements. The results are in the form of a flattened relational table, along with status, error codes, and messages.

The client-server architecture deals with the following components: client interface, protocol, and server interface. First, the *client interface* is the application programming interface described in Chapter 2. It consists of the calling conventions, procedure/function definitions, and the syntax/semantics of the language (usually SQL) passed through the interface. The client interface accepts requests from the application logic and generates the proper protocol to convey them to the server. In Figure 6.4, the client interface is shown as a bar on top of the client application, symbolizing the thin boundary between the application and the rest of the system. At the lowest level, a client interface is a library of procedures invoked by the client application to generate the proper protocol to the server.

The ANSI 89 SQL specification defines most of a client interface with some areas designated as implementation or language dependent. Various vendors offer DBMS products, each of which contains a client interface. For example, IBM offers an SAA Common Programming Interface for SQL that evolves towards a common subset across their four DBMS offerings. In addition, IBM has an even more precise specification for COBOL programs under CICS accessing DB2 data.

Second, the *protocol* is simply a stream of bits flowing on some communication transport between the two interfaces. Within the ISO work, protocol is often referred to as *formats and protocol*, or FAP; this book will use the simpler term. Protocol consists of the sequence of commands and arguments (i.e., data structures). In Figure 6.4, the protocol is shown as being the data flowing within the arrows between the client and server. Note that there is a bidirectional flow.

A simple protocol, for example, would consist of a command from the client to execute immediately the following SQL statement text. The server would respond with the results of processing the SQL statement, such as a status code, number of columns, name and type of each column, data for first row, data for second row, and so on.

In the discussion of open systems in the first chapter, portability and interoperability were described as being dependent on interfaces and protocols, respectively. In other words, compatibility of the interfaces determines the effort to port an application from one platform to another. The compatibility of protocols determines the effort for one system to interact with another. Hence, the interface and protocol are interdependent but should be considered distinct from one another. Any system that understands the protocol can listen to or even generate requests or results, regardless of which interfaces may be used.

Third, the *server interface* is an interface that is a mirror image of the client interface. Instead of responding to procedure calls from the client application, the server interface responds to the receipt of protocol chunks (i.e., blocks or messages). The purpose of the server interface is to accept requests from the client via the transport and pass them onto the database engine.

In most DBMS products, the server interface is hidden inside the database engine, implying that only that vendor's database engine can process requests using the vendor's protocol or the vendor's client interface. In the mid 1980s Sybase Corporation pioneered the concept of the Open Server, in which the server interface was offered as a separate product from the Sybase SQL Server engine. Customers could purchase the Sybase Open Server and develop client-server systems based on the

Sybase architecture but not use the Sybase SQL Server engine to manage the data. Examples could be data processed from real-time sources (such as stock exchange quotas) or from customized ISAM files.

In this section, we have described a client-server architecture as having three critical components: client interface, protocol, and server interface. In the next section, the problems for enterprise database connectivity are discussed when this architecture is used with proprietary interfaces and protocols.

▼ 6.3 PROBLEMS WITH PROPRIETARY ARCHITECTURES

If a corporation is concerned with only one type of client-server architecture (all from a single vendor), many of the problems of enterprise database connectivity disappear, because we are not dealing with federated databases. However, this situation is usually not the case in most corporations today. As discussed in the first chapter, the industry is forced to adopt a more open systems approach. In the context of client-server architecture, the open systems approach implies that the combination of client interface, protocol, and server interface must be an open architecture.

To explore the problems with a proprietary architecture, consider a situation in which an enterprise has purchased two types of servers and developed applications independently to each of those servers. Figure

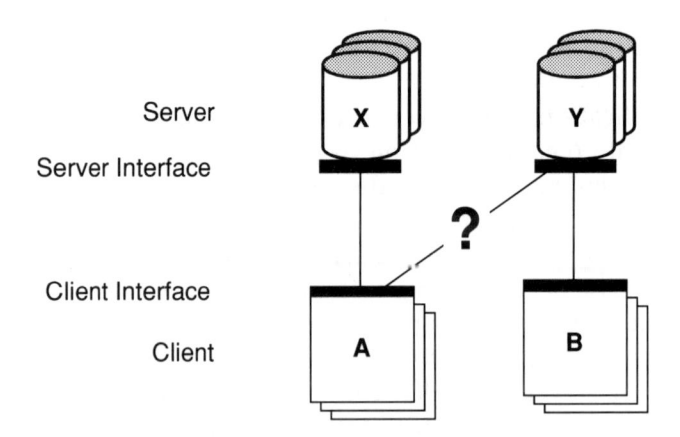

Figure 6.5. *Problems of proprietary interface.*

6.5 shows the two types of servers as X and Y and two sets of applications as A and B. The first application A can access data in any of the databases supported by the type X server; likewise, the second application B can access databases supported by the type Y server.

This proprietary solution can be very effective. What happens, however, when data needs to be shared among different types of database servers? In other words, how does application A access data in server type Y? In today's competitive business environment, the MIS manager who states that application A will never have to access server Y will soon have to recant those words.

In concrete terms, what changes must be made to a client application to retarget from one server to another server? We refer to this situation as *retargeting* an application to another server. For example, if an application has been programming to an Oracle database, what must be done to allow this application to work with IBM OS/2 Database Manager? The problems with data and process transparency covered in the second and third chapters are the same problems encountered in application retargeting:

- database interface and connection
- SQL syntax and semantics
- system catalog tables
- data types and encodings
- status codes and messages
- collating sequences
- data semantics
- transaction boundaries mismatch
- isolation levels mismatch
- user identification and privileges

To solve this new requirement, the application developer would have to program to the client interface of both server type X and server type Y. The developer will probably have to change the application logic so that it is conditional on the server. For example, the SQL statement may be slightly different for each server. The test for the end of result set may be different depending on the status code returned. And if the collating sequence is different, the sort/merge logic of the application will probably be useless, generating confusing results for the user.

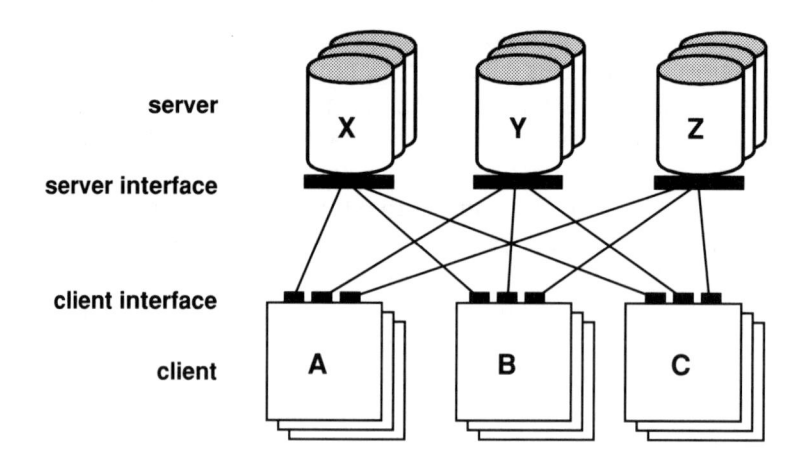

Figure 6.6. *Additional problems with proprietary interface.*

Let's continue the discussion of our application retargeting problem by introducing a third server type. Figure 6.6 illustrates the situation in which data from three different types of database servers must be shared freely among all applications. Using proprietary client interfaces, each application must be written with three different interfaces. Further, we now have nine different types of connections: A-X, B-X, and so on, through B-Z, C-Z.

In general, the number of connection types to be managed is equal to the number of application types *times* the number of server types. This leads to an impossible development and maintenance situation. Consider the difficulty to code and maintain an application that has two embedded client interfaces. The code for each interface must be carefully separated into different source modules, which are then separately precompiled and bind to the respective databases. As a practical guideline, normal applications requiring more than two server types will be impossible to develop and maintain using proprietary interfaces. Vendors who supply database connectivity products certainly add value when they successfully utilize multiple proprietary interfaces in their products. This situation also makes apparent the reasons why these vendors prefer call-level interfaces.

▼ 6.4 THE THREE BASIC APPROACHES

What is the solution to this problem of proprietary architectures? There are three basic approaches (or building blocks) that can potentially alleviate this problem: common-interface, common-gateway, and common-protocol.

The secret to all three approaches is that each approach pivots (or focuses) on one element *that is in common* between the client and server. For instance, the common-interface approach focuses on the interface (either client or server) as common with the various server types. The common-gateway approach introduces a database gateway as the common element. Finally, the common-protocol approach focuses on the protocol flowing between the client and server interfaces as the common element.

Another important aspect of these approaches is that they are building blocks, not pure architecture types. In fact, the actual architecture adopted by an enterprise will usually be some combination of these approaches. And, that is when it becomes more interesting!

A word of warning! No approach or architecture can completely solve problems caused by connectivity among federated databases. Regardless of the standards, interfaces, and protocols, there will always be some problems with retargeting a specific client application to a different server type. The challenge is to anticipate the problems and seek the proper architecture to alleviate them.

For instance, consider the following difficult problem with retargeting applications—the collating sequences used by various database engines. When ORDER-BY or GROUP-BY clauses are used in a SELECT statement, the database engine sorts the result set on the specified columns. But, what is the sequence of this sorting when it involves character data? Character data from IBM DB2 will be sorted in EBCDIC sequence, while character data from any UNIX database will be sorted in ASCII sequence. Further, what about multinational character sets? Realize that the German character set in Germany is sorted differently than the German character set in Belgium! And then, what if character sets are allowed to be mixed in the same column? It may be many years before DBMS vendors will provide flexible and efficient collating sequences based on international standards.

In the next sections, we'll explore each of these approaches in greater detail, remembering that combinations among the approaches have more practical value and that there are limitations to any of these approaches.

6.4.1 Common-Interface Approach

A *common-interface* approach uses the interface (either client or server) as the common element in providing open connectivity. The principle is that the client application programs to one interface specification regardless of the current (or future) server types. That interface assumes the responsibility of transparency from the client to the server. That is, it is transparent to the client if and when the client is retargeted to another server type. The code of the client application does not change. And, hopefully the application works as intended!

The key issue is whether the common-interface specification allows the application logic to be aware of the type or capabilities of the server. This is referred to as being *server-aware* or *capability-aware*, respectively, by the client.

If neither, then the application logic will be independent of the server type or server capability; hence, retargeting should be easily accomplished. However, this implies that the application logic assumes a *least-common-denominator* characterization of the server. In other words, the application logic assumes a minimal set of characteristics that is the intersection of all current (and future) server types.

If server-aware, then the application logic will contain conditional code that is dependent on the server. For example, the application logic could detect through the generic interface that the server is Oracle version 6.12 under OS/2. The application could then generate SQL statements and use data types supported by this server type. Retargeting to other servers will be possible only if the application logic has anticipated those server types. Evolution to future server types is limited to those that are similar to current server types.

If capability-aware, then the application logic will contain conditional code that is dependent on specific capabilities of the server. For example, the application logic could detect whether the server can support an outer join, rather than whether the server is Oracle. This is more desirable than being server-aware since retargeting to a new server can be accomplished by properly profiling the server capabilities. However, the limitation is that someone must be smart enough to specify the appropriate capabilities in the beginning. One reason for new and enhanced servers is that they have new capabilities. These capabilities were probably not anticipated when the interface specifications were released. In section 6.5.7, we will discuss the trade-offs in design decisions with permissive interfaces (i.e., interfaces that allow server or capability awareness).

Although the above principles of a common-interface approach are simple, its realization can become very complex. The common interface consists of two components in general: the generic interface, which the application utilizes, and the driver, which contains specific knowledge of a server. The *generic interface* is the API to which the client application programs. It also resides on the client platform. The vendor for the generic interface may or may not be the same as the vendor for the server. In most situations, the vendor is independent of a specific server vendor and achieves value in supporting a variety of servers. On the other hand, the *driver* is complex code that takes the requests from and results to the generic interface and processes them upon a specific server. The driver contains knowledge of the capabilities (and quirks) of that specific server.

The key design tradeoffs of a common interface involve the driver. In particular, two aspects are important: placement (does the driver reside on the client or server?) and ownership (does the client or server own the driver?). The *placement* of the driver can either be on the client platform (next to the generic interface) or on the server platform (connected to the generic client interface via some private protocol). We will refer to these two cases as being *client-side* and *server-side*, respectively. The client-side case is simpler since the protocol is the responsibility of the server. The server-side case has greater potential since the driver can have a closer coupling to the server.

Likewise, the *ownership* of the driver can either be by the client interface or by the server interface. We will refer to these two cases as being *client-owned* or *server-owned*. In other words, which vendor supplies the driver? Is it the vendor of the generic interface or the vendor of the database server?

With the combination of placement and ownership, we have the potential for four different variations of a common interface, as shown in Figures 6.7–6.10. Let's discuss each of the four variations in turn.

First, the client-side and client-owned variation is a common interface that uses drivers on the client platform and supplies the drivers

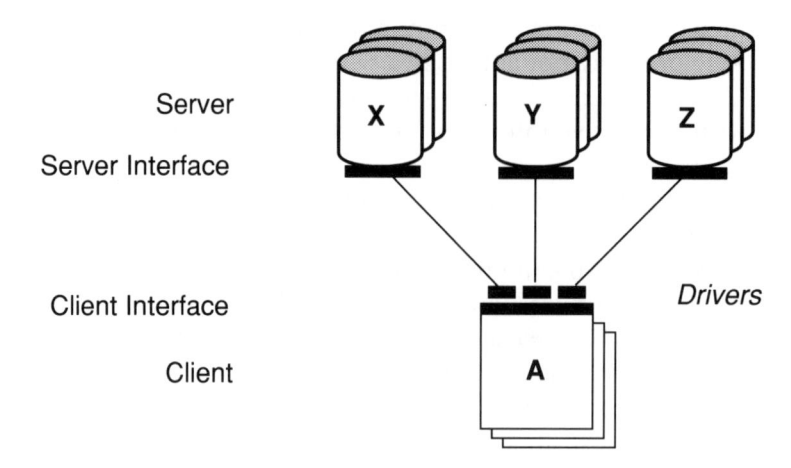

Figure 6.7. *Common interface: client-side and client-owned.*

with the generic interface (Figure 6.7). This implies that the protocol and server interfaces are unique to each of the server types. For instance, application A uses a driver of the generic interface that generates the proper protocol for server type X.

Second, the client-side and server-owned variation is a common interface that uses drivers on the client platform (Figure 6.8). This driver is supplied by the server vendor to reside on various client platforms and attach to various common interfaces. This implies that the protocol is unique (i.e., private) to the server type.

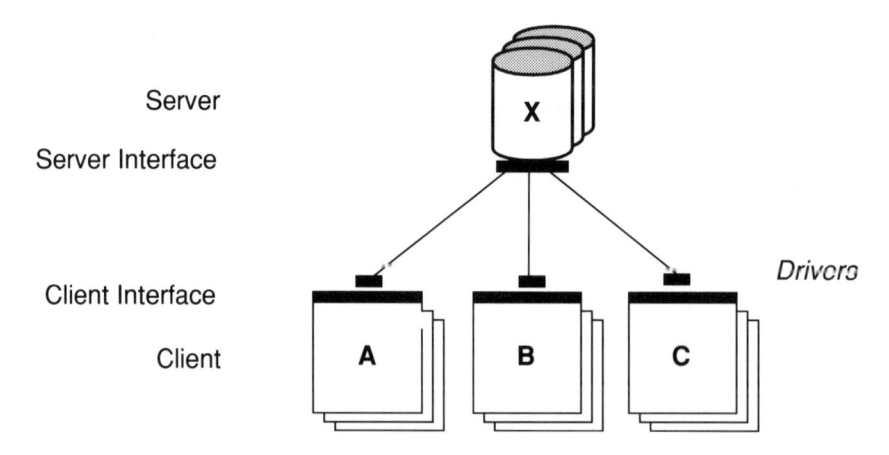

Figure 6.8. *Common interface: client-side and server-owned.*

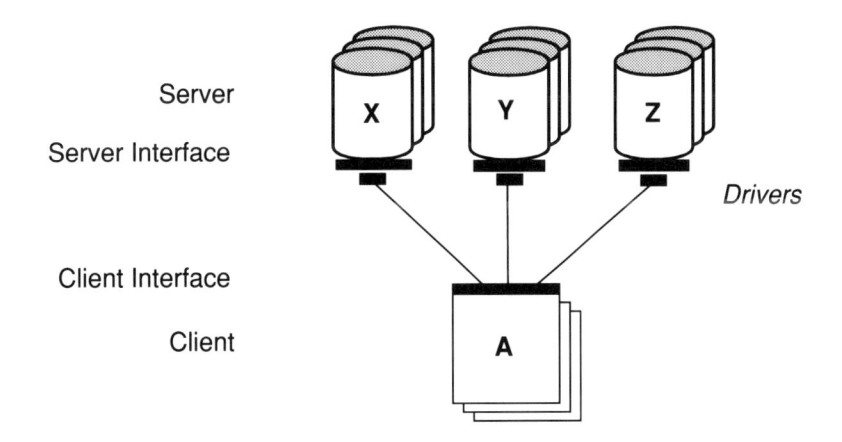

Figure 6.9. *Common interface: server-side and client-owned.*

Third, the server-side and client-owned variation is a common interface that uses drivers on the server platform, rather than the client platform (Figure 6.9). The drivers are supplied by the vendor of the common interface (which is probably different than the vendor of the server). The protocol is private to the interface vendor.

Fourth, the server-side and server-owned variation is a common interface that uses drivers on the server platform (Figure 6.10). These drivers are supplied by the server vendor to connect to various interfaces, each of which have their own private protocols.

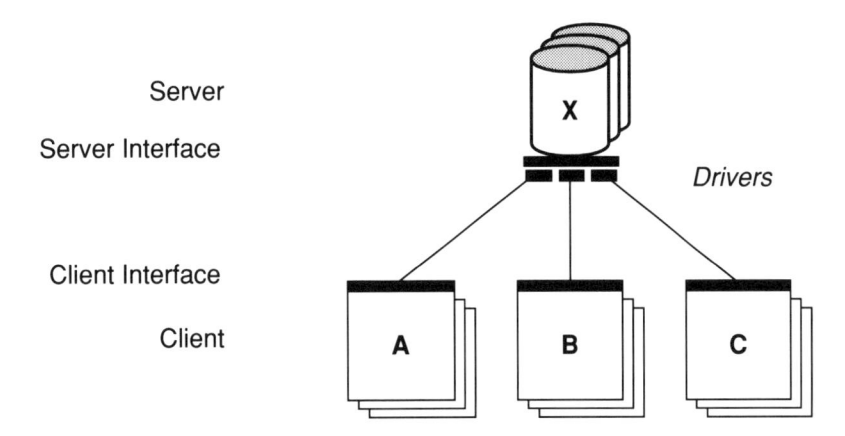

Figure 6.10. *Common interface: server-side and server-owned.*

Over the last three years, many products adopting the common-interface approach have emerged. Examples of these products are Apple Data Access Language (DAL), IBI Enterprise Data Access/SQL (EDA/SQL), and Microsoft Open Database Connectivity (ODBC).

The Apple DAL was a pioneer in the common-interface approach. DAL evolved from the acquisition by Apple of Network Innovations CL/1 product. Along with the usual SQL processing, DAL added a control language to SQL and simple file read/write. This product is a server-side and client-owned variation since most processing is performed on the same platform as the database server.

The IBI EDA/SQL is a newer product, having been announced with the IBM Information Warehouse framework in September of 1991. Its common interface is a restricted call-level API using a simple subset of ANSI-89 SQL (Level 1). Its strong feature is the potential availability of connections to many non-relational data resources. This product also is a server-side and client-owned variation since most of the processing is performed on the IBM MVS platform.

The Microsoft ODBC is the latest product to support a common-interface approach, introduced at a developers conference in March 1992. Its focus is on Microsoft Windows applications, although Macintosh will also be supported. Using the dynamic link library (DLL) mechanism in Windows, the appropriate ODBC driver is loaded when needed to connect to the proper data resource. It is a good example of the client-side common interface that allows a mixture of client-owned (i.e., comes with ODBC) and server-owned (i.e., supplied by the server vendor). See Chapter 7, *Access Management*, for a more detailed description of ODBC.

6.4.2 Common-Gateway Approach

A *common-gateway* approach utilizes a *database gateway* or simply gateway as the common element to alleviate differences among the target server types. The distinction with common-gateway approach is that the server interface of one type is married with the client interface of another type via the gateway. As mentioned in Chapter 5, this marriage extends the two-level client-server architecture into many potential multi-level versions. In Figure 6.11, client A is written to the client interface of server type X. By connecting to the database gateway as if it were a server of type X, client A now has access to database types Y and Z. The server interface of the gateway receives the requests from clients, as if it

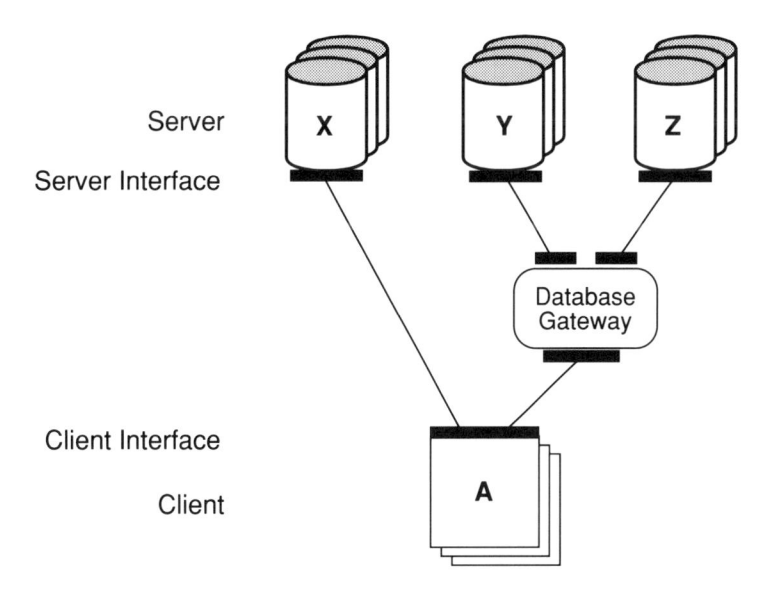

Figure 6.11. Common-gateway.

were a server of type X. The gateway then maps those requests into the proper format for another server type and uses the client interface for that server to resubmit the requests. The opposite mapping occurs to return the results to the client.

The gateway usually operates on a platform separate from the client or server platforms because of its role of mapping many clients to many servers. However, a gateway often resides on the same platform as a server when the gateway is mainly supporting or complementing that one server. Further, there is technically no reason why a gateway can not reside on the client platform, although the economics and administration issues do not justify this.

The effectiveness of the common-gateway approach is dependent upon the value added by the gateway component. When transforming requests for server X into requests for server Y, areas in which value could be added by the gateway are:

- SQL syntax transformation from Type X to Type Y
- detection of semantic differences between X and Y
- conversion of data types
- generic system catalog access

- maintenance of transaction boundaries
- conversion of status code and messages
- mapping user identification and security checks
- load balancing and limits to server
- providing manageable control points for large networks
- mapping LAN transports to WAN transports

In addition, the gateway component could add value in nonconventional areas (as discussed in Chapters 8 and 9), such as:

- stimulating stored procedures against the database
- invoking stored procedures against non-database resources
- interfacing to/from messaging and mail facilities
- transferring bulk data directly between servers
- staging data to workgroup databases
- packaging data for better consumption by users

For each implementation of the common-gateway approach, the question is, "Where is the value-added?" If the cost and overhead of a database gateway is greater than other approaches (e.g., direct connection using a common-interface), then the use of the common-gateway should be closely examined relative to the above areas of value added.

The proper perspective toward the common-gateway approach is that it complements and extends the other approaches. When used with some combination of common-interface and common-protocol, the common-gateway building block often adds flexibility to the system architecture. Because a database gateway operates on a platform that is usually inexpensive and separate from the client and server platforms, losses in efficiency can be minimal.

Products that have adopted the common-gateway approach include IBM Distributed Database Connection Services (DDCS/2), Microsoft Open Data Services (ODS), Sybase Open Server, and MDI Database Gateway for DB2.

The IBM DDCS/2 operates under OS/2 version 2 with the IBM Extended Services (DBM option). For a single user configuration, DDCS/2 acts simply as a client interface to any database supported the IBM DRDA protocol (explained in the following section). However, DDCS/2 acts in the multi-user configuration as a database gateway for clients on OS/2, Windows, or DOS platforms. Since the client interface is based on the SAA CPI for SQL, DDCS/2 provides minimal mapping of the interface characteristics and adds value mainly in configuration, security, and the DRDA protocol.

The Microsoft ODS and Sybase Open Server are not actually gateways but are development tools for building gateways. As mentioned earlier, Sybase pioneered an open version of the server interface with their Open Server; Microsoft then licensed the same technology for the ODS product. These tools are very effective for corporate or custom developers who desire to build generic access to unusual data resources (e.g., real-time stock quotations).

The MDI Database Gateway for DB2 was developed in a joint project between Micro Decisionware and Microsoft, using an early version of ODS. It accepts requests from client applications that use the SQL Server DB-Library interface and mapping the SQL syntax, data types, and so on, between DB2 and SQL Server. MDI now supports other databases than DB2 and stimulates stored procedures under CICS to DB2 and other MVS data resources. MDI also pioneered the transfer function for staging data to and from LAN database servers (see Chapter 8).

6.4.3 Common-Protocol Approach

A *common-protocol* approach utilizes a well-defined open protocol to connect client applications to various server types. Figure 6.12 shows that each client interface accepts requests from the client applications

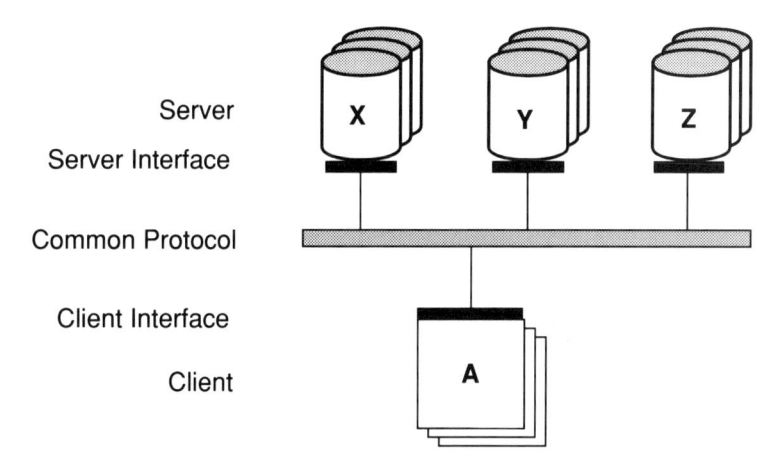

Figure 6.12. Common-protocol.

and translates those requests into the proper common protocol. Likewise, each server interface listens to the common protocol for requests, processes them, and translates the results into the proper common protocol for the clients. As discussed earlier in this chapter, a protocol is simply a stream of bits flowing between the client and server interfaces in both directions. It consists of the following components: transport, request commands and result responses, data encoding and status codes, and SQL dialect (or specialization).

The main benefit of a common-protocol approach is that, as long as client or server interface generates or consumes the same protocol, new client types or new server types can be added in the future without knowledge of the other. The converse of this benefit is that the protocol must be robust enough to handle the diversity of functionality in current and future server types.

Examples of products that use the common-protocol approach are Sybase Tabular Data Stream (TDS), IBM Distributed Relational Database Architecture (DRDA), and ISO Remote Database Access (RDA).

The Sybase TDS protocol is usually not considered an open protocol because it is trademarked by Sybase as a proprietary protocol. However, the protocol can be licensed from Sybase for a reasonable fee and incorporated by any vendor into their products. The protocol was designed to interact with only an SQL Server database engine; hence, there are features in the protocol that are unique only to SQL Server (e.g., COMPUTE rows). On the other hand, the protocol can handle any SQL (or non-SQL) text flowing to the server and has an escape mechanism to handle results of an undefined or user-defined data type.

The IBM DRDA protocol is part of the SAA distributed database strategy to interconnect the four IBM database servers: DB2, SQL/DS, SQL/400, and DBM; it also facilitates the data delivery for IBM Information Warehouse framework. The transport for DRDA is SAN LU6.2 with consideration of also including TCP/IP. The intent of DRDA is to support fully distributed databases; the initial level of DRDA, however, only supports a remote unit of work. With the release of DB2 2.3 (for an MVS client) and OS/2 DDCS/2 (for an OS/2 client), the first examples of an API that generates a common protocol has appeared.

The ISO RDA protocol is an emerging ISO international standard seeking universal data access. The transport for RDA is the ISO Open Systems Interconnect (OSI), with consideration by the SQL Access

Group to extend the transport to TCP/IP. RDA only supports a remote unit of work with dynamic SQL, although an SQL statement can be prepared once and repeatedly executed. In Chapter 7, a more detailed comparison of DRDA and RDA will be presented.

6.4.4 Some Interesting Combinations

Now that we have described the three approaches, let's examine some interesting combinations of these approaches.

First, consider the combination of common-interface and common-protocol, as shown Figure 6.13. In this combination, a client application programs to a common-interface that allows access to a number of server types directly. One of these server types is a common-protocol that allows universal access to yet another group of server types. The advantage to this combination is that the client can use the full functionality of a primary (probably local) server but also have more open access (but with more limited functionality) to other servers.

Second, consider the combination of common-gateway and common-protocol (Figure 6.14). In this combination, the client is always connected to a database gateway, which in turn can connect to multiple common-protocols and hence multiple server types. The common protocols can differ in characteristics (e.g., DRDA versus RDA), in commu-

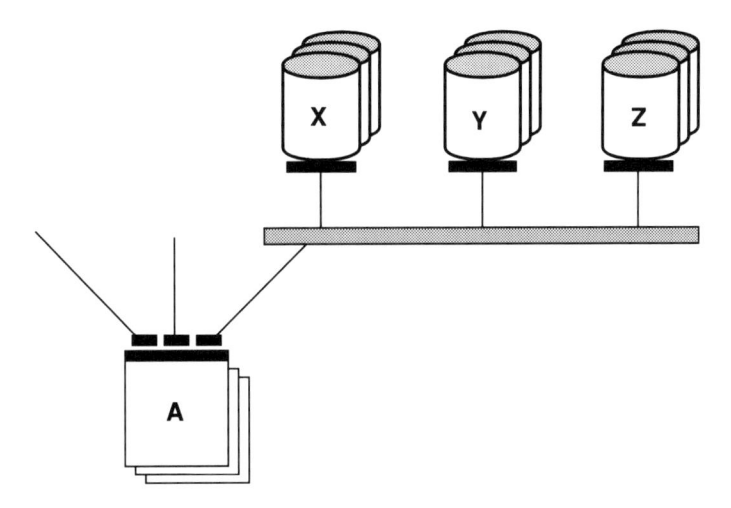

Figure 6.13. Combination #1.

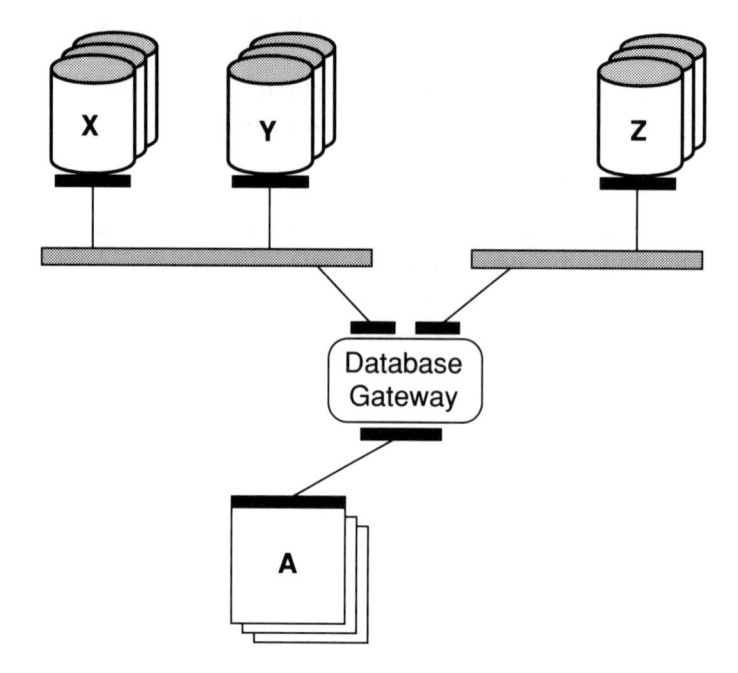

Figure 6.14. Combination #2.

nication networks (e.g., one under TCP/IP versus the other under SNA LU6.2), or in geography (e.g., servers in the United States versus Europe). The advantage to the client application is that the physical and logical location of a certain server is the concern of the gateway in its routing connections among the available common-protocols.

Third, consider the combination of common-interface and common-gateway, as shown in Figure 6.15. In this combination, various clients are written to a common-interface but have only one client driver. That driver is connected to a database gateway. The gateway then manages multiple drivers to various servers (or protocols). The advantage is that drivers do not have to be distributed to or managed on thousands of workstation platforms. Instead, a much smaller number of gateways can consolidate the drivers and provide a simpler system to manage (and control) from an enterprise perspective.

Fourth, consider the combination of common-interface (server-side) and common-protocol, as shown in Figure 6.16. In this combination, the server interface has two drivers, one for each of the common proto-

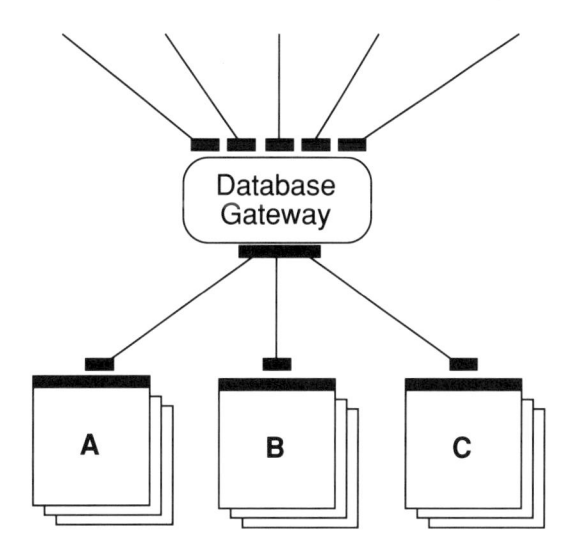

Figure 6.15. Combination #3.

cols. Hence, the server can accept requests from either of the protocols. For example, the Oracle server could be configured in this fashion so that it could accept requests in either the DRDA or RDA protocols.

This covers some interesting combinations of common-interface, common-gateway, and common-protocol approaches to database connectivity; more are possible.

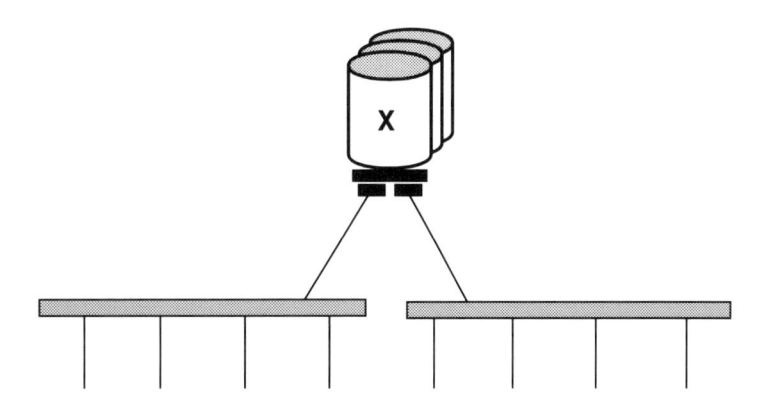

Figure 6.16. Combination #4.

▼ 6.5 COMPARISON CRITERIA

The previous sections described three approaches to open database connectivity among federated databases (i.e., heterogeneous mixtures of clients and servers). By utilizing a combination of these approaches, an enterprise can be aided in developing server-independent applications and using various server products.

The question then arises of how to compare and contrast these three approaches. This section explores the following comparison criteria:

- performance
- transparency
- openness
- manageability
- reliability
- stability
- permissiveness

Let's examine the three approaches in terms of our seven comparison criteria, recognizing that it is difficult to make general statements about architectures without referring to specific products (which in some cases do not yet exist).

6.5.1 Performance

This is an obvious first criterion. If the performance is below a certain level, then a product would be useless to an enterprise regardless of high scores on other criteria. Because of the diversity of applications, there are probably several levels of acceptable performance depending on the primary function. For instance, consider these categories:

- **Simple Extracts.** Retrieval from ad hoc queries for decision support. Small amounts of data to be transferred. Up to several minutes for a response. Failure is noncritical; flexibility is highly desirable.
- **Production Extracts.** Retrieval only for routine end-user applications. Performed on scheduled batch basis. Medium efficiency is needed to transfer large amounts of data. Failures are handled gracefully and automatically rescheduled for recovery.
- **Managed Replicas.** Retrieval and update at several sites of replicated data for production applications, while insuring a single-site update restriction at all times. Medium efficiency.

- **Transaction Processing.** Retrieval and update to several sites, possibly requiring multisite updates and joins. High performance needed with subsecond response. Real-time failure recovery is essential.

It is unlikely that a single EDC architecture would be appropriate across all these categories. It is like building a highway system. Sometimes a four-lane highway is required, while in other cases only a dirt road is needed.

Because performance is highly dependent on implementation details, it is difficult to state general differences among approaches. It will probably be the case that performance will vary more between products of the same architecture than between products across architectures, given the variety of objectives, approaches, and environments.

6.5.2 Transparency

An open architecture must do more than simply connect a client to a server. Actions performed by a client must be transparent as to the server type. In other words, the architecture must allow a client application that operates on one server type to be retargeted to another server type *without* changes to the application. This *application retargeting* was discussed in the second section of this chapter.

The degree of SQL transparency that we could expect among all the approaches will depend on how well the client interface is defined. The common-gateway approach will usually be the highest in transparency, since it is assumed that a specific client interface is utilized (e.g., the interface used by database type X). To the extent that this interface is well defined and relatively permissive, common-gateway products will offer the greatest transparency, with possible difficulties in the areas of system catalog access and collating sequences.

6.5.3 Openness

The third comparison criterion is the degree to which the common protocol is *open*. What is openness? As discussed in Chapter 1, this is a question that the industry has struggled with and debated for over a decade. The extremes are to be avoided. No degree of openness is a closed situation that allows the enterprise no freedom of choice beyond a single vendor. Complete openness is simply chaos. Hence, the desired openness is a balance somewhere between the extremes.

Openness has many complex meanings when applied to interfaces and protocols in client-server systems. Here are some of the aspects of openness as related to comparing EDC approaches:

- Is the documentation on the interface/protocol available?
- Is the interface/protocol documented clearly and adequately?
- Who controls the distribution and usage of the EDC product?
- Is there a licensing contract and fees to use the interface/protocol?
- Who licenses the interface/protocol to other vendors?
- Are there multiple vendors actively supporting the interface/protocol?
- Who controls the evolution of the interface/protocol?
- Is there a verification process that a product is compliant?
- Who sets the verification criteria for compliance?
- Who determines certification of an EDC product?

The potential for high openness exists in all three approaches; however, the common-protocol approach is more likely to have high openness since, once the protocol is adequately defined, vendors developing database servers and customers developing client applications can perform their activities with relative freedom from the other. The openness of the common-interface approach is highly dependent on the openness of server-specific modules that are to be incorporated into the client interface. The openness of common-gateway approach is dependent on the openness of the client interface.

6.5.4 Manageability

Somebody has to manage and control the EDC products within the enterprise. Particularly for large systems, the practical control issues must be addressed within the EDC architecture. For instance, are failures logged so that they can be monitored at a central facility? Can user-level accounting of EDC resources be performed? Can structural changes (e.g., moving certain tables to other servers) be performed without forcing quiescence of the entire system?

From the enterprise perspective, the common-protocol approach offers the highest potential for manageability, but only to the extent that the protocol allows for easy monitoring and centralized administration. The manageability of common-gateway approach is probably conceptually the simplest since all the interoperability is concentrated in the database gateway component. Thus, a specific control element exists to focus monitoring and administration functions. Further, other system management functions, such as data distribution, can be performed within the database gateway since the gateway can act independently from the client or server platforms. The manageability of the common-interface approach is probably the lowest since the interoperability mechanism is dispersed widely on user workstations.

6.5.5 Reliability

Like performance, the EDC architecture must provide an acceptable degree of reliability, depending on the specific function being performed. For some functions, a low degree of reliability may be acceptable, assuming that there is a corresponding means of recoverability. On the other hand, an enterprise that is designing mission-critical applications to be supported by the EDC architecture must have the confidence of high reliability. This criterion is similar to performance; that is, the reliability of operating an EDC architecture will be dependent on its implementation.

6.5.6 Stability

This criterion is interpreted as architectural maturity. The degree to which the architecture is stable (its robustness in handling unusual or unplanned circumstances) is the degree to which products of that architecture will be stable. Stability also involves the mechanism by which the architecture evolves. The architecture has to change over time to incorporate new technologies and requirements. But if the architecture changes too rapidly or in a manner that is not upwardly compatible, then the advantage of cumulative products is reduced or negated.

Stability or architectural maturity can vary widely. The common-gateway approach should offer the highest stability, since the client interface has been predefined and since applications using this interface exist. On the other hand, the stability of a common-protocol approach will be difficult since the protocol will have to anticipate future functionality and allow for it. The common-interface approach can be stable but is highly dependent on a flexible specification for implementing client or server drivers. As an application becomes more server-aware, the stability of that application over time will decline.

6.5.7 Permissiveness

This criterion deals with the lack of a priori restrictions. SQL servers are all different. Motivated by market differentiation, each vendor offers extensions to accent their products. These extensions can be very useful to specific applications (e.g., multimedia), even to the point of permitting the application to be feasible at all. The architecture should allow some degree of permissiveness with regard to these variations and extensions in the various SQL implementations. Being permissive would then allow the enterprise to adopt new technologies for database connectivity without making existing ones obsolete.

There are basically two alternatives to permissiveness with EDC architectures. First, there is the *minimal* approach, which defines the set of capability that is the *least common denominator* intersection among database platforms. Second, there is the *maximal* approach, which defines the set of capabilities that is the union among all database platforms. A typical hybrid approach is to specify a minimal set of capabilities, along with an optional set.

The maximal approach is desirable in general, but there is a problem. The maximal set of capabilities is always changing. Where is the current knowledge of the capabilities of a new server platform? In the custom application? Not unless we redesign it for each new platform. In the interface? Possibly, but it must have a special new module that is easily incorporated for each new platform. In the server platform itself? Possibly, but the protocol must be extended to handle queries about capabilities.

The common-interface and common-protocol approaches can vary widely on this criterion, depending on how the client interface and protocol, respectively, are designed. The common-gateway approach assumes a fixed client interface and, hence, can be relatively low in permissiveness.

6.5.8 Summary of Comparisons

Although it is difficult to make general statements about the EDC approaches, the above comparison invites the following summary: Common protocol has the best potential for openness and interoperability; common gateway has the best potential for portability, acting as the glue for connectivity and decentralized manageability; and common interface has the best potential to complement the other two.

▼ 6.6 RELATION TO EDC FUNCTIONAL LAYERS

In the first chapter, enterprise database connectivity was described as having three functional layers that build upon one another: access management, copy management, and warehouse management. The next three chapters examine each of these layers in terms of the possible EDC architectures. In particular, access management will emphasize the common-interface and common-gateway approaches, while considering common protocols as a future development. Copy management will emphasize the common-gateway approach for transferring relational tables among databases. And, warehouse management covers all three approaches in its framework.

▼ DISCUSSION QUESTIONS

1. What are alternatives to a layered architecture?

2. What are the key conditions for an effective layered architecture?

3. What is a protocol? How does it differ from an interface?

4. What are the pluses and minuses to whether an application is server-aware? And capability-aware?

5. What is the critical component for the common-gateway approach?

6. What functional value can be designed into a database gateway? How does this compare to the typical costs for a database gateway?

7. What is the weak point in the common-protocol approach?

8. Can you think of other interesting combinations of the three approaches?

9. How can one design applications so that they can interoperate with a variety of servers, while retaining all the functionality of any specific server?

10. For your company, rate the priorities on the comparison criteria for EDC architectures.

▼ 7

ACCESS MANAGEMENT

In this chapter, we return to the topic of Access Management with a more practical discussion. The chapter builds on the concepts of client-server architectures and the EDC building-block approaches using illustrations from current products.

Access management is defined as: "managing the architecture for the enterprise to support direct access from any client to any server." It would include combinations of common-interface, common-gateway, and common-protocol approaches as building blocks for a coherent architecture. Access management implies that there is an enterprise-wide agreement on the set of interfaces and protocols to be utilized within the enterprise. In other words, it is more than a simple compilation of installed products.

In this chapter, we will first discuss direct SQL access and then client-server networking. Client-server networking is currently the single most important problem of access management of client-server systems. It deals with laying the infrastructure to support the connection between the set of clients to the set of available servers. To illustrate the three EDC approaches, we will then focus on the following access management products: Microsoft Open Database Connectivity, Micro Decisionware Database Gateway for DB2, IBM Distributed Relational Database Architecture, and ISO Remote Database Access.

▼ 7.1 ALLOWING DIRECT SQL ACCESS

The issue is whether desktop applications (especially generic tools) should be allowed to access directly database tables with SQL statements. After spending most of this book discussing the processing of SQL against some database server, it may seem odd to address this issue now. But, the way SQL is used has changed. . .

In the early days of SQL databases, a user would construct the SQL statement manually and then submit it to the server. The user was usually limited in his/her capacity to construct complex SQL requests. However, generic desktop tools have become very sophisticated in their construction of SQL requests. Hidden from the user, SQL requests are constructed with amazing complexity. These requests are often referred to as *hidden SQL*. The assumption of the desktop tool is that the user has available a local powerful database server. If the database is actually a remote DB2 being used by hundreds of other people, the situation is different.

With a large remote database, the best solution is to allow direct access if the database is primarily used for decision support, there are lots of small tables, good tools that generate smart SQL, and the network is adequate and stable. Otherwise, direct access should *not* be allowed.

What, then, are the alternatives? The first alternative is to grant privileges only for executing stored procedures, rather than DML operations (i.e., SELECT, INSERT, UPDATE, and DELETE). This approach is compatible with the object-oriented data model, in which all objects are encapsulated in methods. The methods (e.g., stored procedures) are the only means of manipulating the objects. The second alternative is to stage data from large remote databases to local (more friendly) databases. The impacts of raw SQL are lessened, while the capacity to respond quickly is enhanced for that user.

The issue of allowing direct SQL access has become a major policy decision in operating larger client-server systems. Let's now examine the ways in which those systems are networked.

▼ 7.2 CLIENT-SERVER NETWORKING

The most confusing aspect of client-server architecture is determining what connects to what and how. Put simply, we have a *plumbing* problem: making sure the pipes are properly connected so that client applications can flow requests to important servers and receive results back!

This problem is very important for many corporations. Having invested huge sums in setting up mainframe, minis, and LAN database servers, these corporations are faced with establishing connectivity architectures and policies for workstation access to the various database servers. Because desktop tools are exploding in variety and complexity, the connectivity requirements are changing constantly. In addition, the reliability of a connection from a specific client application to a specific database server is dependent on many factors and on many vendors.

7.2.1 Fitting the Pipes Together

The basic problem is that certain kinds of things are confused with other kinds of things. It is like comparing apples with oranges, or more like comparing plastic pipes with copper pipes. To unscramble this confusion, we need to consider the following different components:

- development tools (custom and generic) on client platform
- client interfaces on client platform
- local-area transports (both logical and physical)
- wide-area transports (both logical and physical)
- server interfaces on server platform

If we had a ten-dimensional spreadsheet, we could then enumerate all the combinations! Even this would not simplify matters, since we would still have a hard time understanding what is important.

Note that these components fit together in a certain sequence, as shown in Figure 7.1. On the left side, we first start with either a custom development environment or a generic tool, depending on our application requirements. In either case, a client interface is required to accept the client SQL request and process it against a database server. The usual function of this interface is to retrieve a relational result set and return it to the application. All of this resides on a specific client platform.

On the right side, we have the server platform, which is connected through some communication network. Here we have a number of options depending on which database servers are required. Also, with several platforms it is important to specify the telecommunication monitor that is controlling our connection. For example, there are significant differences in connecting to DB2 via TSO or via CICS. Let's now turn our attention to the highlights of each of these components.

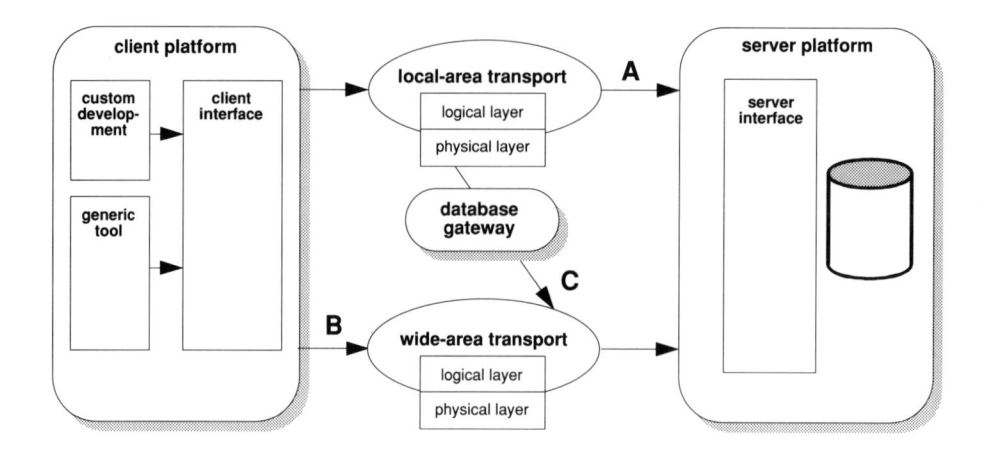

Figure 7.1. Components of client-server networking.

7.2.2 Client Platform

Today's important client platforms (usually denoted by their operating system) are:

- DEC VMS
- DEC Ultrix
- DOS with MS Windows 3.x
- DOS
- HP/UX
- IBM/Microsoft OS/2 v1.x
- IBM OS/2 v2.x

- IBM AIX
- Macintosh
- NCR 3000
- OSF UNIX kernel
- SunOS
- USL UNIX kernel
- Windows NT

Applications under DOS are quite distinct from applications under DOS with Windows. And the Windows environment is rapidly evolving from 3.0 to 3.1 and on to Windows/NT, which will then bring it into the same class as OS/2 and UNIX client workstations. The OS/2 world has experienced considerable turbulence with the disagreements between IBM and Microsoft. There can be significant differences among OS/2 v1.x versions, particularly with LAN support. The long-term viability and MS-Windows compatibility of IBM's OS/2 v2.0 as a client platform is in doubt. The Windows/NT client platform is being positioned by Microsoft as the eventual evolution for Windows applications. Then there is the Macintosh, an oldie but goodie that continues to have significant presence in most corporations. And there are a variety of UNIX workstations, although UNIX as a client platform has had limited penetration, especially in general business settings.

And finally, there are the mainframe platforms acting as clients. The bulk of application software still resides on these platforms, but this fact is often overlooked. Connectivity is lacking between the mainframe platform acting as a client and the new server platforms, however, limiting its potential.

On these client platforms, there are basically two components: development tools and client driver interfaces. As described in Section 2.5, the development tools must be considered as two types: custom and generic. The custom development tools are *used by programmers* to develop the custom applications for a specific business function. There are the conventional 3GL languages (such as C and COBOL) and the newer GUI development tools (including Asymmetrics Toolbook, PowerSoft PowerBuilder, Matesys ObjectView, and Microsoft Visual Basic). The 3GL programming languages usually interface to the client driver via an embedded approach (i.e., precompilation phase to scan for SQL and usually perform an early binding to the database). However, the GUI development tools usually use a call-level approach (i.e., simple procedural calls implying usually a late binding of SQL to the database).

The generic tools are *used by end users* to directly support their ad hoc functions. The reason that this custom/generic distinction is important is that the connectivity options vary greatly based on this factor. In this category, we are blessed with a magnitude of amazing products that enable a user to immediately tap into a database; these products include:

- Asymmetrics Toolbook
- Borland Paradox using SQL-link
- Borland Dbase IV 1.1 Server Edition
- Byth Software Omnis 7
- Channel Computing Forest and Trees
- Cognos PowerPlay
- Cooperative Solutions Ellipse
- DataEase Intl DataEase 4.5
- Datura SQL Commander
- Easel Corp EASEL
- Enfin ENFIN/2
- Gupta Technologies Destiny

- Gupta Technologies SQL Windows
- Intelligent Environments Applications Manager
- Lotus Development Lotus 1-2-3 with DataLens
- Matesys ObjectView
- MDBS Object/1
- Microsoft Access
- Microsoft Excel using Q+E
- Microsoft Excel using ODBC
- Microsoft SQL Server utilities
- Microsoft Visual Basic
- Micro Decisionware PC/SQL-link
- Mozart MOZART
- Open Books OPEN BOOK
- Pioneer Software Q+E and Q+E Library
- PowerSoft PowerBuilder
- Progress Software Application Development System
- Revelation Technologies Advanced Revelation
- Software Products InfoAlliance
- Vanguard DB2 Tools
- Vinzant SQLfile

This list of tools is growing constantly, with new ones added each week. For this discussion, the important point is that each of these generic tools must interface to the database via some client driver that is hidden within that tool. Most driver interfaces are provided (and controlled) by the database vendors, but there is a growing trend to provide more open client interfaces. A few popular client interfaces for specific SQL database servers are:

- IBM SAA CPI for OS/2 Database Manager
- Oracle SQL-net for Oracle
- Sybase/Microsoft DB-library for SQL Server

7.2.3 Server Platform

On the other side, there are the various server platforms. It is important to carefully distinguish whether a platform is for client applications or for database servers. The requirements are quite different. Further, it is not advisable to mix client and server support on the same platform (except for small-scale systems). The most popular server platforms include:

- DEC VAX/VMS
- DOS

- IBM AIX
- IBM DOS/VSE
- IBM MVS via TSO, CICS, IMS/DC, APPC/MVS
- IBM OS/2 v1.3 or v2.0
- IBM OS/400
- IBM VM via CMS, CICS, etc.
- Microsoft OS/2 v1.31
- Microsoft Windows/NT
- NCR 3000 UNIX
- Novell Netware Loadable Modules
- SunOS
- Tandem NonStop
- Windows NT

The more popular database servers on these platforms are:
- DEC Rdb
- Gupta SQLbase
- IBM DB2
- IBM OS/2 Database Manager
- IBM SQL/DS
- Informix
- Microsoft SQL Server
- Oracle
- Sybase SQL Server
- Tandem NonStop SQL
- Teradata DB Computer

7.2.4 Plumbing in the Middle

As mentioned earlier, there are three basic routes for connecting client platforms to server platforms, all of which involve some combination of local-area transport and wide-area transport. For each transport, there is a logical layer (i.e., algorithms for access control, routing, session, etc.) and a physical layer (i.e., nuts-and-bolts cabling). Let's explore the popular alternatives in these categories.

First, alternatives for the logical layer for local-area transports include:
- APPC LOO (LAN-only option)
- AppleTalk
- DECnet
- Named Pipes
- NetBios
- OSI

- SMB (system message blocks)
- SPX/IPX (of Novell Netware)
- TCP/IP

NetBIOS is probably the most universal transport, although it is considered to be a bit out of date. SMB and SPX/IPX tend to be used in most corporate LANs, depending on whether LAN Manager or Netware is used. UNIX LAN tends to use TCP/IP transports of various flavors, with OSI used in UNIX environments that strongly adhere to ISO standards (which are a definite minority). And finally, AppleTalk is used only where Macintosh workstations are dominant.

The situation is more complex with Named Pipes, a higher level transport designed by Microsoft. It can ride upon several of the other transports, such as NetBIOS, SMB, SPX/IPX, and others.

Second, the alternatives for the physical layer for local-area transports include:

- ARCNET (coaxial or twisted pair)
- Ethernet - 10BASE-T (unshielded twisted pair)
- Ethernet - 10BASE2 (thin coaxial)
- Ethernet - 10BASE5 (standard or thick coaxial)
- FDDI fiber-optic cabling
- PhoneNet (unshielded phone cable)
- Token ring - 16Mb Type 1 (thick shielded twisted pair)
- Token ring - 4 Mb Type 3 (thin unshielded twisted pair)
- Token ring - 4 Mb Type 1 (thick shielded twisted pair)

Most of these logical transports can be supported by most of these physical layers. The popular cabling today is either Ethernet 10BASE-T or TR Type 3 because of the convenience and low cost of cabling large buildings. PhoneNet is very simple and inexpensive, but is limited to AppleTalk. Finally, FDDI for fiber-optic cabling is coming on strong as the preferred backbone cabling for all of the above. FDDI may be extended over time to the desktop and into global wide area networks.

Third, there are various network operating systems (NOS) that support both the logical and physical layers to provide such services as Email and printer spooling. The popular options include:

- Banyan VINES
- IBM LAN Server, using SMB, NetBIOS, APPC LOO
- Microsoft LAN Manager, using SMB and Named Pipes
- Novell Netware, using SPX/IPX, supports NetBIOS and Named Pipes

Fourth, choices for the logical layer of wide area networks include:
- APPN
- DECnet
- OSI
- SNA LU2 (3270 data stream)
- SNA LU6.2 APPC
- SONET
- TCP/IP

We need to consider these alternatives if the database platform is remote from our local-area network. Within IBM SNA networks, the LU2 protocol using the EHLLAPI interface is giving way to LU6.2, which is a more reliable and controllable protocol. In UNIX networks, TCP/IP has been extended from LAN into the WAN environment. In DEC networks, there is DECnet, which prides itself on interconnecting smoothly to everything else. Finally, SONET is emerging as the interconnection for global fiber-optic networks.

Finally, some options for the physical layer of wide area networks are:
- FDDI (and CDDI, SDDI) fiber-optic
- fractional T1, full T1, T3
- Frame Relay
- ISDN
- SDLC leased/switched lines
- X.25

Within the IBM SNA networks, SDLC is the dominant protocol with a migration away from leased lines to switched or T1/T3. In international networks, X.25 is often intermixed with SNA. Unfortunately, ISDN is being considered by many to be a failure within the United States. Finally, FDDI cabling on a national or even global scale is being taken seriously by most large corporations, either privately or through long-distance carriers.

As you can see, the plumbing in the middle is messy! To adequately understand and design this plumbing requires a variety of skills. Remember that networking client-server database requires the skills of a database administrator/designer. It has been unusual for this type of person to be involved with this messy plumbing in the middle.

7.2.5 Three Basic Routes

In the middle is the tricky part. First, we need to consider the differences in local area networks (LAN) versus wide area networks (WAN).

The architectures and protocols for LAN and WAN evolved from very different perspectives. Until recently there was poor compatibility between the two types of networks. In every corporation with more than one site, there is some combination of LAN and WAN, in place, to be used for our client-server networking.

As we saw in Figure 7.1, we can connect a client application to a database server via one of three routes:

A. Local area network directly to the server platform. The database server is then called a *local server*.
B. Wide area network directly to the server platform. In this case, we have a workstation that is not attached to a LAN but does have a WAN connection to the server platform. The database server is then called a *remote server*.
C. Local area network to a wide area network and then to the server platform. In this case, the workstation is attached to a LAN that provides the WAN connection.

What are the trade-offs among the three routes? Route A seems the simplest, and Route C seems the more complex.

LAN transports do provide higher bandwidth and reliability than WAN transports because of the inherent design constraints of using long-distance telecommunications lines. Moving data across the LAN can be 10 to 100 times faster and more reliable than across the WAN. Hence, the protocols for connecting applications to databases can provide a closer coupling between the two. Scrolling cursors across a vista of GUI-style list boxes is difficult and inefficient with a 9600-baud switched SDLC line.

Historically, Route B is the oldest, stemming from the VT100-like asynchronous terminals, to 3270 synch terminal via bisynch lines, and then to coax-attached PC via SNA LU2. Even today, Route B is the largest installed base in most corporations. However, Route A is rapidly gaining ground with the percentage of LAN-attached PCs increasing daily. Further, Route C is the IBM-suggested alternative, with SNA forming the corporate backbone to interconnect the token-ring LANs via TIC-attachments on cluster controllers.

What is the best route? The trend is away from remote servers (as defined above) and towards local servers because of the requirements of greater bandwidth to the desktop. In most corporations, however, the issues of integrating with legacy systems and deploying enterprise-wide

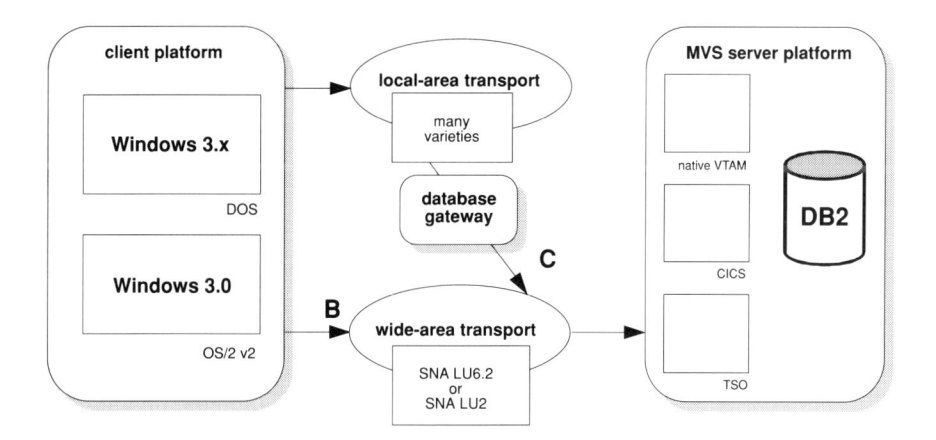

Figure 7.2. Connecting Windows clients to DB2.

applications weaken the argument for the one-big-happy-LAN design. Route C is being adopted as the compromise architecture for consolidating resources on the LAN and for providing only one point of connect into the WAN. For consolidation and manageability, Route C is preferred by many corporations despite its greater complexity.

7.2.6 Connecting Windows Clients to DB2

An excellent example of client-server networking is the challenge of connecting DB2 directly to desktop applications, especially front-end database tools operating in the Microsoft Windows environment. As usual, the plumbing problem is complex.

Figure 7.2 illustrates the important components. Note that only two routes are possible: B for WAN only and C for LAN/WAN combination via a gateway. Route A (i.e., LAN only) is not possible because there is no method for directly connecting a LAN protocol into an MVS teleprocessing monitor; all connections must by handled by VTAM using an SNA protocol.

First, there are two environments in which Windows applications can operate: DOS with Windows 3.x and OS/2 version 2 with Windows 3.0. The OS/2 environment does provide "Windows better than Windows" in terms of preemptive multitasking and memory protection. However, OS/2 Windows applications require more resources on the client platform and do not yet have support for the new extensions released in Windows 3.1.

Second, there are usually three routes between the client and server platforms; however, this figure shows only Route B and Route C which both involve the WAN transport. To connect to DB2, an application must at some point connect into the WAN transport of SNA, either as LU2 (3270 data stream) protocol or as LU6.2 (APPC) protocol. Therefore, DB2 cannot technically be designed as a local server (according to our previous definitions), although it can be an expensive workgroup server.

Third, the WAN transport cannot connect directly into the DB2 database engine. Another subsystem (e.g., CICS, TSO, or a native VTAM task) must exist, running a server interface locally to the DB2 subsystem. Even the Distributed Relational Database Architecture (DRDA) Application Server that comes packaged with DB2 V2R3 runs as a separate VTAM task under MVS/370. As an aside, whatever happened to using APPC/MVS direct attach to DB2? It exists, but no vendor is touching it, including IBM.

Let's examine the two routes to DB2 in more detail. Route B (WAN-only) is simpler but supports less function and reliability. Since the LU6.2 protocol stack requires over 250 Kb of main memory, most DOS platforms are unable to support LU6.2 as a direct WAN transport to DB2; thus, the reliability of the APPC syncpoint mechanism and efficient buffering schemes cannot be utilized. Further, the VTAM/NCP configuration of LU6.2 to lots of PU2.1 machines is very tricky!

In contrast, the LU2 protocol has been omnipresent in large corporations, but the program-to-program interaction has been notoriously unreliable. Logon sequences must be performed manually from a 3270 emulation screen. Critical time delays and broadcast messages have been a universal headache of LU2 applications. Data transfers can be reliable (e.g., IND$FILE) but must be packetized with checksums on top of the EHLLAPI functions. Therefore, this WAN-only route to DB2 must use a proprietary protocol over LU2. The bottom line is that the WAN-only route is only for simple, light-duty, noncritical applications by users who are familiar with the mainframe and willing to tolerate its quirks.

Route C (the LAN-WAN combo) requires a gateway platform (usually under OS/2 or UNIX) to convert into the WAN transport. The important issues involve: What is the added value of this gateway platform? If it only is providing a LAN-to-WAN transport conversion, then the over-

Client-Server Networking ▼ 179

Client Interface	LAN Transport	Gateway	WAN Transport	Server Interface
Microsoft Open DB Connectivity	n/a	n/a	SNA LU2	MDI CICS/TSO Access Server
IBI EDA/SQL API	n/a	n/a	SNA LU2 or LU6.2	IBI EDA/SQL Server
Microsoft Open DB Connectivity	n/a	n/a	SNA LU2	IBI EDA/SQL Server
IBM SAA CPI	NetBIOS	IBM Distributed DB Connection Services/2	SNA LU6.2	IBM DRDA Appl. Server for DB2
Sybase/Microsoft DB-Library	Named Pipes	MDI DB Gateway	SNA LU6.2	MDI CICS Access Server
Microsoft Open DB Connectivity	Named Pipes	MDI DB Gateway	SNA LU6.2	MDI CICS Access Server

Table 7.1. *Products that provide connectivity.*

head may not justify the additional complexity. We need to investigate the support for consolidation of resources (e.g., LU6.2 protocol stack, SQL translation) and a point of control (e.g., load balancing, additional security).

Some of the available products that provide connectivity between a Windows client and DB2 are shown in Table 7.1. The first three alternatives use Route B (WAN only), while the latter three use Route C (LAN gateway to WAN). The earliest method used the DB-Library API through the MDI Database Gateway to the MDI Access Server under CICS. The Microsoft ODBC interface allows several methods of accessing DB2: either LU2 or LU6.2 (preferred) and either from MDI or IBI. Traditional COBOL applications under Windows have only one method, the IBM DDCS/2 gateway. The Microsoft ODBC, MDI Database Gateway, and IBM DDCS/2 will be described in later sections of this chapter.

7.2.7 Requirement for Network Integration

How is the above discussion useful to you? Let's assume that you are responsible for determining enterprise policy for client-server networking.

One possible tactic is to specify the important end points, and then work through the combinations that may link those end points.

In particular, specify the important client tools and platforms. Then specify the important database targets. Finally, work through each potential linkage from one to the other. Carefully note the "I-gotcha" situations in which most of the linkage is present but critical pieces are missing. Through vendor questioning and focused prototyping, investigate those features and capabilities that will be critical to your requirements. For example, certain development tools may be excellent for clients using DOS or Windows but may lack support for Macintosh clients. It is possible, but difficult, to formulate an enterprise policy; having no policy results in an unmanageable situation.

As is apparent from the above discussion, there is an urgent requirement to integrate the various LAN and WAN protocols, especially among SNA (LU6.2), TCP/IP, and OSI. Various groups have considered matching the higher layers of OSI with the lower layers of TCP/IP. One proposal, called RFC 1006, does accomplish this objective and has been implemented in products by several companies. In addition, IBM has submitted a proposal to X/Open called Multi-Protocol Transport Networking (MPTN) and has announced their new SNA blueprint based on a Common Transport Semantics (CTS). The major components of this blueprint are shown in Figure 7.3.

The current IBM networking offerings are shown along the left side of the figure. Common Programming Interface for Communications (CPI-C) with Advanced Program-to-Program Communication (APPC) has been part of the System Application Architecture (SAA) since the early days and is the basis of many current products from IBM and others. The new pieces of this picture are the support for Remote Procedure Calls (RPC) with the OSF Distributed Computing Environment (DCE) flavor; Message Queuing Interface (MQI); TCP/IP; and OSI.

The MQI component is interesting. MQI is a mail facility for an application to send a message to another application *with guaranteed message delivery and recovery.* Instead of establishing a continuous connection between a client and server, a client application could send (using MQI) a request message and continue with other processing until a result message is received. The MQI specification is fairly simple and supports mixtures of the following data types: character strings, bit strings, binary integers, packed-decimal integers, and floating-point numbers. Surpris-

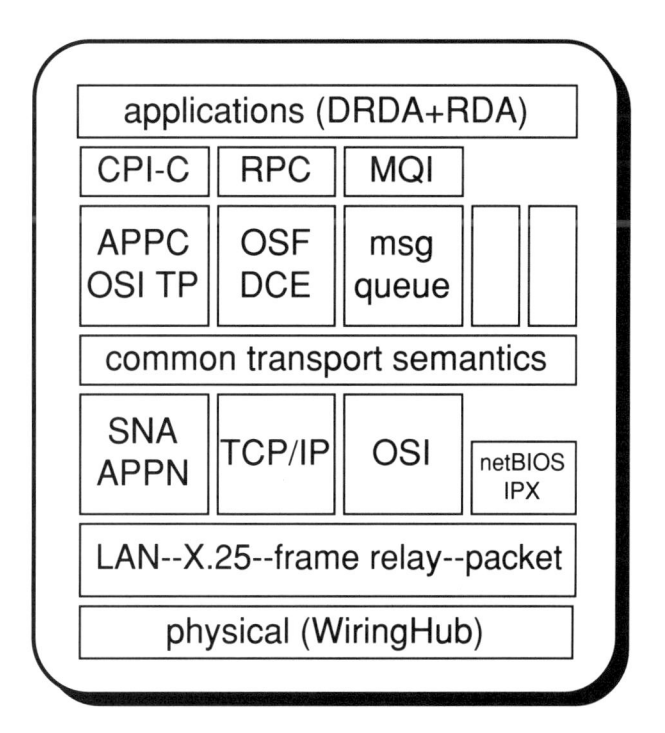

Figure 7.3. New IBM SNA blueprint.

ingly, IBM is positioning MQI for high transaction processing environments, such as banking and securities.

In summary, the current situation for client-server networking is a mess for the large enterprise. Through careful architectural planning, it is possible to have a coherent client-server network; there will be limitations, however, on the diversity of clients, servers, and protocols supported. Hopefully, an integration of networking alternatives can evolve from such efforts as the MPTN proposal to X/Open.

In the next sections, we will examine details of some EDC products. First, the Microsoft ODBC is a good example of a common-interface approach. Second, the MDI Database Gateway is a good example that pioneered the common-gateway approach. Third, the IBM DRDA and ISO RDA are good examples of the common-protocol approach. The chapter ends with a comparison of DRDA and RDA.

▼ 7.3 INDEPTH: MICROSOFT OPEN DATABASE CONNECTIVITY

The Microsoft Open Database Connectivity (ODBC) is an example of the common-interface approach since it offers a generic API to application programs for access to a variety of data sources. ODBC is now compatible with Windows 3.x and will be bundled into future versions sometime in 1993.

ODBC is designed for Microsoft Windows and Windows NT for use by a C program using a call-level (rather than embedded) SQL interface. Although there is some commitment for ODBC on the Apple Macintosh, there is no commitment for plain DOS, PM, COBOL, Motif, etc. Releasing the ODBC API as part of Windows is a bold move by Microsoft to strengthen its theme of "Information at your fingertips." Although Microsoft can make a legitimate claim that ODBC is a vendor-neutral API based on emerging standards, this positioning is aimed at advancing Microsoft Windows towards the dominant client platform.

ODBC is Microsoft's interpretation and productization of the SQL Access Group Call-Level Interface (SQLCLI) specification, which is being passed onto the ANSI SQL committee for their consideration. Currently, X/Open has published SQLCLI as a snapshot document.

The SQLCLI specification forms the core level of ODBC, which is roughly half of the ODBC functions. There are 51 functions defined for ODBC, 22 of which are in the core. The ODBC core is intended to track the SQLCLI specifications as it evolves through the ANSI standards process. The other half of ODBC are unique extensions by Microsoft. Some of these extensions are generic and should have been in the SQLCLI, such as obtaining information on servers, tables, columns, datatypes, etc. The other extensions (which are needed for Windows applications) are scrollable cursors, multiple row retrievals/updates, asynchronous calls, extended data types, and multiple result sets.

A number of vendors have announced ODBC drivers to provide access to IBM DB2, DEC Rdb, Microsoft SQL Server, Borland Paradox, Oracle, Xbase, Excel XLS, and normal text files. The unusual aspect of these drivers is the access to data that resides on the client platform, such as Xbase files.

An ODBC Software Developer Kit (SDK) includes the reference material and libraries required to develop applications and drivers using ODBC. Included in this SDK is an ODBC Driver Test Utility.

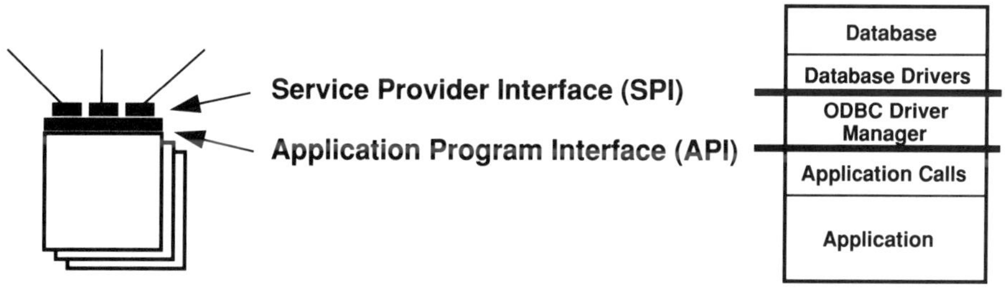

Figure 7.4. Common interface and ODBC.

7.3.1 Windows Open Service Architecture

ODBC is an example of what Microsoft calls the Windows Open Service Architecture (WOSA). The objective is to define specifications for a set of services, such as data access (with ODBC), multimedia, or electronic mail. Then, any software vendor can freely add its value as a service provider to Windows applications.

Let's examine the ODBC architecture from the WOSA perspective. Figure 7.4 illustrates how the common-interface approach relates to the ODBC architecture. The common interface has a generic interface plus various drivers. As expected, the interface between the application and the generic interface is called the Application Programming Interface (API). As a new component, the interface between the generic interface and drivers is called the Service Provider Interface (SPI).

As seen in Figure 7.5, the specification of the SPI can open up the market for vendors to develop drivers independent of the application and of the driver manager. The application programmer would program to the API, while the service provider (i.e., driver developer) would program to the SPI. The analogy in Windows is the current support for printer drivers and the emerging support for multimedia devices. To an application programmer, the ODBC API is just part of the huge Windows API library. To a database vendor, ODBC appears as a SPI to program an ODBC driver to access the database. The Dynamic Link Library (DLL) capability of Windows plays a key role in loading ODBC drivers as needed.

184 ▼ Access Management

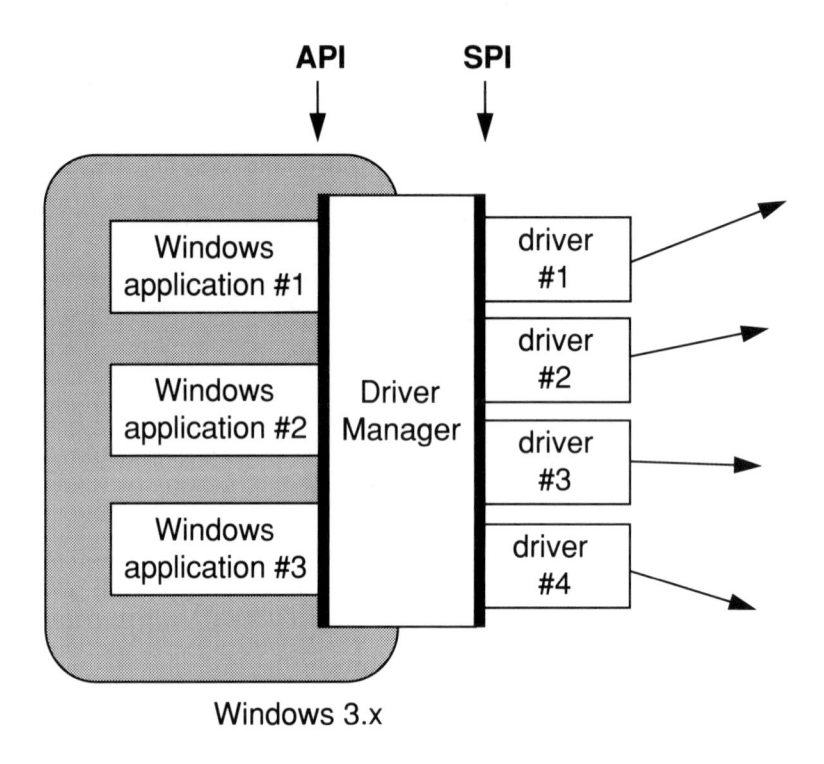

Figure 7.5. Microsoft Windows Open Service Architecture.

The trick is that any Windows program (either generic tools or custom applications) requiring a particular service should use the proper WOSA API. Then, the user has the freedom to purchase and install the proper WOSA driver to supply that service. Microsoft controls the particular WOSA specification and the driver management piece that links the internal Windows program to the external WOSA driver. Theoretically, any vendor can freely play on either side.

ODBC is a first test of the WOSA concept. Technically, there is no doubt that it will work. The challenge will be whether the marketplace will respond positively in both directions: Windows programs using the proper WOSA API, and software vendors using the WOSA SPI to provide a rich array of services. The message from Microsoft to a software vendor is clear: "If you want access to any external structured data from Windows, use ODBC!"

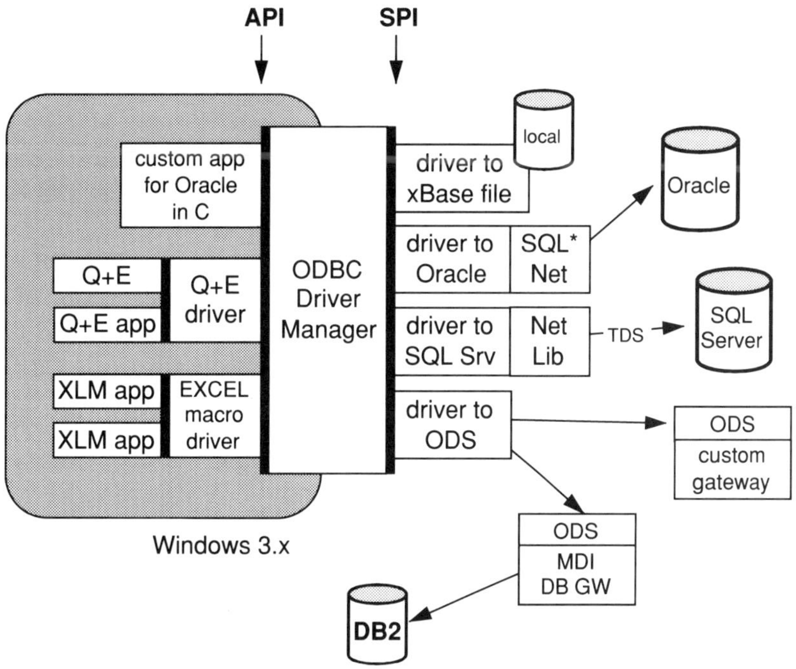

Figure 7.6. Examples of using ODBC.

7.3.2 Examples of Using ODBC

How does ODBC actually work in the Windows environment? Consider the examples in Figure 7.6. On the left are various Windows applications requiring data from external sources. On the right are ODBC drivers that connect to these data sources. In the middle is the ODBC driver manager, which provides the linkage between the API and SPI and loads the proper drivers when needed.

For example, suppose that we write a custom application in C to target the Oracle database. We could use the Oracle-supplied API (called the Oracle Call Interface); however, there is a possibility of retargeting the application to another server in the future. To maintain this transparency, the ODBC API is used instead. When the application is executed, the ODBC driver manager loads the driver for Oracle (which will use SQL-net internally). In the application logic, we ask the ODBC API whether we are connected to an Oracle server (i.e., being server-aware). If so, the logic invokes unique features of the Oracle server, thereby reducing the ability to retarget. With ODBC, the application developer could make the design decision as to whether the application should be server-aware.

In another example, we have some tools (Q+E and Excel) that require data access from a variety of sources, such as a local xBase file. Note that both tools have their own higher-level APIs.

On the driver side, there is an example of using SQL Server with an ODBC driver to emit the private protocol (i.e., TDS) of that database server. Also, an ODBC driver is available to handle the Open Data Services (ODS) so that various Windows applications can use gateways, such as the custom gateway shown. Finally, the MDI Database Gateway for DB2 can be used by ODBC applications via the same ODBC driver.

7.3.3 Brief Overview of ODBC Programming

Now let's explore some simple details of programming with ODBC. First, the ODBC specification consists of over fifty functions. These functions are divided into the core functions (i.e., those that adhere to the SQL Call-Level Interface of the SQL Access Group, as described later), and two levels of Microsoft-unique extensions, in roughly a 50-50 ratio. Appendix A lists these functions, along with a description. Note especially the functions that obtain information about the server.

As shown in the Figure 7.7, an application must first allocate an ODBC environment, then allocate one or more connections, and finally allocate one or more statements within each connection. This forms a

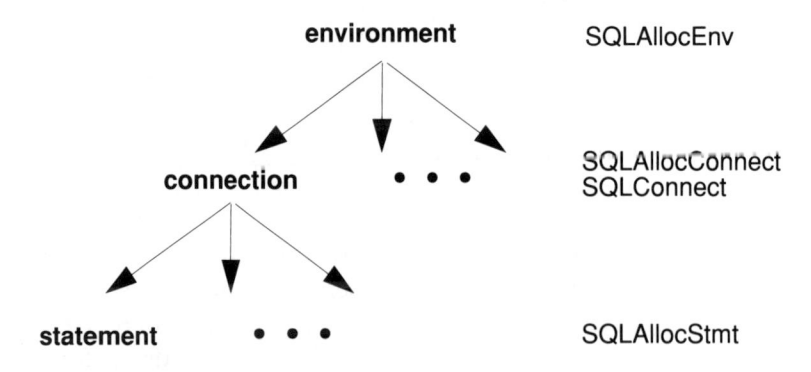

Figure 7.7. ODBC context hierarchy.

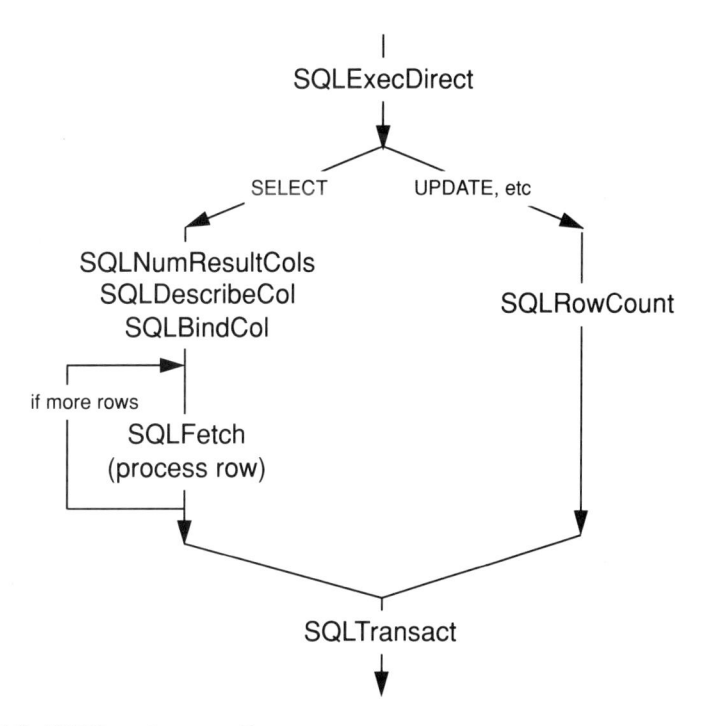

```
            SQLExecDirect
           /            \
     SELECT          UPDATE, etc
       /                    \
  SQLNumResultCols
  SQLDescribeCol         SQLRowCount
  SQLBindCol
      ↓
  if more rows
   SQLFetch
  (process row)
           \            /
            SQLTransact
```

Figure 7.8. ODBC one-time execution.

neat hierarchy of environment-connection-statement. By executing SQLAllocConnect and SQLConnect, the connection is established that enables the application to access one data source. Likewise, by executing SQLAllocStmt, the application can submit an SQL statement to the database for processing.

To execute a statement, there are two choices: one-time execution or repeated execution. The program for one-time execution of an SQL statement is shown in Figure 7.8. In this case, the program first executes SQLExecDirect. Then, there is a choice between SELECT statement with results, non-SELECT with the number of rows affected, or DDL statement.

If we are performing a SELECT, then we determine the number of columns with SQLNumResultsCols, the description for each column with SQLDescribeCol, and the C variable to contain the value for each column with SQLBindCol. This is performed once; the program loops for each row in the result set and processes it.

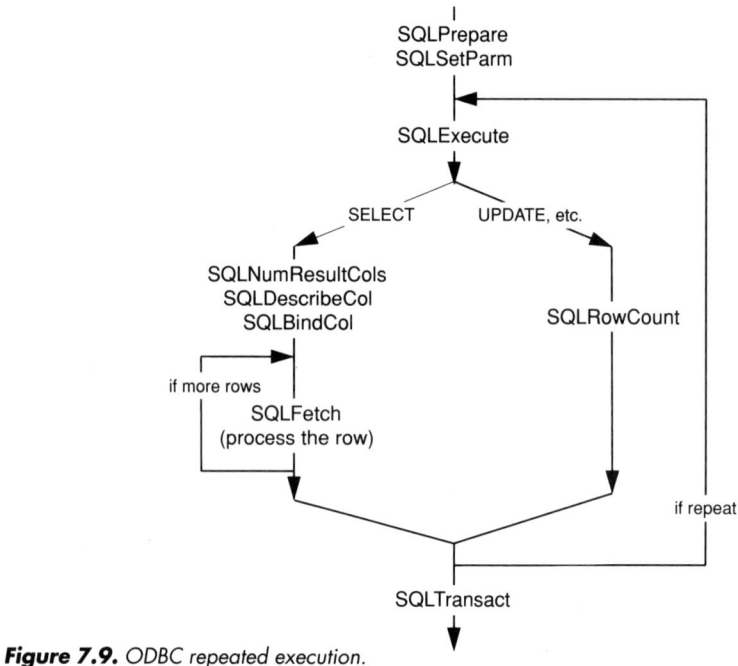

Figure 7.9. ODBC repeated execution.

The program for repeated execution of an SQL statement is shown in Figure 7.9. The program first executes the following three statements:

- SQLPrepare to parse and optimize the SQL statement
- SQLSetParm to place any parameters into the statement
- SQLExecute to actually execute the SQL statement

Again, we have the choice between a SELECT and non-SELECT statement, with the subsequent processing as before.

Note that ODBC can only handle dynamic SQL, implying that an SQL statement is parsed and optimized each time a program is executed. We can prepare a statement once, however, and then execute it several times within the context of the current program execution, as described above.

▼ ▼ ▼ ▼ ▼ ▼

For Further Information: Contact the ODBC group at Microsoft (206/936-2655). Ask for the ODBC Software Developers Kit (which will eventually be part of the Windows Software Developers Kit). See the Microsoft ODBC Interface API Reference, along with the Applications Programmer's Guide and Driver Programmer's Guide.

▼ 7.4 INDEPTH: MICRO DECISIONWARE DATABASE GATEWAY

The Database Gateway (DG) from Micro Decisionware Inc. (MDI) adopts the common-gateway approach to providing access between client applications using the SQL Server DB-Library interface and mainframe database management systems (such as IBM DB2, Teradata Database Computer, or IBM SQL/DS). In addition, it performs several other functions:

- mapping of LAN named pipes instances to SNA LU6.2 conversations
- SQL syntax transformations
- conversion of data types
- generic system catalog procedures
- maintenance of transaction boundaries
- conversion of status codes and messages
- balancing request loads to server
- enforcing limits to server
- CICS applications as clients initiating requests
- direct bulk transfer between mainframe and LAN databases
- invoking stimulated stored procedures under CICS
- data compression of result sets to client

The MDI DG also supports access to DB2 by a number of front-end tools vendors, such as Pioneer Q+E, Borland Paradox, Powersoft PowerBuilder, and Channel Computing Forest and Trees.

As shown in Figure 7.10, there are three components involved with the MDI DG:

- client application at the user workstation
- MDI Database Gateway on the LAN server platform
- DB2 database access via the MDI CICS/DB2 Access Server

The first component—the client application—is programmed to the SQL Server DB-Library (either from Sybase or Microsoft) or to the Microsoft ODBC interface. The application can reside on any platform supported by the two interfaces. Either interface performs the following functions for the client application:

190 ▼ Access Management

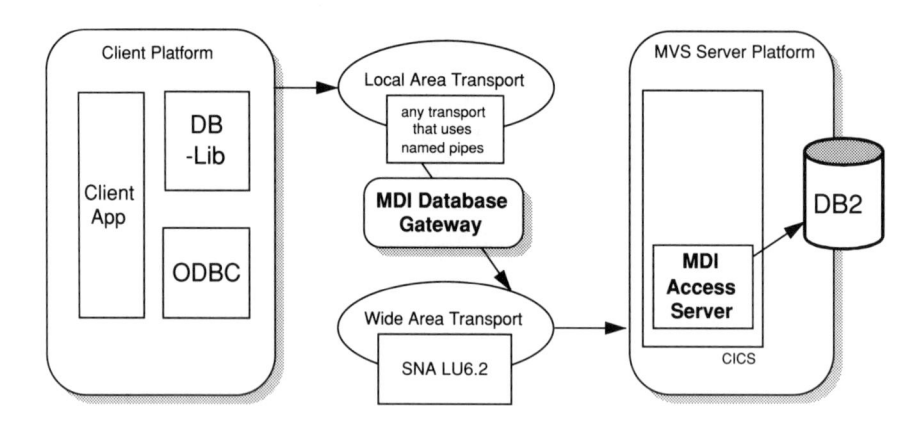

Figure 7.10. Components of Database Gateway.

- establish a connection to a database or gateway
- construct and process an SQL request
- retrieve status codes and messages
- retrieve the result data
- terminate the connection

The second component—the MDI Database Gateway—receives the requests using the Microsoft Open Data Services (ODS). Between the client and gateway, requests can flow over named pipes or several other LAN logical transports using the tabular data stream (TDS) protocol. The ODS interface is a classic server interface, which is event-driven by requests from clients. It is implemented by using a single process thread for each connection. The events handled by ODS are simply open connection, execute request, and close connection. The gateway can reside on the same server platform with Microsoft SQL Server, IBM Database Manager, or other OS/2 database systems.

To the client application, the Database Gateway appears as a local SQL Server but it processes the requests on DB2 by using SNA LU6.2 conversations. An optional Huffman compression algorithm can be enabled to reduce data transfers for both requests and results. The server platform is identified as an SNA Type 2.1 logical unit capable of multiple, parallel APPC sessions to the CICS region residing on the MVS/370 mainframe. The physical link to the mainframe is SNA SDLC using leased/switched lines or using token-ring to a TIC-attached cluster controller.

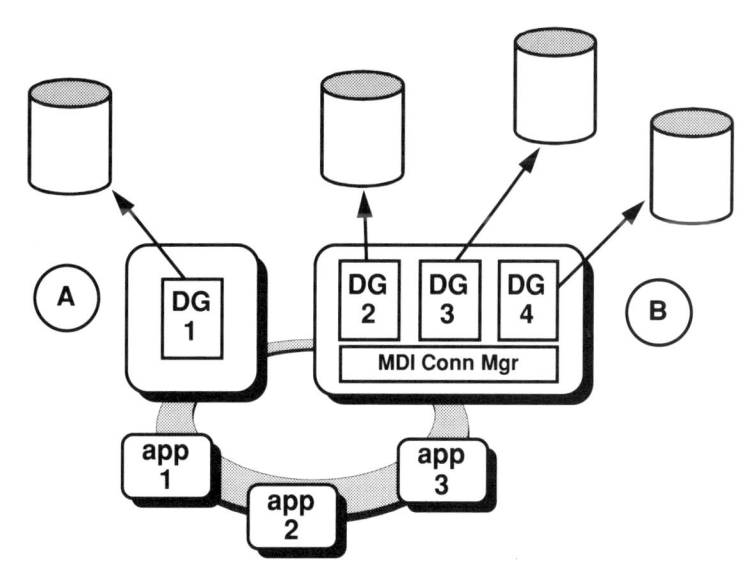

INDEPTH: Micro Decisionware Database Gateway ▼ 191

Figure 7.11. *Handling multiple clients and servers.*

The third component—the MDI Access Server under CICS—receives the requests from VTAM via the LU6.2 conversations. Security is verified by the usual security package (e.g., RACF, ACF-II, or Top Secret) through VTAM using APPC conversational-level security. Optional validation exits can be used for additional security checks. User identifications are passed from the client and are used for both the CICS ID/password and the DB2 user privileges. The MDI Access Server submits the request to DB2 using the normal CICS client interface for DB2 and retrieves the results from DB2. The results can be spooled directly back to the client (via the gateway) or collected in temporary CICS storage. By spooling to temporary storage, DB2 resources can be released as soon as possible.

There are several additional features of interest to the MDI Database Gateway. As shown in Figure 7.11, one client application can connect to the same or different gateways multiple times since each connection is maintained on a unique process thread with separate data segments. Further, several instances of the gateway can be operating on the same platform (shown in B), allowing access to multiple mainframe databases concurrently. An MDI Connection Manager provides load balancing among multiple gateways to the same database in production environments. Likewise, multiple CICS instances (i.e., transaction IDs) of the

192 ▼ Access Management

MDI Access Server under CICS can run, allowing for different CICS operating characteristics.

A CICS transaction program can be written by the mainframe-knowledgeable user to act as a stored procedure to DB2. The client application would invoke this stored procedure in the same manner as one within SQL Server. The gateway routes the request to execute the stored procedure to CICS, which invokes it with a CICS LINK operation. The results from this transaction program can be flowed back to the client as if the data were retrieved from DB2.

Figure 7.12 shows how this CICS Remote Stored Procedure feature allows access to DB2 using static SQL and also to any CICS data resource (e.g., VSAM data sets, IMS databases, IDMS databases, etc.). In A, an SQL request was executed directly by the MDI Access Server against DB2 as dynamic SQL. In B, a user-written RSP was invoked instead, which could have executed the same SQL request, but this time it is static SQL. In C, a user-written RSP is utilizing data from another CICS data resource. In D, a CICS transaction program can be written to request services from the LAN servers with the mainframe acting as a client. The requests flow through the MDI Access Server via an APPC allocation to the LAN server platform to be processed by SQL Server or by the Database Gateway. Hence, the mainframe-based clients can process the same requests as the LAN-based clients can.

As is explained further in the Copy Management chapter, the MDI

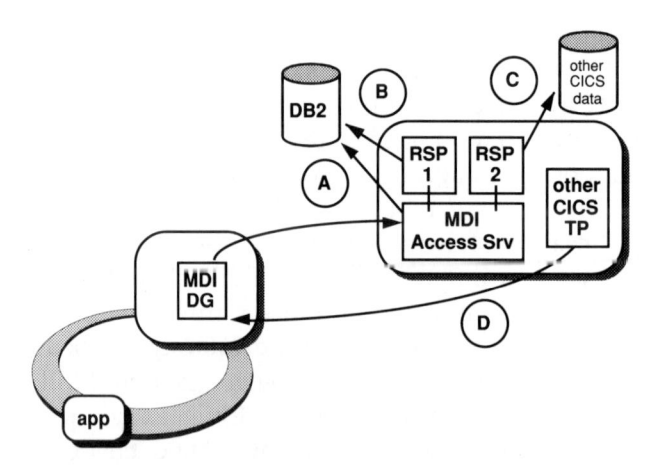

Figure 7.12. Remote Stored Procedures and client services.

Database Gateway can transfer bidirectionally relational tables from these databases to several mainframe databases (e.g., DB2). In addition, SQL Server can internally invoke the gateway through a remote stored procedure from either another stored procedure or a trigger. Hence, an update can flow to DB2 whenever triggered by similar data being updated in SQL Server.

▼ ▼ ▼ ▼ ▼ ▼

For Further Information: Contact Micro Decisionware at 303/443-2706. See the Database Gateway Reference and Installation Guide.

▼ 7.5 INDEPTH: IBM DISTRIBUTED RELATIONAL DATABASE ARCHITECTURE

The IBM SAA Distributed Relational Database Architecture (DRDA) is a common-protocol architecture that links together the IBM (and potentially other) database platforms. The major components involved with the DRDA protocol are shown in Figure 7.13.

The client interface is called the *Application Requester* (AR), and the server interface is called the *Application Server* (AS). The protocol be-

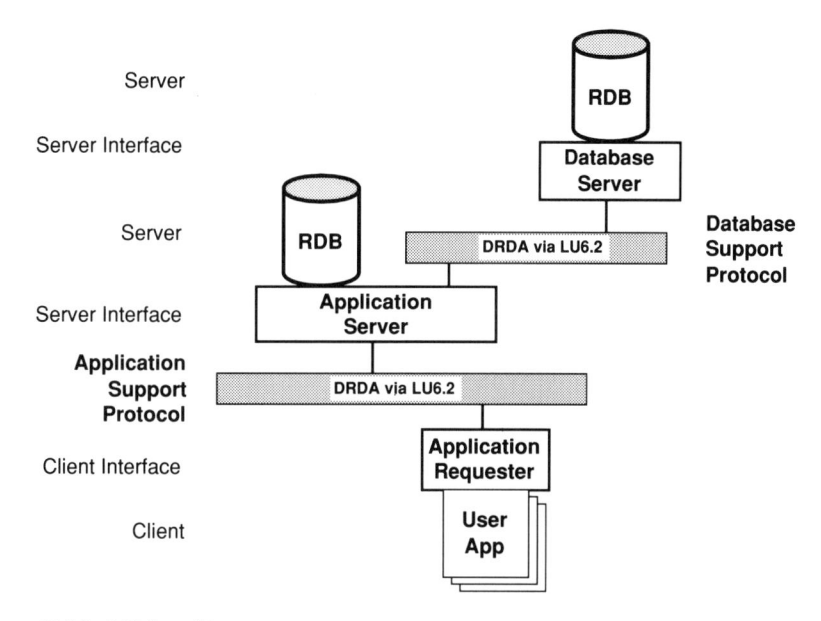

Figure 7.13. DRDA architecture.

tween the AR and AS is called the *Application Support Protocol* since it focuses on supporting the client application. The DRDA transport mechanism is based on the basic verb set of Advanced Program-to-Program Communications (APPC) which uses the SNA LU6.2 network protocol; however, the new SNA blueprint indicates that DRDA could operate over TCP/IP and OSI protocol stacks in the future.

An interesting feature of DRDA is that a second layer to the protocol is planned. The AS can emit another version of DRDA called the *Database Support Protocol* that links together the AS with the *Database Server* (DS). This second layer enables the AS to route requests or sub-requests on to other databases. Note that the AS is then acting as a gateway with a hidden client interface into the second layer.

As described in Chapter 5, IBM has defined four levels of distributed database transactions:

- **Remote request**: *one* statement to *one* database
- **Remote unit of work**: *many* statements to *one* database
- **Distributed unit of work**: *many* statements to *many* databases but only *one* database per statement
- **Distributed request**: *many* statements to *many* databases and each statement can refer to *many* databases.

The important distinction is that the *many* statements are handled as a unit in a single logical unit of work.

The current DRDA specification (DRDA/1) has defined functions for only a remote unit of work. IBM is working on the other levels and the Database Support Protocol, but they have not been finalized. The next level will support a distributed unit of work that can span databases and will distinguish whether the AR or AS directs the distribution of work among databases.

In general, DRDA has had to cope with the significant heterogeneity among the SAA database platforms. Figure 7.14 shows that various combinations of clients and servers are possible within the DRDA environment.

IBM is committed to providing complete interconnection among the four SAA database platforms: DB2 2.3, SQL/DS 3.3, SQL/400 2.1.1, and DBM. Existing IBM products provide that complete interconnect, except for DBM. OS/2 Database Manager (DBM) is supported with a DRDA AR (using DDCS/2), but no DRDA AS is available yet for DBM. In other words, an application remote from OS/2 cannot currently access data

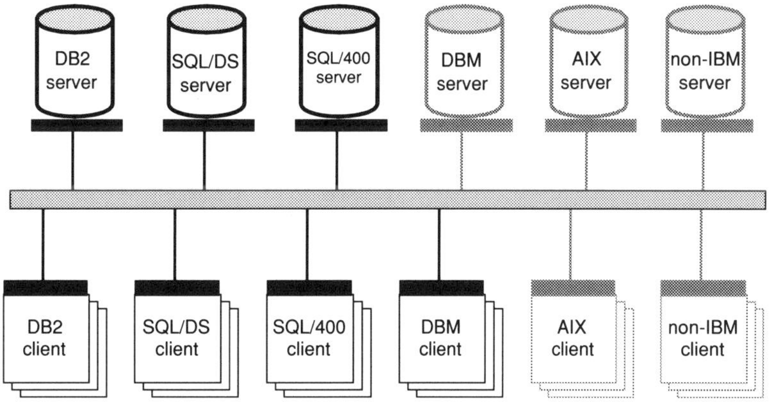

Figure 7.14. DRDA combinations.

contained in the DBM database via DRDA. The intent to support the new AIX database has been announced.

IBM is soliciting other vendors to support their products with as either a DRDA client or DRDA server. The companies that have publicly expressed commitment to develop either a DRDA AR or AS in various environments are: Borland International, Cincom Systems, Computer Associates, Gupta Technologies, Informix, Micro Decisionware, Oracle, Sybase, and XDB Systems. As of this time, Micro Decisionware, XDB, and Object Technology have announced DRDA-compliant products.

As an EDC architecture, DRDA is permissive in its tolerance of SQL syntax and data types. It has full support of a bind function, implying that static SQL is the normal mode of processing SQL statements. Various efficiency issues have been addressed, such as sending data in its native format and converting at the receiver only when necessary. DRDA also supports single-row fetch with updatable cursors or multiple-row fetches for efficiency. Finally, DRDA supports various system management features, such as generation of NetView alerts and collection of accounting information.

7.5.1 DRDA Components

As mentioned above, the AR and AS glue the client application together with the server database using a common protocol. In simple terms, this protocol consists of three layers:

196 ▼ Access Management

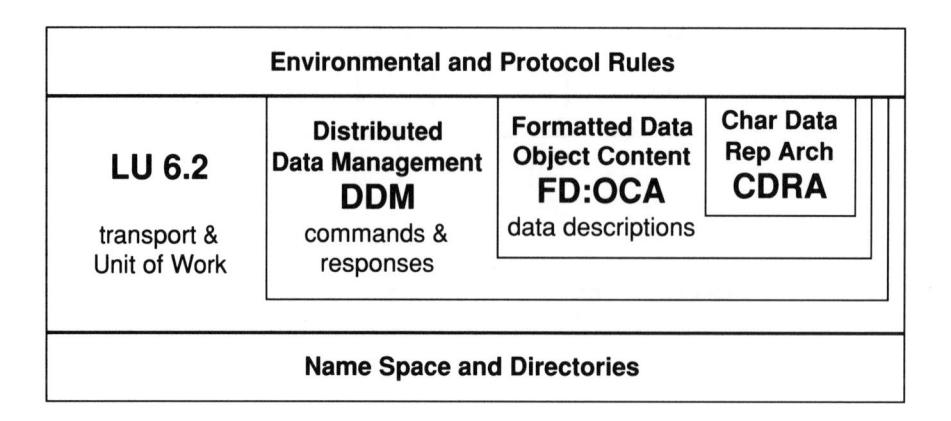

Environmental and Protocol Rules				
LU 6.2 transport & Unit of Work	**Distributed Data Management** **DDM** commands & responses	**Formatted Data Object Content** **FD:OCA** data descriptions || **Char Data Rep Arch** **CDRA**	
Name Space and Directories				

Figure 7.15. DRDA components.

- transport
- commands
- data formats

The actual DRDA components are shown in Figure 7.15. LU6.2 provides the transport and maintains a unit of work across remote nodes in an SNA network. The *Distributed Data Management* (DDM) specifications provide the basic command definition that DRDA specializes for database connectivity. All data is described and represented using the *Formatted Data: Object Content Architecture*, or FD:OCA (pronounced "fa-doe-ka" by insiders). Finally, character data is given special treatment with the *Character Data Representation Architecture* (CDRA) that specifies all the various single-byte and double-byte character sets in the world.

Within the LU6.2 transport is also the support for transaction (UOW) management to provide commit and rollback functions. Flowing through the LU6.2 conversation are data structures composed of the other DRDA components: DDM, FD:OCA, and CDRA. The Distributed Data Management (DDM) commands provide the basic functions of connecting to databases, binding SQL statements, fetching result rows, opening cursors, etc. Whenever data flows between the AR and AS (usually when a result set is returned to the AR), the data is described using the FD:OCA and, in the case of character data, the Character Data Representation Architecture (CDRA).

Establish Connection
    Access Database   establishes a path to a named RDB
Bind Packages
    Begin Bind   starts package bind into RDB
    Bind Statement   binds a single statement to package
    End Bind   indicates that package is complete
    Drop Package   deletes an existing package
    Rebind Package   rebinds an existing package   #
Execute SQL
    Prepare SQL   binds to existing package
    Execute SQL   executes existing package section
    Execute SQL Immediate   executes statement sent with command
    Describe SQL Results   gives definition of result columns
    Open Query   starts cursor open & fetching
    Continue Query   continues to fetch result data
    Close Query   terminates cursor processing
Retrieve Catalog Information
    Describe Table Columns   defines columns of a table   #
    Describe Privileges   defines privileges of executor   #
Control Transactions
    Commit Transaction   commits current unit of work
    Rollback Transaction   aborts current unit of work
    Interrupt Request   stops current running request   #

NOTE: # indicates DDM commands that are optional for DRDA/1.

Figure 7.16. DRDA DDM commands.

Shown in Figure 7.16 is a list of DDM commands used in DRDA flows. Remember that a package must be created prior to executing SQL, even in the case of dynamically executing SQL.

7.5.2 An Example

It is very easy to get lost in the DRDA forest, with its complex of terminology and multiple layers. There is nothing better than an example to allow one to hug a tree in this forest!

Let's consider a simple example of printing a list of customers. Assume that we have a table in some remote SAA database (supported by a DRDA AS) called CUSTOMER. This table contains the customer number, name, and state, along with other information. Also assume that we have to select customers based on their state; that is, we need only to print customers residing in a specific state.

7.5.2.1 *Program preparation and execution*

To understand the way in which DRDA works, let's briefly review the usual steps for handling embedded SQL programs. There are two distinct steps that we must perform to obtain our customer list: program preparation and program execution.

Program preparation is typically accomplished by a programmer within the company's Information Services organization. In consultation with the database administrator, the programmer would code, in COBOL perhaps, the program to generate the customer list. Note that, according to the SAA specifications, we could have used other languages, such as C, PL/1, or FORTRAN, depending on the SAA platform.

After the programmer has coded the program into a source file, the program is passed through a precompiler that strips the SQL-specific statements and substitutes normal CALL statements in their place. The program then proceeds through the usual compile and link processing.

As noted in Chapter 2, the important part of program preparation is what happens to the SQL statements. They are placed in a bind file (or sometimes called a database request module), which is bound to the database containing the required data. This important part of program preparation is called *bind processing*, which involves:

- parsing the SQL syntax
- checking security
- validating the table and column names
- optimizing the algorithm for accessing data

Within the DRDA context, the result of bind processing is the creation of a *package* within the database. The intent of bind processing is that a significant portion of the database processing is performed *once*, so that program execution (which is performed many times) will be more efficient.

The second step, *program execution*, is performed by a user when he/she desires the customer list, sometime after the program preparation has been completed. During execution, the program refers to the package previously created and invokes it with the required parameters.

Now let's look at some real COBOL code:

```
ID DIVISION
       PROGRAM-ID.         EXAMPLE1.
       AUTHOR.             RD HACKATHORN.
ENVIRONMENT DIVISION.
    ...
WORKING-STORAGE SECTION.

01 CUSTOMER-TABLE.
    10 CUST-NO             PIC S9(9) USAGE COMP.
    10 CUST-NAME           PIC X(20).
    10 CUST-STATE          PIC X(2).

01 STATE                   PIC X(2).

    EXEC SQL                                            #1
        INCLUDE SQLCA
    END-EXEC.

PROCEDURE DIVISION.

100-MAIN.
    DISPLAY '*** BEGIN EXECUTION OF EXAMPLE 1'

    EXEC SQL                                            #2
        CONNECT TO DALLAS02
    END-EXEC.

    IF SQLCODE NOT = 0
        PERFORM 300-HANDLE-ERROR THRU 300-EXIT
        GO TO 400-FINISH.
    DISPLAY '*** AS INFORMATION = ' SQLERRP.
```

```
    EXEC SQL                                                    #3
        DECLARE CURSOR1 CURSOR
        FOR SELECT CUST-NO, CUST-NAME
            FROM CUSTOMER
            WHERE CUST-STATE = :STATE
    END-EXEC.

    MOVE 'CO' TO STATE.

    EXEC SQL                                                    #4
        OPEN CURSOR1
    END-EXEC.

    IF SQLCODE NOT = 0
        PERFORM 300-HANDLE-ERROR THRU 300-EXIT
        GO TO 400-FINISH.

    DISPLAY '*** DISPLAY COLORADO CUSTOMERS'

    PERFORM 200-FETCH THRU 200-EXIT
        UNTIL SQLCODE NOT = 0.

    DISPLAY '*** END OF LIST'

    EXEC SQL                                                    #5
        CLOSE CURSOR1
    END-EXEC.

    GO TO 400-FINISH.

200-FETCH.
    EXEC SQL                                                    #6
        FETCH CURSOR1
            INTO :CUST-NO, :CUST-NAME
    END-EXEC.
```

INDEPTH: IBM Distributed Relational Database Architecture ▼ 201

```
        IF SQLCODE NOT = 0
            PERFORM 300-HANDLE-ERROR THRU 300-EXIT
            GO TO 400-FINISH.

        DISPLAY 'CUSTOMER NUMBER = ' CUST-NO.
        DISPLAY 'CUSTOMER NAME = ' CUST-NAME.
        DISPLAY ' '.
    200-EXIT. EXIT.

    300-HANDLE-ERROR.
        DISPLAY '*** ERROR = ' SQLCODE.
    300-EXIT. EXIT.

    400-FINISH.
        DISPLAY '*** END EXECUTION'
        GOBACK.
```

The COBOL program shown above contains six sections of SQL-specific statements (in bold). These SQL sections are numbered #1 through #6.

Section #1: INCLUDE SQLCA is very simple. It copies in the declaration for the SQLCA structure which includes general status variables. For instance, SQLCODE tells us the status of the previous SQL operation. If it is not zero, then some type of error condition has occurred. In an actual program, error checking and handling would be much more extensive. As we will see later, this section has no effect on the DRDA flows, since it is a local declaration.

Section #2: CONNECT is perhaps the most interesting section. The CONNECT statement distinguishes this program as using DRDA to connect to a remote database for RUOW processing. If this section had been omitted, then the program would access data on the local database, rather than on a remote database. The SQLERRP field contains information about the AS to which we have connected.

Section #3: DECLARE CURSOR is another declaration section that defines the SQL statement to be executed. It is a simple SELECT of customer data restricted to only those customers in a specified state. The value is contained in an input *host variable* called STATE.

Section #4: OPEN CURSOR is where the action really begins. At this point, the package (as defined in Section #3) is invoked with the proper STATE value, and the remote database generates the desired result table.

Section #5: CLOSE CURSOR terminates the use of the cursor, releasing any database resources, such as the result table. Note that an explicit commit of the RUOW is not necessary for retrieval. However, if we were updating the remote database, an additional COMMIT section would be required.

Section #6: FETCH CURSOR retrieves a single row from the result table and places the data into the proper output host variables, which can then be displayed to the user. Note that this section is executed multiple times from the PERFORM statement as long as no error condition occurs.

7.5.2.2 *What happens under the covers?*

The programmer sees the program being compiled and bound. The user sees the program displaying the desired data. But the data is at some remote database. What happens under the covers? Let's examine the DRDA flows that occur, first during program preparation and then during program execution.

During program preparation, the AR for the precompiler will need to:
- Establish the connection
- Do the bind processing
- Terminate the connection

During program execution, the AR for our COBOL program will need to:
- Establish the connection
- Process the query and retrieve data
- Terminate the connection

Note that our COBOL program does not generate or even know anything about any DRDA flows. It is only the AR at our local site that is involved with the DRDA flows. On behalf of first the precompiler and then our COBOL program, the AR takes care of those complex details, as descied in the following sections.

7.5.2.3 *Establishing the connection*

Note that establishing and terminating the connection is essentially the same, although the context (program preparation versus program execution) is very different.

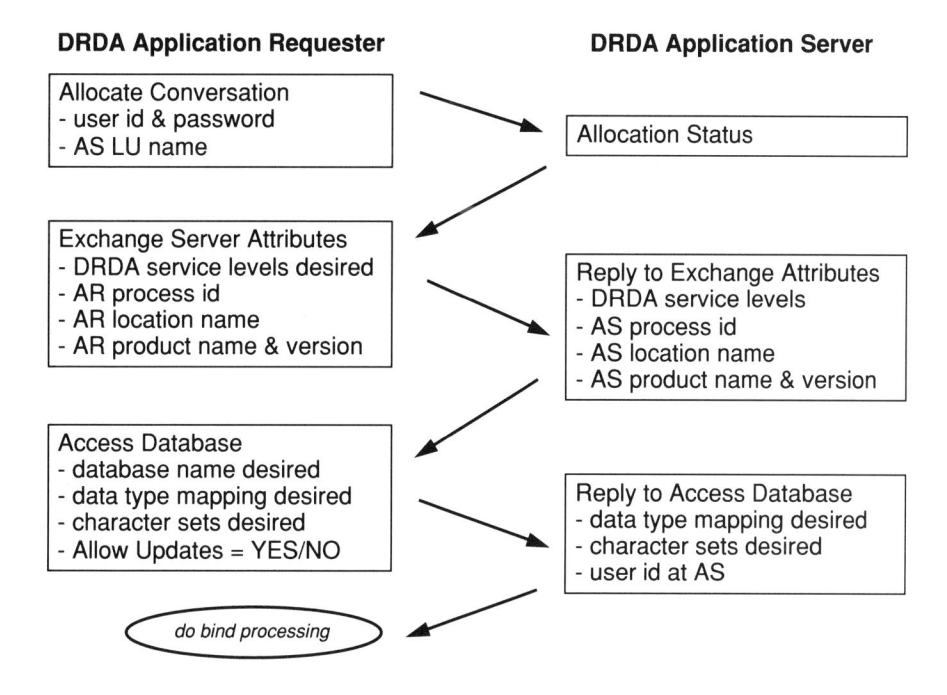

```
DRDA Application Requester                    DRDA Application Server

┌─────────────────────────────┐
│ Allocate Conversation       │──────────┐
│ - user id & password        │          ↘  ┌─────────────────────────────┐
│ - AS LU name                │             │ Allocation Status           │
└─────────────────────────────┘          ↙  └─────────────────────────────┘
                                     ┌──
┌─────────────────────────────┐      ↙
│ Exchange Server Attributes  │
│ - DRDA service levels desired│─────────┐
│ - AR process id             │          ↘  ┌─────────────────────────────┐
│ - AR location name          │             │ Reply to Exchange Attributes│
│ - AR product name & version │             │ - DRDA service levels       │
└─────────────────────────────┘             │ - AS process id             │
                                         ↙  │ - AS location name          │
                                    ┌──     │ - AS product name & version │
┌─────────────────────────────┐      ↙      └─────────────────────────────┘
│ Access Database             │
│ - database name desired     │
│ - data type mapping desired │──────────┐
│ - character sets desired    │          ↘  ┌─────────────────────────────┐
│ - Allow Updates = YES/NO    │             │ Reply to Access Database    │
└─────────────────────────────┘             │ - data type mapping desired │
                                            │ - character sets desired    │
              ╭─────────────────╮        ↙  │ - user id at AS             │
              │ do bind processing│◀──         └─────────────────────────────┘
              ╰─────────────────╯
```

Figure 7.17. Establish connection.

What is needed to establish a connection? In the Figure 7.17 we see the sequence of DRDA flows required. On the left side are commands generated by the Application Requester and sent to the Application Server, which generates the appropriate replies.

The first command, Allocate Conversation, requests the allocation of an APPC conversation. In the situation of accessing DB2 on an MVS mainframe, VTAM would check the user id and password through host security, allocate the required conversations, and invoke the AS to respond to subsequent commands. The location of the remote database is determined from the database name in the CONNECT statement (e.g., DALLAS02), which is converted into the appropriate LU name.

The second command, Exchange Attributes, is a dialogue where the AR tells who it is to the AS and the AS tells who it is to the AR. It is a relatively simple exchange but a very important one that determines whether a proper DRDA connection can be established.

The third command, Access Database, is the AR asking to use a specific database. On some SAA platforms like VM/ESA, there can be many databases available for remote access, so that the AS LU name is not sufficient. The mapping of SQL data types to the binary representations for the AR platform is specified, along with the desired representations for the character sets. Finally, a flag indicates whether updates to the database will be allowed during this connection.

In response, the AS replies with the mapping of SQL data types and character sets on the AS platform. It is important to note that data is sent in its native format, implying that the receiver must convert it (if necessary). For example, consider the situation where DB2 is returning the customer number (which is INTEGER inside of DB2) to an AR on OS/2. The customer number will be in S/370 four-byte integer format. The AR must convert this value into the proper Intel 80x86 format before giving it to our COBOL program. Likewise, when our COBOL program under OS/2 asks for all Colorado customers, the "CO" value for CUST_STATE will be sent as an OS/2 character set and must be converted to the appropriate S/390 character set by the AS for DB2. These FD:OCA and CDRA specifications become very tricky for multilingual applications.

That's all that is needed to establish a connection between a DRDA AR and DRDA AS! Actually, the details are a bit complex, but IBM or another DRDA vendor has taken care of these details.

7.5.2.4 *Doing the bind processing*

Figure 7.18 illustrates the sequence of DRDA flows to bind our SQL statements into the target database. The DRDA AS accepts the bind request and binds the SQL statements into a package that is physically stored within the target database.

The first command, Begin Bind, identifies the package and sets various bind options (e.g., isolation level). Packages are identified roughly as follows:

- package or plan name (e.g., LISTCUST1)
- consistency token (e.g., timestamp at precompilation)

The Begin Bind command also specifies the user id that owns the package and thus has the proper database privileges. For instance, the owner id must have SELECT privileges against the CUSTOMER table; however, the user id that executes this package only needs EXECUTE privileges for the package.

INDEPTH: IBM Distributed Relational Database Architecture ▼ 205

DRDA Application Requester

Begin Bind
- package id
- various bind options
- user id owning package

Bind SQL Statement
- package id
- section number

Specify SQL Statement
- "SELECT CUST-NO ..."

Specify Input Host Variable
- descriptions (e.g., :STATE)

End Bind
- package id
- max number of sections

terminate connection

DRDA Application Server

establish connection with updates allowed

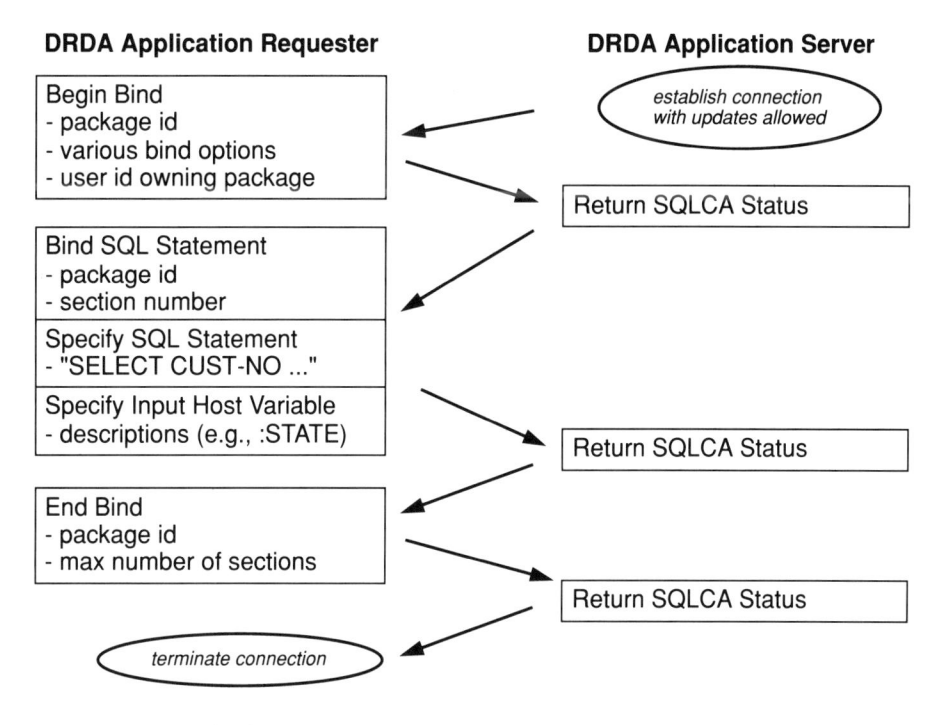

Return SQLCA Status

Return SQLCA Status

Return SQLCA Status

Figure 7.18. *Do bind processing.*

The second command, Bind SQL Statement, specifies the new section within the package for the following SQL statement and its input host variables (as contained in the third and fourth commands).

The final command, End Bind, simply ends the bind processing for this package. For our COBOL program, only the single DECLARE CURSOR statement needs to be bound. The CONNECT, OPEN, FETCH, and CLOSE statements are not part of the package and flow commands at program execution.

7.5.2.5 Terminating the connection

To complete program preparation, we need to terminate the connection. As shown in Figure 7.19, connection termination simply commits the logical unit of work and deallocates the APPC conversation. Since we update the target database (by creating a new package), we must perform an explicit commit before completing bind processing.

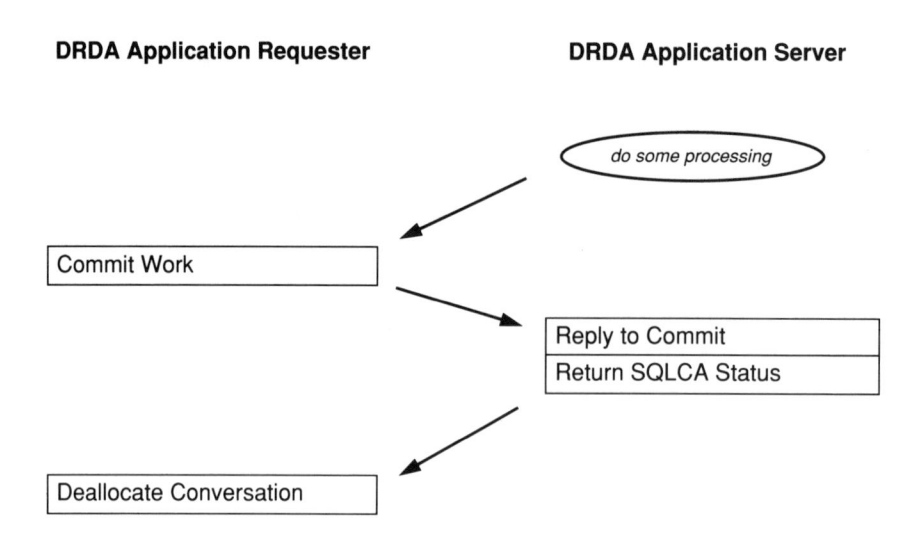

DRDA Application Requester　　　　　　　**DRDA Application Server**

```
                                           ( do some processing )
        ┌─────────────────┐              ↙
        │ Commit Work     │
        └─────────────────┘  ↘
                                ┌──────────────────────┐
                                │ Reply to Commit      │
                                │ Return SQLCA Status  │
                                └──────────────────────┘
        ┌────────────────────────┐  ↙
        │ Deallocate Conversation│
        └────────────────────────┘
```

Figure 7.19. Terminate connection.

7.5.2.6 Doing the query processing

Now let's consider the program execution. As shown in Figure 7.20, establishing and terminating the connection is the same, except that updates are *not* allowed for our simple retrieval application.

The connection is established when the AR is invoked by the CONNECT statement (in section #2). The INCLUDE SQLCA and DECLARE CURSOR sections are actually not going to invoke the AS, and hence no DRDA flows will occur at these points during program execution.

When the OPEN CURSOR (in section #4) is executed, the AR will send an Open Query command to the AS requesting the answer set from the target database. The package id plus the section number specifies our SELECT statement that was previously bound. In this example, the SELECT statement does not allow updates (i.e., no FOR UPDATE clause was specified). Data can, therefore, be retrieved in the more efficient block mode, rather than one row at a time.

As part of the OPEN CURSOR, the value for the input host variable (:STATE) is passed through the AR to the AS. When the package is executed at the remote database, the value of "CO" can qualify the query to retrieve only Colorado customers.

In reply, the AS will send a description of the answer set. For exam-

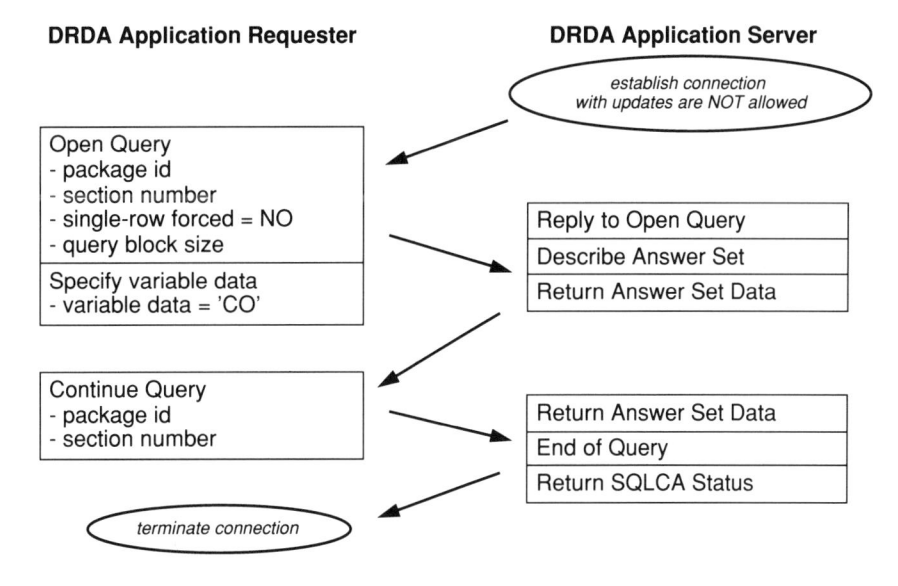

INDEPTH: IBM Distributed Relational Database Architecture ▼ 207

Figure 7.20. Process query and retrieve results.

ple, this description would consist of two columns; the first column is CUST-NO as INTEGER; the second column is CUST-NAME as CHAR(20). Then, the first block of data rows for the answer set will be sent to the AR.

If the answer set is small, the entire answer will be sent back in this first flow. If not, subsequent Continue Query commands from the AR will retrieve the remainder. Note that most FETCH operations in our COBOL program will obtain data immediately from local buffers.

7.5.3 OS/2 Distributed Database Connection Services/2

To extend the above example into concrete product terms, consider the use of the IBM OS/2 Distributed Database Connection Services/2 (DDCS/2). It is a DRDA AR from IBM and acts as an extension of the OS/2 Extended Services/2 (ES/2) package. The IBM database servers supported currently by DDCS/2 are shown in Figure 7.21.

At the top are the various IBM database servers supported by a DRDA AS, such as DB2 2.3; SQL/DS 3.3; and SQL/400 2.1.1. Note that DDCS/2 cannot access an OS/2 DBM database remotely via DRDA; however, an OS/2 application can access an OS/2 DBM database that is logically con-

208 ▼ Access Management

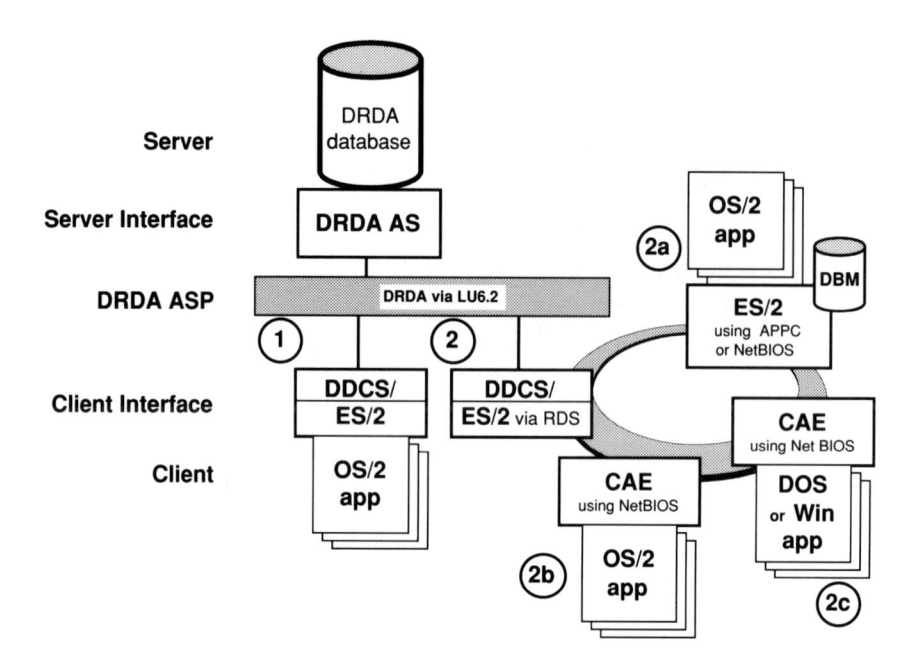

Figure 7.21. DDCS/2 configurations.

nected to the same LAN via ES/2 Remote Data Services (RDS), which does not use the DRDA protocol. In all other cases, DDCS/2 uses the LU6.2 services of SNA to establish the conversation with the various DRDA AS.

The figure also illustrates the use of DDCS/2 in two configurations: single-user stand-alone and multi-user gateway. First, the single-user, stand-alone configuration (Case #1) supports access from a single OS/2 workstation to the various DRDA AS databases. OS/2 v2.x is required, along with OS/2 ES/2 and the separately packaged DDCS/2. The workstation must have a SNA PU2.1 capability to establish LU6.2 conversations with the remote host.

The OS/2 application is programmed to the SAA CPI for SQL (i.e., an embedded API) in COBOL, C, etc., using either the common SAA subset of SQL or in the unique SQL dialect of the target database—an important design choice! During program preparation, a DRDA connection is established to the target database, and the SQL is bound to that database. Security is handled by the OS/2 User Profile Management (UPM) and passed to the remote site via the LU6.2 conversation-level security mechanism.

Second, the multi-user gateway configuration (Case #2) supports access through a gateway platform from OS/2, DOS, and DOS Windows clients. As the figure shows, these client workstations are connected on the same logical LAN as the gateway platform, which is the only platform requiring LU6.2 connection to the remote hosts.

There are three different ways of configuring the clients through the multi-user gateway:

- OS/2 *full-function* application using ES/2 (Case #2a)
- OS/2 *limited-function* application using CAE (Case #2b)
- DOS or DOS Windows application using CAE (Case 2#c)

First, the OS/2 application requires ES/2 and uses the RDS protocol over APPC or Net BIOS to connect to the DDCS/2 gateway. This client has available the full functions of a client application on the DDCS/2 platform (as in #1). Also, this client application can have an OS/2 DBM database on that same platform as a private database or on another platform on the LAN as a shared database. The manner of programming the application is the same as in Case #1.

Second, the OS/2 application requires the Client Application Enabler (CAE) component from the ES/2 DBM RDS. This component can be copied to the required platforms "under license" of the ES/2 agreement (supposedly for no additional fee). CAE consists of a limited set of services for database, communications, and user verification required for DDCS/2 access. This smaller CAE reduces the resource requirements for the client platform. CAE uses NetBIOS to connect to the DDCS/2 gateway.

Third, the DOS or DOS Windows application requires CAE, as above. On a platform running only DOS or DOS Windows, the reduction of resources (e.g., memory and disk) are very important. In addition, the DOS and DOS Windows application can be executed under OS/2 v2.x (as described in Cases #2a or #2b) and use CAE to access the DDCS/2 gateway.

Installing and configuring the above DDCS/2 configurations is quite complicated. The installation of OS/2 v2.x, ES/2, and DDCS/2 on the same platform requires multiple passes. The Database Connection Services (DCS) directory of DDCS/2 must be linked properly with the usual system database directories, DBM configuration files, volume directories, and workstation directories. Fortunately, there is a Directory Tool to assist in this directory configuration.

▼ ▼ ▼ ▼ ▼ ▼

For Further Information: Contact your local IBM office. See the Distributed Data Library and red International Technical Support Center (ITSC) documents. Note especially the DRDA reference manual (SC26-4651) for general DRDA and the ITSC manual, *Distributed Relational Database: Using OS/2 DRDA Client Support with DB2* (GG24-3771, May 1992).

▼ 7.6 INDEPTH: ISO REMOTE DATABASE ARCHITECTURE

Contrasting in many ways with DRDA, the Remote Database Access (RDA) common-protocol architecture was initiated as an ISO/IEC standards effort of the Joint Technical Committee WG3 in 1985. In 1991, RDA became an ISO Draft International Standard, with the expectation that RDA would be a full International Standard by 1993.

The RDA specification consists of two parts: generic RDA (ISO/IEC DIS 9579-1) and the SQL specialization (ISO/IEC DIS 9579-2); it is extremely tedious reading. As stated in these specifications, RDA is "positioned in the application layer of the Open Systems Interconnection (OSI) Basic Reference Model. . . . The goal of RDA is to allow, with a minimum of technical agreement outside the interconnection standards, the interconnection of applications and database systems:

- from different manufacturers;
- under different managements;
- of different levels of complexity;
- exploiting different technologies."

The specification continues by stating "an application may itself be a database system, and therefore RDA can be used to support multi-database system interworking." As shown in Figure 7.22, RDA provides connectivity from the client application to a *data resource*, which is defined as "a named collection of data and/or capabilities on the database server." (An interesting side note is that a data resource "may be nested, with subordinate resources grouped within their parent resources." However, the RDA SQL specialization does not support hierarchical data

INDEPTH: ISO Remote Database Architecture ▼ 211

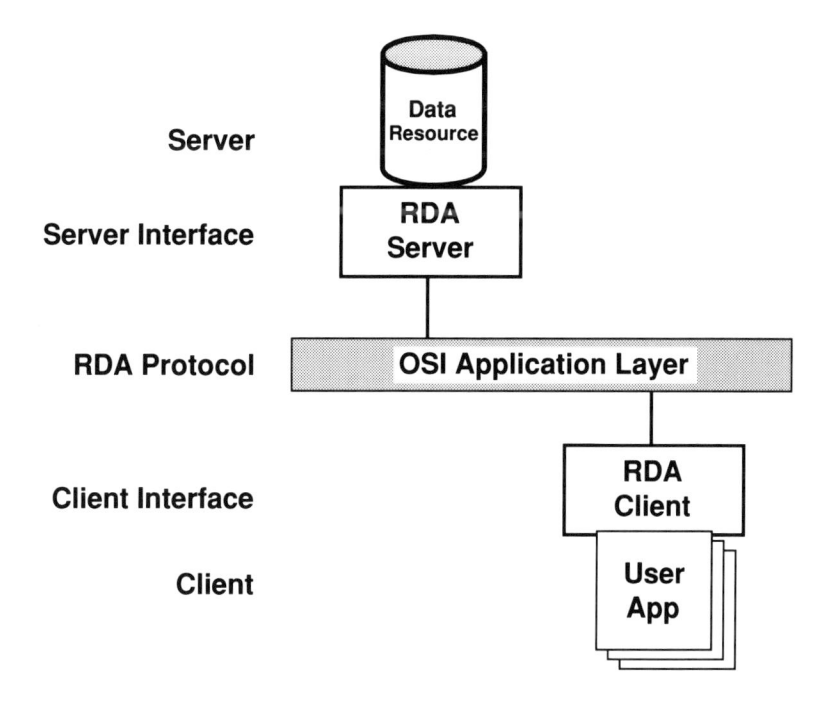

Figure 7.22. ISO RDA.

resources.) The client interface is referred to as the RDA client, and the server interface is called the RDA server. This RDA server is specialized to conform to the SQL database model defined in ISO/IEC 9075 (referring to both SQL 89 and SQL2).

The transport mechanism is the application layer of any OSI-compliant communications stack (which is not TCP/IP).

An RDA *dialogue* is defined as a "cooperative relationship between an RDA Client and an RDA Server," with a unique identifier assigned when the dialogue is first established. An *RDA Transaction* is a unit of work being processed within *one* RDA Dialogue.

The list of *RDA Services* (i.e., commands) is shown in Figure 7.23. The RDA Services support only a remote unit of work and dynamic SQL (although repeated executions of prepared statements are supported). The data encoding is specified with the *Basic Encoding Rules* (BER) for *Abstract Syntax Notation One* (ASN.1), which are ISO 8825:1989(E) and ISO 8824:1989(E) standards, respectively.

The above description of RDA seems a bit boring until we consider

Dialogue Management
    R-Initialize
    R-Terminate
Transaction Management
    R-BeginTransaction
    R-Commit
    R-Rollback
Control
    R-Cancel
    R-Status
Resource Handling
    R-Open
    R-Close
Database Language (immediate execution)
    R-ExecuteDBL
Database Language (stored execution)
    R-DefineDBL
    R-InvokeDBL
    R-DropDBL

Figure 7.23. RDA services.

the vendors who will be developing RDA products when RDA becomes a full ISO International Standard. This is where the SQL Access Group is involved.

7.6.1 SQL Access Group

The *SQL Access Group* (SAG) is "an association of leading systems and software vendors committed to defining and prototyping database interoperability and portability specification" as stated in a SAG press release. The objective is to generate specifications compatible with the ongoing ISO and ANSI standards activities (primarily RDA and SQL2) to enable SQL-based products from multiple vendors to work together. It was founded in 1989 and is a nonprofit corporation whose membership is open to all parties (primarily vendors) as either producers or reviewers. The list of members as of September 1992 is shown in Figure 7.24. Note that all major database vendors are members, except one: IBM. IBM's position is that its energies are better focused on the international/na-

Apple	Metaphor
Boeing Computer Services	Micro Decisionware
Borland International	Microsoft
British Telecom	Mimer Software
Bull HNCincom Systems	MUST Software
Cognos	NCR/Teradata
Computer Associates	Novell
Computer Corp of America	Oracle
Digital Equipment Corp	Progress Software
Dupont	Retix
Fujitsu	Revelation Technologies
Fulcrum Technologies	Siemens Nixdorf
Gupta Technologies	Software AG
Hewlett Packard	Sybase
Information Builders	Tandem
Informix	Unify
Ingres	Unisys
JYACC	Vmark Software
Lotus Development Corp	X/Open

Figure 7.24. SAG membership list.

tional standards activities; however, IBM has attended SAG meetings as an X/Open observer.

SAG has produced draft specifications for its interpretation of RDA as the protocol and on ANSI SQL as the database language for the client interface. These specifications are under review by X/Open for future publication as a Portability Guide. This intent is to complement the ISO specifications in areas that are unclear (e.g., implementor defined).

The relationship of SQL Access (as the output from SAG) is shown with several other activities in Figure 7.25. The two ISO standards (for RDA and SQL) are considered, along with X/Open SQL refinement, the U.S. NIST implementor agreements (i.e., further fine tuning), and the X/Open Formats and Protocols (FAP) specifications. Besides RDA, the second area of SAG concern has been the language specifications to assist SQL2 to become an international standard.

A high point for SAG was a press-only conference in New York in July 1991. The conference showed a successful proof of concept to RDA by

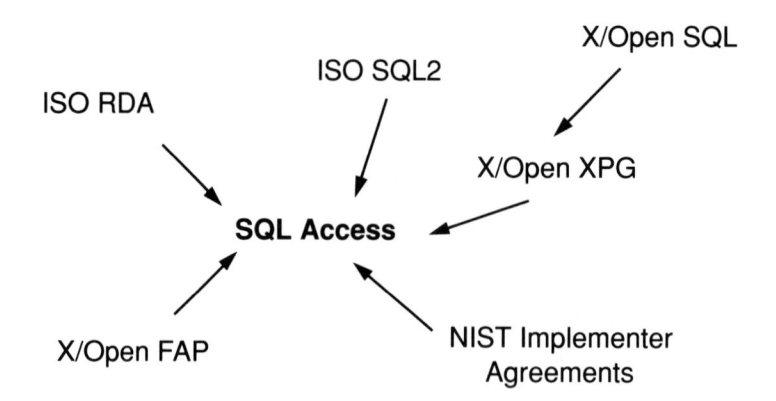

Figure 7.25. ISO RDA and SQL access.

demonstrating several servers (e.g., Oracle, Teradata, and Sybase), all interacting with various clients (such as Excel) via RDA over an OSI network. RDA-compliant products have yet to appear, however. As of May 1992, the following vendors have announced specific RDA-compliant products: Digital Equipment Corp announced SQL Access Server for Rdb/VMS, SQL Access CLI for RDA interoperability, and SQL Access Format and Protocol to generate the RDA protocol. MUST Software International, vendor of NOMAD, announced an open API based on SAG accessible from NOMAD applications, available in late 1992. Retix announced two products: TP-920 for OSI TP support compliant with X/Open Distributed Transaction Processing (DTP) model; and RD-930 for RDA Protocol Services. Both are OEM products to be incorporated into other products. RD-930 is compatible with both OSI and TCP/IP, supports the SAG CLI, and ported to UNIX SVR4, OSF/1, and Sun OS4.

The third area that SAG has explored is the specification of a *SQL Call-Level Interface* (SQLCLI or simply CLI)), which is functionally equivalent to the embedded SQL (dynamic only) described by the X/Open SQL specifications. The objective is to simplify the use of SQL by avoiding the use of a preprocessor for embedded SQL. The SQL functions are to be invoked directly by the statements in the application program. The intent is to enhance the ability of a tool developer to distribute generic software packages. SQLCLI is used by Microsoft as the basis of its ODBC specification. (See Appendix A for the SQLCLI functions that form the core of the Microsoft ODBC interface.)

Other areas of concern for SAG members have been: two-phase commit to support a DUOW; RDA over other transports, such as TCP/IP; and stored procedures or other persistent SQL objects.

▼ ▼ ▼ ▼ ▼ ▼

For Further Information: The ISO documents are available through several sources. Unfortunately there is not currently a good technical summary of the RDA specifications. Information on the SQL Access Group can be obtained through its public relations firm, Hayes/Gardiner at 408/988-3545. Also, see the X/Open publications related to RDA, SQL, and SQLCLI. Contact X/Open at 415/323-7992 in the USA and +44 734 508311 in the UK.

▼ 7.7 COMPARISON OF IBM DRDA AND ISO RDA

In the previous two sections, we described the common-protocol architectures and products for IBM DRDA and ISO RDA. It is appropriate now to draw some direct comparisons in a constructive fashion. The purpose is to aid general understanding in the industry since many view these two architectures are in direct opposition to one another, which is not a fair assessment.

Let's compare the components of the two architectures, shown in Figure 7.26. The components are separated into four categories: transport, command set, data encoding, and SQL specialization. Notice that com-

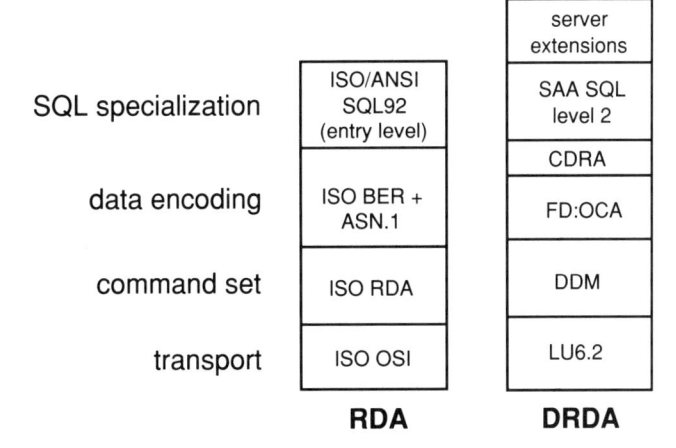

	RDA	DRDA
SQL specialization	ISO/ANSI SQL92 (entry level)	server extensions / SAA SQL level 2 / CDRA
data encoding	ISO BER + ASN.1	FD:OCA
command set	ISO RDA	DDM
transport	ISO OSI	LU6.2

Figure 7.26. *Comparison of DRDA and RDA components.*

ponents do not exactly compare to one another in these categories. In other words, we must be careful not to compare apples with oranges. For example, ANS.1 is a more generalized data encoding, while CDRA extends data encoding into the assortment of character sets used globally.

The major issues to focus on are:

- full-duplex OSI versus half-duplex LU6.2
- dynamic SQL versus static SQL
- data encoding to canonical form
- data descriptor on result set
- bulk data retrieval
- SQL dialect permissiveness
- openness of architecture

First, the transports for each are different in origin and features. OSI is an international standard that has minor market presence, especially relative to TCP/IP. It has long-term potential, but the question is when OSI would become widely adopted. OSI is a full-duplex transport, implying that the client and server can concurrently send data to each other.

SNA LU6.2 is an IBM proprietary transport with strong market presence where SNA is widely used (i.e., very large DP shops). LU6.2 has been adopted as the preferred industry-grade transport by IBM and IBM-related vendors. However, LU6.2 is not TCP/IP, which is the preferred transport in the non-IBM world (most other DP shops). LU6.2 is basically a half-duplex transport, implying that only one (i.e., either the client or server) can send data at the same time. However, an application using LU6.2 can establish two APPC conversations between client and server and achieve full-duplex. Hence, it would be plausible that the DRDA AR and AS using LU6.2 would evolve to support full-duplex internally if there were significant performance or functional advantages. In any case, the effort to support the APPC API (as used by DRDA AR and AS) over TCP/IP and OSI in the MPTN proposal would seem to be a smart move by all concerned.

Second, the RDA standard does not yet support static SQL, implying that production applications executed repeatedly by many clients would be significantly hindered. Support for static SQL (via stored procedures or some other persistent SQL object) is a high priority item for the RDA (and SAG) folks. DRDA was designed from the beginning with *packages* as a central feature. In fact, even pure dynamic SQL must have an empty package bound to the target database before execution. This is a major difference, but remember that RDA does support repeated executions of an SQL statement that is bound once within the scope of the program execution. Hence, bulk INSERT statements would be as efficient in either.

Third, a distinct design difference is the use of a canonical form for data encoding. RDA specifies that all requests and results must be encoded using the BER form of ASN.1. This ensures that diverse platforms can interoperate in a uniform fashion. A particular client or server must only have the ability to convert its native format (i.e., floating point numbers) into and from ASN.1. However, for every exchange, the client must encode the request that must be decoded by the server, and the server must encode the results that must be decoded by the client.

In contrast, DRDA only converts when necessary. In other words, the sender (i.e., either client with a request or a server with results) sends the data in its native format (which is properly tagged as such). The receiver "makes it right"; that is, the receiver converts, if necessary, into its native format. If the client and server have the same native formats (e.g., DB2 on MVS S/390 and SQL/DS on VM S/370), no conversion is performed. The obvious advantage is performance for high data volumes. The disadvantage is that the DRDA AR and AS must be able to convert anything that they expect to receive. This conversion code is nontrivial to do correctly. If a new platform with unusual formats is added to the DRDA environment in the future, the DRDA AR and AS for this new platform would be forced to convert to a predefined format.

Fourth, the use of ASN.1 in RDA is specified so that each data element is tagged with its encoding. For example, we are retrieving a thousand rows of ten-column data. Each data cell in each row (all ten thousand of them) would be tagged with the proper typing information. If the typing information is two bytes, and the data is an average of eight bytes, this is a 25 percent increase in data transmission. (This needs to be fixed in the RDA specifications.) On the other hand, DRDA in FD:OCA allows the descriptor information to flow once regardless of the number of data rows.

Fifth, the mechanism for retrieving bulk data is different. In RDA, multiple rows of data can be retrieved in a single request using the repetition count in R-ExecuteDBL or R-InvokeDBL. DRDA has defined an elaborate blocking mechanism in which the DRDA AR can specify a size (in bytes) to buffer the retrieved results. From the program's perspective, this is more controllable since row sizes are unpredictable in general. On the other hand, the DRDA specification seems tainted with low-level program details.

Sixth, RDA carefully specifies a common subset of the ISO/ANSI SQL standards as the SQL dialect that should flow between client and server. Supposedly, a server receiving statements that do not conform to this common subset would reject the request. The advantage is that all servers know clearly what is expected of them. In contrast, DRDA is permissive in specifying its SQL dialect. DRDA suggests that the SQL dialect should be the SAA CPI for SQL (or ISO/ANSI SQL) to maximize interoperability of client applications. On the other hand, if the client application knows about the specific server and wants to utilize special SQL features unique to that server, DRDA allows any SQL statements to flow to the server for processing. This client application, which is now server-aware, has limited interoperability with other servers. If a new DRDA AS for some enhanced database server is released by IBM or others, applications can be immediately developed to avail themselves of the new functionality, as opposed to RDA, which incurs a multiyear cycle through the standards process to incorporate new functionality.

Finally, is RDA open? Is DRDA open? These questions often border on a religious debate. If open is narrowly defined based on the presence of a de jure standard, then clearly RDA is open and DRDA is not. RDA is now an ISO International Standard. DRDA is definitely a proprietary specification trademarked by IBM with explicit architectural licensing arrangements. Although they are listening to a few serious DRDA implementors, IBM clearly controls the future evolution of the DRDA specification.

If open is more loosely defined based on standards adopted by many vendors (either de jure or de facto), then RDA may be open, and DRDA may be open. RDA may be open, but we have yet to see a diversity of the products from many vendors. Several hurdles remain for RDA: OSI broadened to include TCP/IP; serious vendors with stable products; some performance and manageability enhancements. Likewise, DRDA may be open because its status as a de facto standard is in doubt. IBM

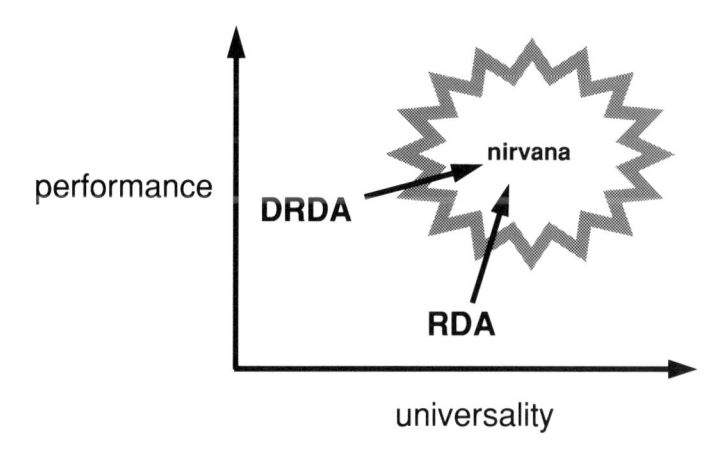

Figure 7.27. Migration paths for DRDA and RDA.

should aggressively pursue other vendors to broaden the product base for DRDA; if this effort is not successful, then DRDA is deceased (except for a few very large DP shops).

In summary, consider Figure 7.27, which shows that both DRDA and RDA fall short of an "interoperability nirvana." DRDA is judged high on performance, while RDA is high on universality. Both strive towards high ratings in both categories. In the near term, DRDA and RDA have basically different design objectives by their respective clientele, which implies that both could be successful. If so, the market positioning of DRDA and RDA could evolve similar to that of SNA and X.25. Just to make this discussion a bit more interesting, note that IBM is in the best position in the industry to deliver both DRDA and RDA products in a variety of environments over various transports. In any case, it will be one or two years before rational judgements are possible.

▼ DISCUSSION QUESTIONS

1. For your company, should you allow direct SQL access to your data? If so, why and what data? If not, why and what data?

2. Sketch the networking plumbing for one of your critical client-server systems, either operational or proposed. Explain it to a colleague. If you had to explain it to top management, could you?

3. How does your company connect applications using Microsoft Windows to a mainframe database, like IBM DB2? Is this connection important?

4. Explain what a Service Provider Interface (SPI) is. Why is this important to Microsoft? To a custom application developer? To a generic tool vendor? To a database vendor?

5. Contrast ODBC and a specific database API (e.g., DB-Library for Sybase/Microsoft SQL Server or SQL-net for Oracle). Which is better?

6. Is the MDI Database Gateway a database gateway? Why?

7. What is the difference between a remote stored procedure and a remote procedure call?

8. What is the relationship between the IBM SAA Common Programming Interface for SQL and the IBM Distributed Relational Database Architecture (DRDA)? Are they the same? Do they work together?

9. Is it possible for DRDA to use TCP/IP instead of SNA LU6.2? To use OSI?

10. What is the relationship between the SQL Access Group and the ISO Remote Database Access (RDA)?

11. For your company, which is better—DRDA or RDA?

8

COPY MANAGEMENT

This chapter examines copy management with a more practical discussion using illustrations from current technology. *Copy management* is defined as "managing the architecture to support copying of data (or processes) between any two servers." Note that we are dealing with *server-server architecture*, rather than client-server architecture.

Copy management focuses on the execution, scheduling, and monitoring of copies from one database to another for the purposes of data staging. With current technology, copy management deals with the distinction between extracts and replicas, refreshing volatile data, and re-synchronizing replicas. Copy management includes the approaches of common interface, common gateway, and common protocol as the building blocks for a coherent architecture.

As described in Section 5.4, a copy is any duplication of data or process, usually in the context of placing that copy on another platform. If a copy is intended for read-only usage, the copy is called an *extract*. If a copy is intended for update, the copy is called a *replica*. This distinction is important as to how we handle the copy.

In this chapter, we will discuss the mechanics of copy management, the single-site update policy, various techniques for copy management, and descriptions of the TRANSFER feature of the MDI Database Gateway and Digital VAX Data Distributor.

▼ 8.1 MANAGEMENT OF COPY MANAGEMENT

In complex enterprise systems, managing any copy is a nasty activity. It is best to avoid copies and retain data (and processes) in a single centralized database, as we will see later. However, such a database can impose too many restrictions.

Here are some reasons for copying data (adapted from White, 1992):

- **To improve performance**: move data to a platform that has greater processing capacity or greater bandwidth to the desktop.
- **To avoid disruption of production systems**: move data off production systems to avoid unpredictable performance degradation.
- **For better data security**: move non-sensitive data to a platform that can be made more available, while tightening security on original platform.
- **For better data consistency**: move data from production systems where data is constantly changing to a platform where data can be more consistent as to a moment in time.
- **For better data integrity**: move data to a platform so that it can be "cleaned up" by detecting and correcting inaccuracies.
- **For better data consumption**: move data to a platform so that it can be packaged to better suit the needs of various users (see Chapter 9).

For one or more of the above reasons, we often seek solutions involving the staging of data from primary source databases to various target databases. This staging is not to be performed on an ad hoc basis, but it should be part of the ongoing operations of the information system. In other words, *it should be managed*. Simply providing access to various enterprise databases leads to extract chaos in which each person's data is inconsistent with that of everyone else.

Ideally, the technology of distributed database systems should manage the staging of data and processes among platforms. In other words, the distributed database would perform any required copying internally so that a single, consistent logical image of data is maintained for the user and application programs. Except in limited situations, this is not possible with current technology. Therefore, this chapter explores the simpler techniques for copy management which can be implemented on an application-dependent basis.

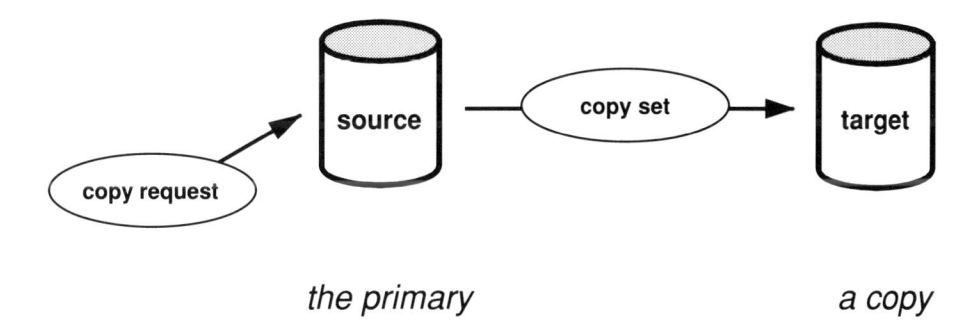

Figure 8.1. Copy management, simple case.

▼ 8.2 MECHANICS OF COPY MANAGEMENT

The simple case of copy management consists of two basic operations: the retrieval of copy set from source database, and the placement of copy set into target database. As shown in Figure 8.1, the key terms are: a *copy request* is executed against the *source*, resulting in the *retrieval* of a *copy set* and followed by the *placement* of the copy set into the *target*.

For every copy operation, there is a source and target. In addition, we can indicate that a source is the *primary*, or master copy (i.e., one unique copy). Likewise, the target can be referred to as a *secondary* copy, or one of possibly many copies. Let's examine the operations of retrieval and placement in greater detail.

8.2.1 Retrieval of Copy Set

With a relational database, the request could be a SELECT statement of arbitrary complexity, and the results could be a relational table (with its full structural information). In other words, we are implying more than a simple sequential file, which has limited structural information.

Note that the retrieval operation is not limited to a single SELECT statement. The copy request could be multiple SELECT statements that generate multiple relational result sets. In addition, the copy request could be a stored procedure that may also generate multiple result sets. Hence, there can be considerable processing performed in preparation of the copy set and considerable complexity in the copy set.

To specify the copy set adequately, the concepts of *object class* and *object instances* (from the object-oriented data model in Chapter Two) are useful. It is often the case that a cluster of relational tables should be copied in unison, since this cluster represents a single object class, such as accounting data for all customers in Dallas. Each instance of an object class requires a unique identifier (e.g., customer number). Therefore, we will refer to a copy set as the general case, and to a result set as the simple case of a one-table result.

8.2.2 Placement of Copy Sets

The copy set is then placed into the target database via one of several modes: append, replace, update, create, or "other."

Let's assume that we are dealing with a simple copy set consisting of a single relational table. The *append* mode—the simplest placement—means that the copy set is inserted into an existing table at the physical end of existing rows. The *replace* mode means that the copy set is inserted into an existing table after all existing rows in that table have been deleted. The *update* mode means that the data in each row of the copy set updates a specific existing row in the table, based on matching primary keys. This mode requires that additional information be specified in the copy operation, such as the primary key, columns for update, whether new rows are to be inserted, and whether old rows can be deleted. The *create* mode means that a new table is created (based on the copy set structure) and new rows are inserted into that table from the copy set.

In addition, there can be a variety of other placement modes that may be customized to the application. In the section covering MDI TRANSFER (Section 8.4), we will examine an open-ended way of specifying placement.

8.2.3 General Case of Copy Management

We have described the basic operations of copy management; however, the general case of copy management can be more complex, including such additional operations as:

- performing transformations on copy set
- monitoring and logging transfer events
- recovering from failures
- maintaining and scheduling copy requests

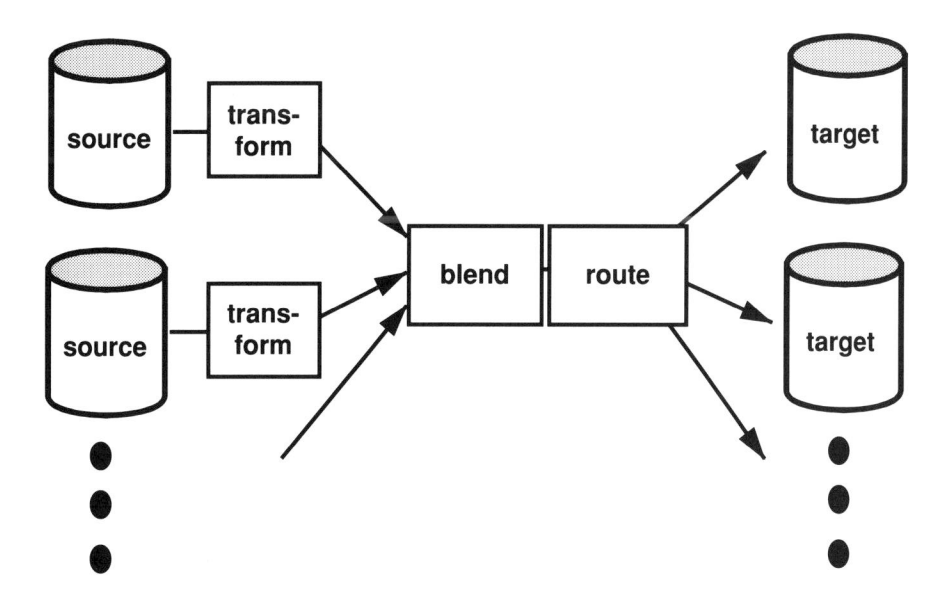

Figure 8.2. Copy management, general case.

- blending multiple sources
- routing to multiple targets
- refreshing of extract or replica from primary
- resynchronizing of replica to primary

These additional operations are illustrated in Figure 8.2.

Copies can be generated from multiple sources. *Transforms* can be applied to each copy set, such as aggregation, grouping, extrapolation of missing values, conversion of structures, and sampling. The transformed copy sets can then be *blended* into a single copy set, usually through simple concatenation. The final copy set can then be *routed* to multiple targets.

An important aspect of copy management is consideration of transaction boundaries and failure points. As explored in Goldring (1990b), the transaction boundaries can include the entire process or portions thereof. Possible failure points for copy operations can be during retrieval, transmission, routing, etc. The detection, monitoring, and recovery of failures is vital to any reliable system invoking copy management.

Another issue is whether the copy is *pushed* from the source or *pulled* from the target (as described in White, 1992). When a copy is pushed, the retrieval and placement operations are performed on the source platform; hence, the source pushes the copy to the target. When a copy is pulled, the retrieval and placement operations are performed on the target platform; hence, the target pulls the copy from the source. These terms do not adequately describe the situation where the operations are split between the platforms. The terms are useful, however, for describing situations involving mainframe databases *pushing* a copy to workgroup databases and workgroup databases *pulling* a copy from mainframe databases.

8.2.4 Factors for Evaluating Copy Management

Three factors can be used to evaluate techniques for copy management. They are fragmentation, updateability, and volatility.

8.2.4.1 *Data fragmentation*

The first factor, *fragmentation*, implies the degree of difficulty in partitioning the database design into appropriate fragments. Such partitioning can be performed either horizontally (i.e., certain rows are grouped together) or vertically (i.e., certain columns are grouped together). An example of horizontal partitioning is to group customers by the principal branch office that should serve that customer; an example of vertical partitioning is to group customer data for all customers depending on whether it is used for ordering, billing, or shipping. In actual situations, some combination of both partitioning options may occur. Note that in either case of partitioning it is important that: (1) data is copied from a well-defined object class; (2) a distinct primary key is defined for the object class; and (3) data for an object instance is contained in joining a small set of relational tables.

8.2.4.2 *Data updateability*

It is relatively easy to handle data in a read-only mode for analysis and decision support. It is quite a different situation to use data that you intend to change and share the changes with others). A further consideration is whether these updates are isolated to a local site (e.g., group, individual, or department) or whether these updates should be permitted from multiple sites.

8.2.4.3 *Data volatility*

The third factor is *volatility*, or the degree to which the data changes during normal usage. Volatility has several considerations. Consider the probability that data on a specific object has changed within a specific time period. For example, if every hour, significant data changes for ten customers out of a database of one thousand customers, then there is a 1 percent probability that a specific customer's data is wrong within an hour after a copy is made from the primary database. Another consideration is the stability of its volatility, or significant changes in volatility depending on data characteristics. For example, the volatility of aircraft occupancy data is fairly low until the hour of the flight departure; then, its volatility is very high until the flight departs.

The objective is to measure the business value of data and how this value changes with time. In particular, the situation is that we may copy this data from a production database to another platform and then indicate the decline in its value with time.

Try the following experiment with an associate. Obtain $100 in new $1 bills. After determining the data requirements for a specific application, invite the person responsible for the application to discuss the volatility of the application's data. Place all the money between the two of you.

State the situation as: "Assume that you are willing to pay $100 for direct access to the production database. Now, we will copy the relevant data to a local database for your usage. At certain time intervals (e.g., seconds, minutes, hours, days, weeks, etc.), the data will be refreshed from the production database. Also assume that all other aspects are equal between directly accessing the operational data and accessing the local copy."

Start with a short refresh interval (e.g., one second) and ask how much money the copy is worth. Continue to ask about longer intervals until the value reaches zero.

How much would the person pay for the copy? Less than $100? If so, how much less? And, it should be dependent on the refresh interval in some way. This subjective estimate by the user is the *business* value of the data, related to the benefit received for business activities.

Consider Figure 8.3, which shows the value of the data with various refresh intervals. It is hypothesized that in general the relationship is as follows: The copy is immediately devalued from the live data by a cer-

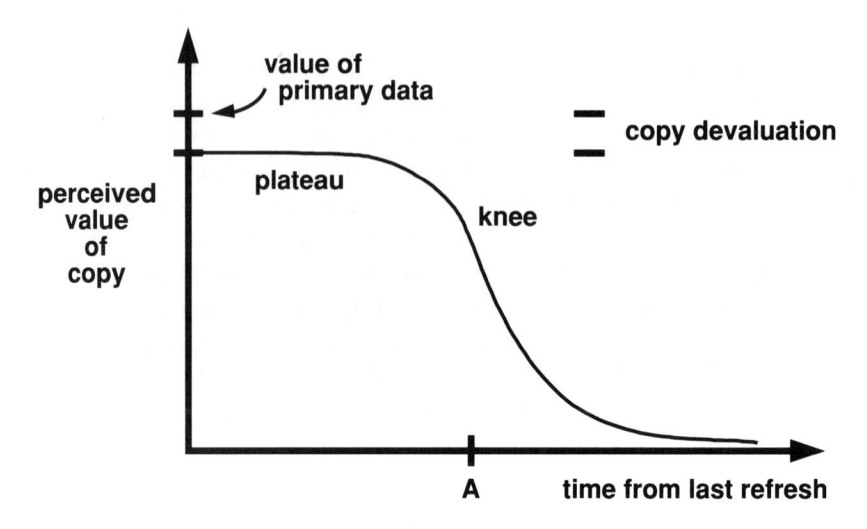

Figure 8.3. Well-behaved data volatility.

tain amount; this is the *copy devaluation*. The user is then indifferent up to a certain refresh interval, or *plateau* of data volatility. After the plateau, the user starts to consider whether the copied data is really worth the plateau value since the production data has probably changed in some significant ways. Roughly at point A with the copy, the user struggles with using cheap old data or expensive current data. After point A, the value drops rapidly since business decisions based on very old data may be wrong.

There are several special cases of data volatility: historical copy, event-dependent copy, and unpredictable copy. The *historical copy* is a copy taken at the end of a specific period (quarterly, for example) and used to monitor performance and to forecast trends. In general, it makes little sense to refresh the copy since the production data has changed significantly. In fact, a refresh of the historical copy would diminish its value. A historical copy is actually new data that should be treated independently from the production data. The original data may have been inaccurate, however, so that corrections to the historical copy must be made, for legal or accounting reasons. In a real situation, historical copies should not be considered as perfectly nonvolatile.

The *event-dependent copy* is a copy whose value depends on its relation to a certain event. Consider seating assignments of a specific airline flight. This data is fairly static up to a month prior to the flight departure. As the departure becomes closer, the volatility increases. In the hour prior to departure, the volatility is very high especially on crowded flights. When the door to the airplane is closed, data on seating assignments instantly becomes nonvolatile.

A copy can be *unpredictable* because its value is perceived to be influenced by a number of factors (in addition to time) that are uncertain or unknown. This is a special case, because, if a user feels that the copy value is unpredictable, the only alternative is direct access to the current production data.

8.2.5 Living Without Distributed Updates

Multisite distributed updates are very demanding on database systems, as we discussed in Chapter 3. Although in specific homogeneous situations the technology that supports distributed updates may be feasible, we are usually limited to a remote unit of work capability when dealing with most (federated) databases.

The implication of a remote unit of work is that only one site can update an object instance. For instance, suppose that we have made copies of a specific customer account to various regional offices from the headquarters' database. Who can update that customer record? Everyone could! However, if everyone does, then we have an impossible task of resynchronizing the copies back into the primary database, because we have no indication as to whether one change is any more or less valid than any other change. The usual mechanism for resynchronization is the time sequencing of the transaction commit. The last transaction wins! But how do we know which is the last transaction among multiple sites? This reasoning leads into some complex analysis (see Barghouti and Kaiser, 1991; Pu and Leff, 1991). We will limit the following discussion to the capability of a remote unit of work and, hence, of updating only at a single site.

We can, however, shift the site at which we update through time (if we are careful). This situation is called the *single-site update policy* and is defined as "the enforcement of only one update site at any specific time for any object instance." As you will see in the next section, we can be creative as to where and when that update site can be.

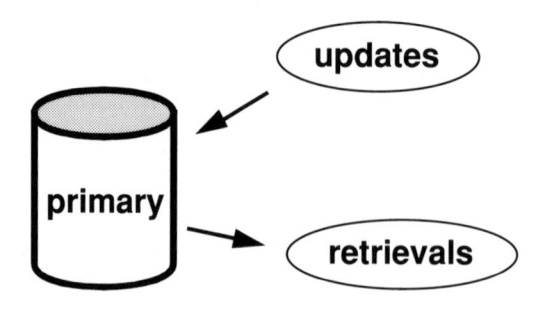

Figure 8.4. *Centralization.*

▼ 8.3 TECHNIQUES FOR SIMPLE COPY MANAGEMENT

This section will describe various techniques for staging data via copy management using the single-site update policy, which are: centralization, partition, simple extract, timestamp extract, checked extract, refreshed extract, periodic replica, continuous replica, and check-out replica.

8.3.1 Centralization

The first technique is to centralize the data into a single database, which distributes the use of data but not the data itself. This is often the best technique because it is the simplest and avoids copying data completely. All applications must access the single database either locally or remotely (via RUOW). Control and maintenance is simplified. Note, however, that centralized databases do not have to reside on mainframe platforms. A LAN database server can act as a centralized database for many client-server systems. In summary, a centralized database should be your first consideration.

8.3.2 Partition

The next technique is to divide the primary database into separate databases without any overlap in data instances. In other words, no data is duplicated in more than one database. With the partition technique, there now are multiple primary databases.

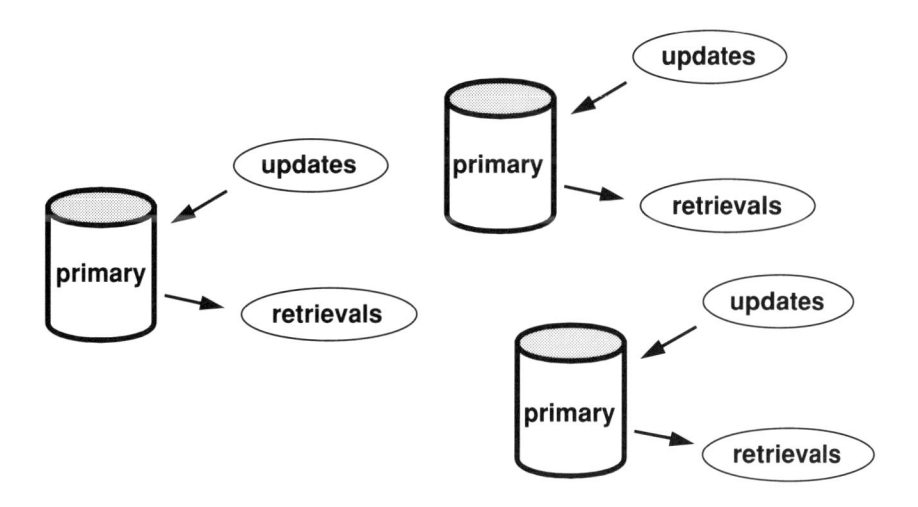

Figure 8.5 Partition.

For example, a customer database could be partitioned into branch databases depending on which branch services a particular customer. The assumption is that each customer is serviced by one and only one branch. This partitioning is called a *horizontal partition* since it divides the database horizontally based on rows.

Next, consider the same customer database, but this time with customer data divided into a checking database, saving database, loan database, and so forth. This is called a *vertical partition* since it divides the database vertically based on columns. Note that each column of the primary database is contained in one and only one database, except for the primary key (e.g., customer number) which must be duplicated at each site. In both horizontal and vertical partitions, a single-site update policy is maintained since, for any specific object instance, it can be updated at one and only one site.

The difficulties with the partition technique are twofold: First, an object instance is maintained at one specific site. If retrievals or updates are needed by another site, then requests must flow to the primary site for that object instance. For example, if a customer requests service from a branch office that is not his/her primary site, then those requests must be submitted remotely to the proper branch office. Second, if the primary key of an object instance changes, then the object instance must

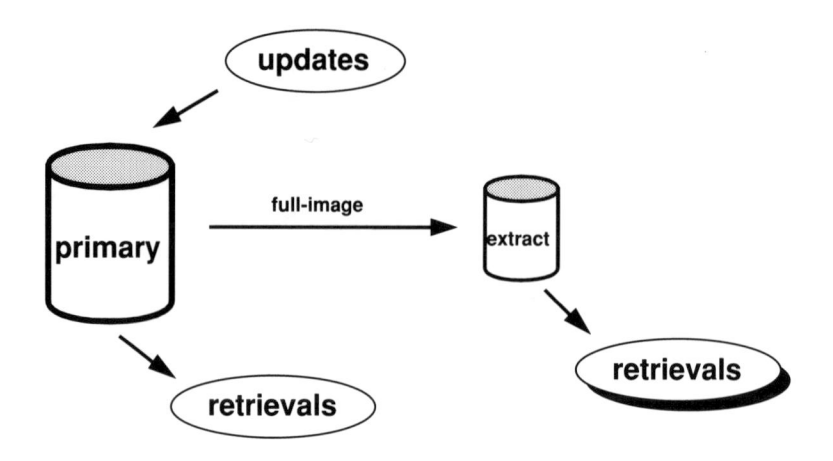

Figure 8.6 *Simple extract.*

be moved to the proper site. For example, if a customer opens another account and is issued a new customer number, the primary site for that customer data may now be at a different site.

The IBM term for the partition technique is a *distributed table* according to the IBM SAA Distributed Data Architecture.

8.3.3 Simple Extract

The next technique is to identify a single primary database and only allow *simple extracts*, or copies that will not be updated, from that database. The simple extract is the way that most corporations currently support analysis and other decision support activities at an intelligent workstation. The simple extract is excellent for historical data and for low-volatility data.

For the case of a copy set consisting of one table, the IBM term for a simple extract is an *extracted table* according to the IBM SAA Distributed Data Architecture.

Current wisdom concerning simple extracts is that these extracts should be clearly defined and documented to avoid misinterpretation of the data. Further, most important extracts should be performed by MIS operations and placed in a *data warehouse* (as discussed in the next chapter). Otherwise, the situation with simple extracts often degrades into *extract chaos*, in which everyone has his/her own extract of what

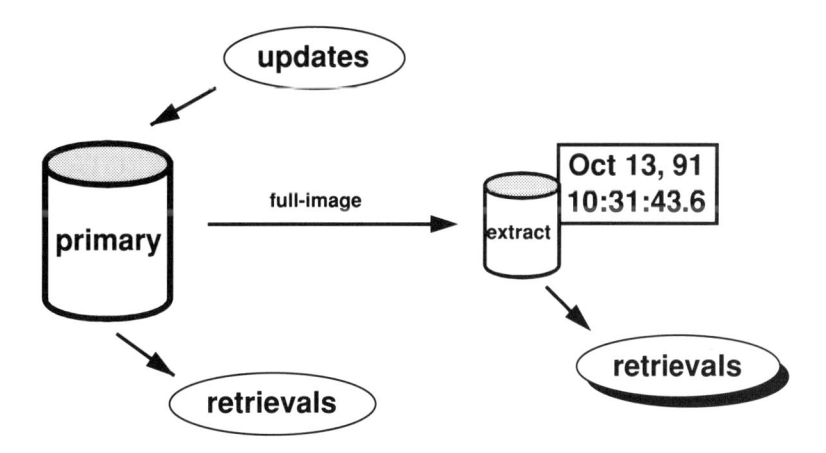

Figure 8.7. Timestamp extract.

they think is the same information but in fact is totally inconsistent.

Note that, for a simple extract (and other extracts discussed later), the single-site update policy is maintained since there remains one and only one database to which all updates are directed.

8.3.4 Timestamp Extract

The next technique is to perform a simple extract in which a timestamp is associated with the extract. The application directly (or the user indirectly) can make a judgment based on the timestamp as to whether the extract data is valid. If intelligent enough, the application could initiate another extract if the data was considered invalid for the current business function. A timestamp extract is also useful because of cyclic nature of most enterprise processing. Doing an extract in the middle of a business day may not be as valid as an extract at the end of the business day. For example, customer balances may be more valid if extracted after batch updates, rather than around noon.

8.3.5 Checked Extract

The next technique is a simple or timestamp extract that includes an aggregated value about the object instance. For example, a checked extract on the customer data on savings accounts would also include the total of all accounts. Then, if the validity of the extract was in question, a

234 ▼ Copy Management

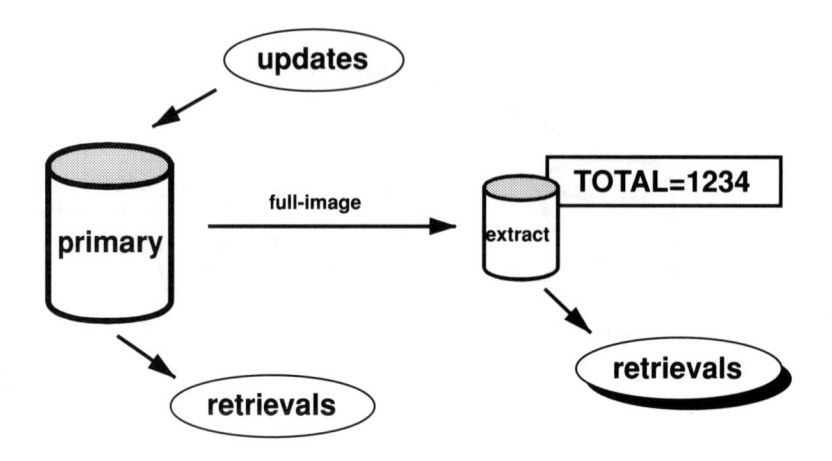

Figure 8.8. Checked extract.

total of account balances in the primary database could indicate whether the extract was valid enough for the specific business function.

8.3.6 Refreshed Extract

The next technique is a simple extract that is performed automatically at specified intervals. Therefore, the user knows that the extract is valid as of the specific time of refresh. There are two methods for creating a

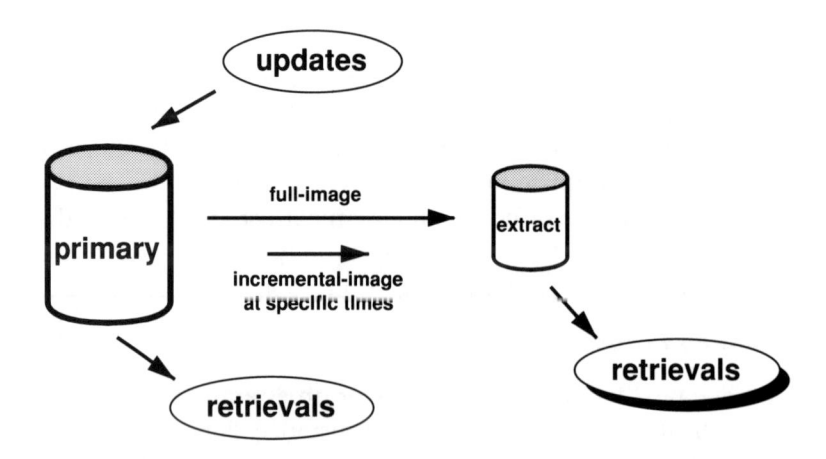

Figure 8.9. Refreshed extract.

refreshed extract. The first is to perform a full-image copy to the secondary database at each interval. This method is simplest and may be preferred for small extracts. The second method is to perform a full-image copy once and then perform incremental images at each interval. This is the preferred method in most cases since it minimizes data flow.

For the case of a copy set consisting of one table, the IBM term for a refreshed extract is a *snapshot table* according to the IBM SAA Distributed Data Architecture.

8.3.7 Periodic Replica

The next technique involves a replica, which is a copy for which updates are allowed. The assumption is that, at the instant a replica is performed, the locus of update shifts from the primary database to the replica database, thus maintaining the single-site update policy. In other words, the primary database only allows retrievals to the object instances that were copied to the replica database.

The critical aspect of any replica technique is that the changes to the replica must be migrated back to the primary database. This process is called *resynchronization*.

The question is when and how the resynchronization occurs. For periodic replica, the resynchronization occurs periodically at predefined intervals. For example, the customer data for a branch is replicated (full-image) to the branch in early morning. Updates occur to the replica

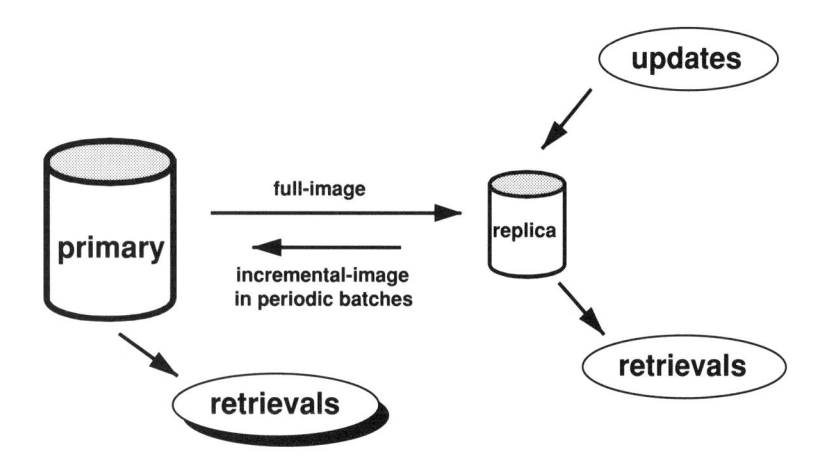

Figure 8.10. *Periodic replica.*

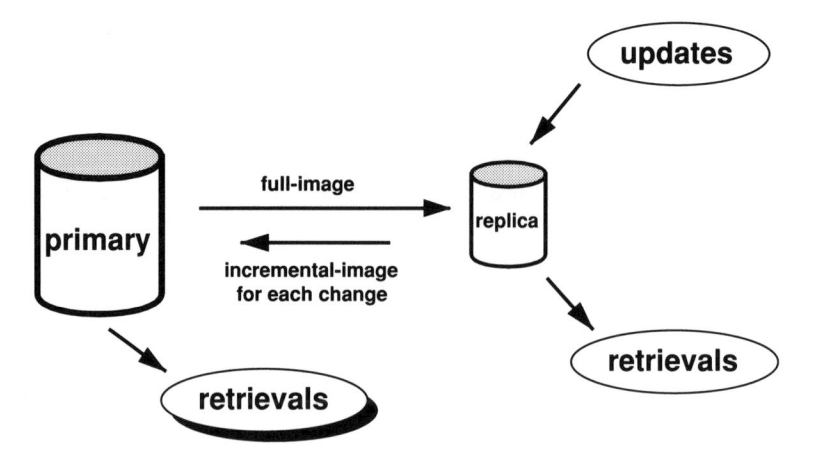

Figure 8.11. Continuous replica.

database during the day, and then the changes (incremental-image) are resynchronized with the primary database in the evening. Over the night, various batch jobs can process all customer data. And, the cycle repeats.

For the case of a copy set consisting of one table, the IBM term for a periodic replica is a *replicated table* according to the IBM SAA Distributed Data Architecture.

8.3.8 Continuous Replica

The next technique is a replica that resynchronizes continuously with the primary database. In other words, a full-image copy is performed initially to the replica database. Then, as each change occurs, each change migrates back to the primary database as an individual transaction. This has the advantage of maintaining consistency with the primary database, subject to the delay in applying each change image. The initial copy from the primary database needs only to be performed once, assuming everything works correctly. The disadvantage with the continuous replica technique is that failures may cause the loss of changes to the primary database. The recovery and restart of the individual change transaction is critical to maintaining synchronization between the replica and primary databases. In actual situations, some combination of periodic and continuous replica techniques may be more practical.

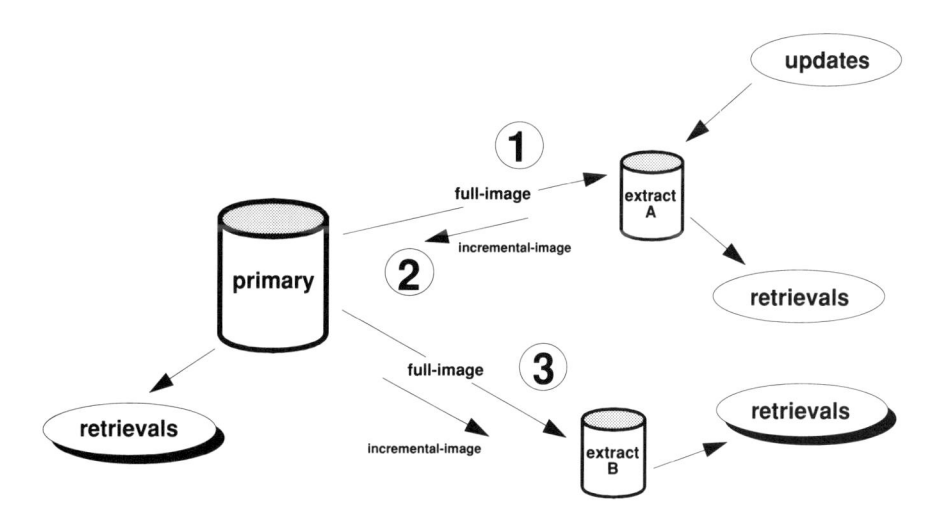

Figure 8.12. Check-out replica.

8.3.9 Check-out Replica

The final technique is called a *check-out* replica because the site of update can change among databases according to whom desires to update the specific object. The name comes from the similarity between this procedure and checking out a book from a library. This technique is particularly useful when one can not predetermine which database objects should be copied to secondary databases.

As shown in Figure 8.12, the first step is to copy a full image to the requesting replica site. The site of update shifts from the primary to the replica site. The users of the replica can now update the object as desired. The second step is to resynchronize periodically the replica with primary database, since the object may be checked out for relatively long periods. The third step is an optional full-image copy (plus any incremental updates) to another extract site, allowing this site retrieval access to the object.

As an example of the check-out technique, engineering drawings are quite complex involving megabytes of data. An engineer at his/her workstation could check out a specific engineering drawing and work on its for several days. Once checked out, no updates would be allowed by the primary database. When finished, the engineer would check in

	Fragmentation	Volatility	Updateability	Method
A	hard	n/a	n/a	centralization
B	easy	high	local-site	partition
C	easy	none	no	simple extract
D	easy	low	no	timestamp/ checked extract
E	easy	medium	no	refreshed extract
F	easy	low	local-site	periodic replica
G	easy	medium	local-site	continuous replica
H	easy	high	local-site	check-out replica
I	easy	high	multi-site	centralization

A When it is difficult to fragment data, a centralized database approach is suggested. In this case, data concerning a specific database object may be very complex, involving joins among numerous tables, various levels of aggregation, or timing dependencies. In fact, the definition of the object class may be uncertain.

B When data is easily fragmented but data has high volatility, partitioning the database, either horizontally or vertically, among multiple sites is suggested. There is no duplication of data. A specific object instance exists at one and only one site, and updates occur only at that site.

C When data is easily fragmented and is updated only at the primary database, one of the three extract cases (C, D, or E) is suggested. If the data has no volatility, a simple extract is suggested. This is an ideal case since there is no requirement for update or for refresh.

D If the data has low volatility, the extract should be time-stamped or checked to insure its validity. The user of the extracted data must make a judgment whether the extracted data is still valid.

E If data has medium volatility, the extract should be refreshed at specific intervals to insure its validity. The intervals should be determined based on the business judgment of the volatility knee.

F When data is easily fragmented and is required to be updated at the local site, one of the three replica cases (F, G, or H) is suggested. If the data has low volatility, a periodic replica is suggested. The intervals to resynchronize with the primary should be determined based on the business judgment of the volatility knee.

G If the data has medium volatility, continuous replica is suggested, in which the updates are continuously streamed back to the primary.

H If the data has high volatility, the check-out replica is suggested. This case is also suggested for ultra-long transactions involving complex object instances.

I When many sites must be able to update the data and the data has high volatility, we suggest returning to a centralized database. The effort to maintain, refresh, and resynchronize is too great for the high volatility of the data.

Figure 8.13. Comparison of copy techniques.

the specific drawing, along with resynchronizing the incremental changes with the primary database. The site of update returns to the primary database. Depending on retrieval and notification rights, there are several variations on the check-out replica technique.

8.3.10 Comparisons Among Techniques

After discussing the above techniques, the obvious question is, "What are the advantages and disadvantages of these techniques?" Considering the factors of fragmentation, updateability, and volatility, when should one technique be used instead of another? Some general points can be made:

- If the data structure is difficult to separate into clean object classes, the centralization technique is preferable.
- If data is highly volatile, only centralization or partition should be considered. The latter is preferred if updates can be confined to a single local site.
- The other techniques (i.e., extracts and replicas) are applicable only if volatility is at a reasonable level.

Figure 8.13 summarizes the various cases. These comparisons should only be used as general guidelines; specific application situations will dictate other criteria that may outweigh the above considerations.

▼ 8.4 INDEPTH: MDI DATABASE GATEWAY TRANSFER

This section examines the TRANSFER feature of the Micro Decisionware Database Gateway (DG). Although the product can support other database products, we will focus on its usage for copy management between the IBM DB2 and Microsoft SQL Server databases.

The components related to the TRANSFER feature are shown in Figure 8.14. From some client application, a TRANSFER statement is submitted to the database gateway for processing. This application can reside on the gateway platform, on the mainframe (using MDI Client Services), or within SQL Server (using the remote stored procedure feature). The TRANSFER statement is parsed at the gateway, initiating a copy operation in either direction between DB2 and SQL Server. The copy set does not flow through the client but flows directly between the two databases via the gateway.

There are two forms of the TRANSFER statement: bulk and template. The bulk form assumes that rows of data are to be inserted into an exist-

240 ▼ **Copy Management**

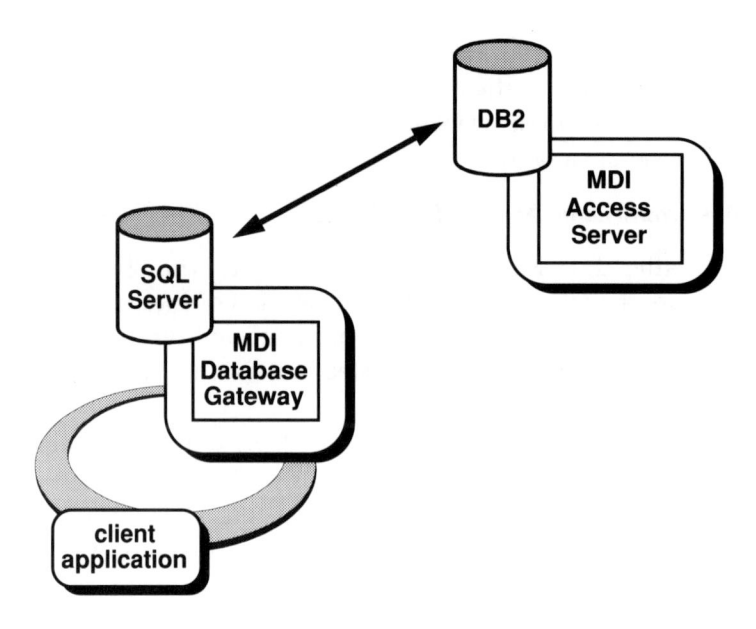

Figure 8.14. *Database Gateway TRANSFER.*

ing table at the target, using the most efficient mechanism possible. The template form allows more flexibility by passing any statement (not just an INSERT statement) to the target database. A template is specified and values from each data row are substituted at appropriate places within this template. For each data row, an instance of this template is passed to the target database.

The usage of the TRANSFER statement will be explained more fully through the following examples.

8.4.1 Centralized Database Case

Let's consider an example of a large corporation in the service sector that has hundreds of branch offices internationally. They are managing fairly complex customer data, and each branch office needs quick access to their respective customer data.

Let's consider some typical numbers. Assume that the company has one million customers with an average of 1000 bytes of data on each customer. In other words, our database is handling about one gigabyte of critical enterprise data.

Also, assume that there are 500 branch offices that are connected via leased 56,000 bps telephone lines. On the average, there are 2,000 customers per branch; however, some branch offices have 50,000 customers, while many others have only have 500. On a typical eight-hour business day, let's assume that 5 percent of the customers have inquiries while only one percent of the customers have changes, and then only 10 percent (on the average) of that customer's data is affected.

In the first case, let's assume that a centralized operational database, such as IBM DB2, has been in place for several years. Employees use IBM 3270-type workstations to handle inquiries and updates.

With a little arithmetic, we can determine that a large branch is moving 2.5 megabytes of customer data for inquiries to its workstations each day. The leased line can handle 25 megabytes per hour at full utilization. So, on the average, our system should perform adequately, assuming that peak periods are not a problem.

8.4.2 Simple Extract Case

As a second case, consider the same corporation, but now the centralized DB2 database is not sufficient to handle the enormous load of querying this complex data in a timely fashion. The peak periods have gotten too severe. It happens that 30 percent of customer inquiries occur during the lunch hour, resulting in slow response time. However, updates to the customer data, which are handled adequately, are sent directly back to the centralized database. So, now what?

One solution would be to extract the customer data based on the assigned branch office and copy that data to a local LAN-based database at that office. The primary database at headquarters allows retrievals and updates to itself. In addition, a full-image copy—for retrieval only—is made of the customer data for a branch to the extract database. Note that retrievals against the extract are out-of-synch with the primary. Whether these inconsistencies are important is a business-specific decision. In our example we will assume that it is sufficient to have customer data current at the start of business day.

How would we implement this solution?

Again, we would use the Database Gateway to connect into the DB2 database; however, instead of retrieving information from the DB2 database, each workstation queries the customer data locally via the LAN from Microsoft's SQL Server. This local connection to the customer data permits much more extensive displays to be supported by the workstation.

Overnight, a fresh copy of customer data is copied from the DB2 database into the SQL Server database. The actual copy operation from DB2 to SQL Server of the customer data is performed with the TRANSFER statement, as follows:

```
transfer to "Denver Hack hello"
select cus_no, cus_name, ... from customer
    where branch = "Denver";
insert into customer (cid, cname, ...)
    values (?, ?, ...);
```

This statement will transfer all the branch data to the local database, overnight as a single operation. It is a "transfer to" implying that the source database is DB2 and the target database is SQL Server, which is locally accessible somewhere on the LAN. The service name for this SQL Server database is "Denver," as is the branch office name in the customer table. The customer data is selected from the DB2 database based on the branch. This data is then transformed into a stream of INSERT statements that are applied to the SQL Server database.

For example, assume that the following data is retrieved from DB2:

```
123  Patch    ...
234  Wood     ...
345  Grass    ...
```

Then, the following INSERT statements would be automatically applied to the SQL Server database:

```
insert into customer (cid, cname, ...)
    values (123, "Patch", ...);
insert into customer (cid, cname, ...)
    values (234, "Wood", ...);
insert into customer (cid, cname, ...)
    values (345, "Grass", ...);
```

Note that character data is properly quoted, as contrasted with the numeric data which is not. There are optional qualifications for handling value substitutions of date, time, and so forth.

The INSERT statement that is specified in the transfer is completely arbitrary; any SQL statement appropriate for the target database can be given, as will be illustrated in the section on final TRANSFER examples.

There is an alternative way of specifying the transfer statement, which uses the bulk copy processing of SQL Server. For simple insertion of new data, the bulk copy version is five to ten times more efficient. An example of this transfer statement is as follows:

```
transfer to "Denver Hack hello"
    with insert into customer;
select cus_no, cus_name, ... from customer
    where branch = "Denver";
```

Note that the INSERT statement is not specified, since it is assumed. The new data would be appended to any existing data in the customer table. However, if the clause *with insert* were changed to *with replace*, the existing customers in the local table would be deleted and replaced with the new data.

Let's consider the numbers again. We can determine that the company is moving the entire one gigabytes of customer data each night with full-image copies. It takes roughly two minutes to move one megabyte of data to a branch. For a large branch, the time would be about two hours, while a small branch would require only one minute. Further, the entire one gigabyte would require a total of forty hours if there were only *one* connection. But, with our large system, all 500 leased lines are handled concurrently.

8.4.3 Refreshed Extract Case

Now let's assume that management wants to investigate some down-sizing alternatives. Specifically, several million dollars per month can be saved by replacing the leased lines with switched lines operating at 9600 bps using V.32 modems. Connections are established between a branch office and the central data site only when data is required. However, moving daily copies of all customer data to every branch office would be too great for this network.

Consider this alternative: what if you transferred only the data that is changed? Thus an incremental image, rather than a full image, would be transferred.

Let's do some further calculations. If only customers whose records have changed need to be transferred, then just ten megabytes, rather than one gigabyte, will be moved each night. Our lines now only have to transfer 4.3 megabytes per hour, instead of 25 megabytes per hour. For large branches, 500 customers would be transferred, requiring just seven minutes of connection time.

How can we transfer only the incremental image of this customer data? First, the primary database must maintain special tables containing the incremental image. In this case, DB2 would maintain through application logic two special tables—cust_chg and cust_del—containing the updates to existing rows and deletions to existing rows, respectively.

Second, two separate transfer statements are required to apply these two special tables to the target database, the local SQL Server database at each branch office. The first statement handles the changes to existing customers:

```
transfer to "Denver Hack hello"
select cus_name, ..., cus_no from cust_chg
    where branch = "Denver";
update customer
    set cname = ?, ...
    where cid = ?;
```

The second statement handles customers that need to be removed from the database:

```
transfer to "Denver Hack hello"
select cus_no from cust_del
    where branch = "Denver";
delete from customer
    where cid = ?;
```

Note that the proper UPDATE and DELETE statements are generated and applied to the local database based on each row of data retrieved from the DB2 incremental image tables.

Third, the incremental image for a specific branch must be deleted when the transfer is successfully completed. The DELETE statements to accomplish this are:

```
delete from cust_chg
    where branch = "Denver";
delete from cust_del
    where branch = "Denver";
```

WARNING: The above description has been simplified. Handling of new customers is not mentioned through the transfer of INSERTs as in the previous case. And more importantly, the problem of the ordering of UPDATE, DELETE, and INSERT statements is not addressed, so that it reflects accurately the transaction flow in the primary database.

8.4.4 Periodic Replica Case

Let's extend our example a bit further. Assume that updates to customer data from branch offices increase dramatically so that updates directed to the centralized DB2 database are not feasible.

Our extract now becomes a replica. In other words, a full-image copy is transferred to the SQL Server database. During the business day, updates are no longer allowed to customer data on the DB2 database; updates are only allowed on the SQL Server database. This restriction maintains the single-site update policy.

The changes to the replica data are then transferred to the primary database at the end of the business day, by using the following transfer statements:

```
transfer from "Denver Hack hello"
select cname, ..., cid from cust_chg;
update customer
    set cus_name = ?, ...
    where cus_no = ?;
transfer from "Denver Hack hello"
select cid from cust_del
delete from customer
    where cus_no = ?;
```

These statements are similar to the refreshed extract case, except that the transfer is FROM the local database, rather than TO the local database. Note that the qualification on branch is not needed and that SQL Server must maintain the incremental image in the special tables—cust_chg and cust_del—probably using its trigger mechanism.

8.4.5 Continuous Replica Case

The final case to explore is called the continuous replica, implying that changes are transferred back continuously to the primary database as they occur.

In our example, SQL Server would capture each change in a trigger stored procedure and invoke the Database Gateway as a remote procedure call. The UPDATE and DELETE statements would be as shown in the periodic replica, but processed individually for each change. Therefore, the primary database is only out-of-synch for the duration of transaction flow.

To support this close synchronization between the primary and replica databases, the additional burden is twofold: First, there is the requirement to maintain connection between the mainframe and LAN during business hours. Second, there is the additional code for recovery and restart of the transaction flow for the incremental images.

8.4.6 Final TRANSFER Examples

The above examples using the TRANSFER statement illustrated copy operations manipulating data values (i.e., DML operations). The final examples will illustrate how copy operations can perform some database administration functions.

First, consider the following way of administering authorizations:

```
transfer to "server1 sa password"
select priv, table, person from dba_priv
    where server = "server1";
grant ? on table ? to ?;
```

The above transfer assumes that DB2 contains a special table called "dba_priv." This table has the columns containing database privileges, table name, person for grant, and server name. The SELECT statement retrieves the privileges for a specific server.

```
select    customer    patch
delete    inventory   wood
select    account     grass
```

The GRANT statements are then generated based on the row values and passed to the SQL Server database. The statements processed by SQL Server would appear like this:

```
grant select on table customer to patch;
grant delete on table inventory to wood;
grant select on table account to grass;
```

Second, consider the following way of performing schema changes:

```
transfer to "server1 sa password"
select change_stmt from dba_changes
where server = "server1";
?N;
```

The above transfer assumes that DB2 contains a special table called "dba_changes". This table contains the text of SQL statements (of any form) that are to be processed against the specific server. For example:

```
create table ...
create index ...
```

The SELECT statement retrieves the character string value for each row in the table, qualified on "server1". This stream of character strings is then substituted for the question mark in the template. The "N" qualification specifies that the value is to be treated as a numeric value; hence, no quotes are placed around the character string, as is desired.

This last example illustrates that copy operations can be quite generalized, performing database administration functions in addition to simple data transfers.

▼ ▼ ▼ ▼ ▼ ▼

For Further Information: Contact Micro Decisionware, Inc. at 303/443-2706. See the *Database Gateway Reference and Installation Guide*, Chapter 6.

▼ 8.5 INDEPTH: DIGITAL VAX DATA DISTRIBUTOR

Another product example of copy management is the VAX Data Distributor of Digital Equipment Corporation. Released about five years ago, it is one of those products that was ahead of its time, in the positive sense.

The Data Distributor manages operations called *transfers* which define what data and data definitions are to be moved from a *source* to a *target*. The source can be the VAX Rdb/VMS database, or any database that can be accessed via Digital RdbAccess interoperability products. These databases currently include DB2, Oracle, RMS, and VSAM. The target can be only Rdb/VMS.

There are three types of transfers:

- **Extraction**: transfer of a database or a set of tables from one source to one target. Extracts can be updated but the updates are not reflected back to the source.
- **Extraction rollup**: same as extraction, with the extension that there be more than one source.
- **Replication**: same as extraction, with the extension that the target can be refreshed with updates to the source, rather than complete rebuild. No updates are allowed directly to the target.

For every transfer, a *schedule* can be defined specifying the time to execute the transfer, along with general procedures that can be executed before and after a transfer.

▼ ▼ ▼ ▼ ▼ ▼

For Further Information: Contact Digital Equipment Corporation for product materials on the VAX Data Distributor.

In the next chapter, we will explore how copy management combined with access management can create the infrastructure for warehouse management.

▼ DISCUSSION QUESTIONS

1. Why copy any data? Are any of these reasons pertinent to your company?

2. What responsibilities do you incur when you make an extract? When you make a replica?

3. Which is better—to push copies from the source or to pull copies from the target?

4. For data familiar to you, describe the behavior of its volatility?

5. For situations in your company, compare and contrast the usage of the techniques for simple copy management.

6. How does the TRANSFER feature of the MDI Database Gateway support the copying of meta-data?

9

WAREHOUSE MANAGEMENT

This chapter examines the topic of warehouse management, building on the material on access management and copy management. The thesis is that warehouse management is only viable if the systems to support access and copy management are in place and stable. Enabled by access and copy management, warehouse management adds an important layer that focuses on the business justification for EDC technology.

Warehouse management is defined as "managing the architecture to support consumption of data (or processes) by a business community." In a way, this is a *server-client architecture*, in which the server takes a proactive role in collecting, packaging, and disseminating data to client platforms. This definition contrasts with production database systems that support consumption of data by collection of application programs, rather than a community of business people.

In this chapter, we will discuss the definition for a warehouse, a warehouse example, some of its characteristics, major issues in design and operation, and then an INDEPTH description of the IBM Information Warehouse framework.

▼ 9.1 WHAT IS A WAREHOUSE?

The concept of a data warehouse started to emerge in the literature in the early 1980s. The early writings of W.H. Inmon (1981, 1984, 1986) discussed the issues concerning the system of record, atomic data, decision support databases, and so on. J. Martin (1982) described Class IV databases for "searching and fast information retrieval" as the basis for user-driven computing. Devlin and Murphy (1988) described an IBM internal project consisting of "an integrated warehouse of company data based firmly in the relational database environment." This warehouse was accessed by end users with "a consistent set of tools . . . supported by a business data directory that describes the information available in user terms." In September 1991, the IBM announcement of its Information Warehouse framework was a critical event that sparked much interest in the industry.

The term data warehouse has been used in the industry for ten or more years. Similar terms are often used interchangeably with data warehouse, such as information warehouse, informational database, decision support database, historical data archive, and business information resource. We will use the shorter term "warehouse" in subsequent discussions.

9.1.1 A Definition

In general, the concept of the warehouse is quite simple. Yet there has been much confusion and even controversy over what constitutes a warehouse, since its characteristics fluctuate with each writer on the subject. The following discussion is yet another humble attempt to clarify this subject.

For our purposes, a *warehouse* is defined as "a collection of data objects that have been packaged and inventoried for distribution to a business community." The collection of data objects is usually assumed to be relational tables or views in a relational database system. This database is contrasted with the production databases used by production applications that contain constantly changing atomic-level data. The act of packaging and inventorying implies that the data is organized for better consumption. Finally, the business community is assumed to be end users (rather than application programmers) who are performing management-level business functions. As shown in Figure 9.1, the anatomy of a warehouse consists of three major components: data resources, back office, and front office.

First, the data resources are of two types: internal and external. The internal data resources are usually production systems containing the

What Is a Warehouse? ▼ 253

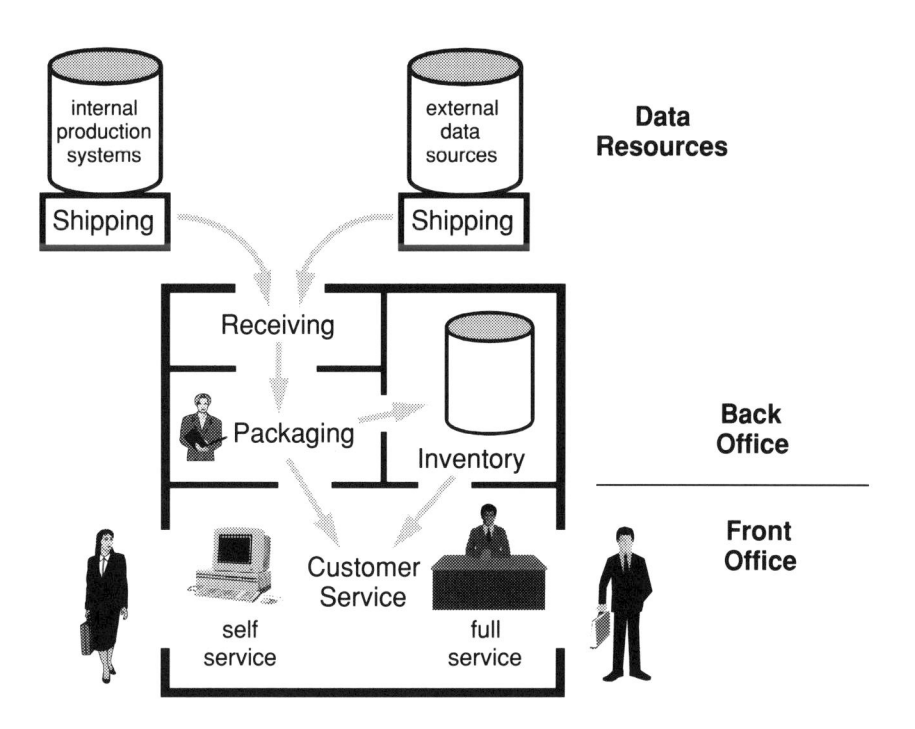

Figure 9.1. Anatomy of a warehouse.

detailed live data of the enterprise. This data may be contained in relational databases, nonrelational databases (of various sorts), and simple files. The external data may be contained in a variety of sources from public to fee-based databases, dealing with industry trends, competitors, market dynamics, population demographics, etc. Each year, there is a growing breadth and quality to these external sources.

With all the data resources, there is a Shipping Department that is responsible for copying the appropriate data and shipping it to the warehouse. This is where the infrastructure built upon access management and copy management are relevant. With this infrastructure, we have a viable distribution system to support the warehouse.

Second, the Back Office of the warehouse consists of the following departments: Receiving, Packaging, and Inventory. The Receiving Department checks the quality of data and marks its arrival time and characteristics. The Packaging Department transforms the raw data into a more palatable form (as discussed later). The Inventory Department stores the packaged data in an *informational database* for delivery to customers.

Note two important aspects of the Back Office. Packaged data can be delivered either from the Packaging Department directly to the customer or from Inventory. The method depends on requirements for data currency. Unlike other departments that are fully automated, the Packaging Department has a person to supervise and direct the packaging process. Martin (1982) described this person as a data coordinator who has the skills of a database administrator, knowing the technology and structures of available data resources.

Third, the Front Office of a warehouse is where the action is. The customer (i.e., business-oriented user) can enter in one of two ways: full-service, or self-service. The full-service option involves a person usually called an information analyst, who knows the contents of the informational database and interacts with the data coordinator if additional or more timely data is required. The self-service option involves an information access tool operating on the workstation. This tool accesses the informational database in a flexible manner, delivering data into a variety of other analysis tools.

9.1.2 An Example of a Large Warehouse

At an International DB2 User Group (IDUG) conference, Nate Lyman (1992) of the Travelers Corporation gave a presentation describing the characteristics of two warehouse databases. His company handles a variety of insurance products, with 127 years in the business and more than 35,000 employees.

The MIS staff has about 3,250 employees. Their mainframe platforms have about 1,000 MIPS of processing power, 67 terabytes of storage, about 200 product applications, 12 million online transactions per day, from 31,100 personal computers (with 3,200 being OS/2) and 11,000 CRT terminals, and finally connected to 300 LANs. They first installed DB2 in 1984. Their goal statement for the warehouse is: "The overall function for a warehouse system is to provide the tools and facilities to manage and deliver complete, timely, accurate, and understandable business information to authorized individuals for effective business decision making."

The first warehouse application consists of 24 tables and 30 indexes, with a total database size of 150 gigabytes. The largest table contains

244 million rows (with 104 bytes per row) and 26 columns. There is a weekly batch update from production systems, 40-100 nightly queries and ad hoc retrievals using DIS and FOCUS.

The second warehouse application consists of 29 tables and 32 indexes, with a total database size of 180 gigabytes. The largest table contains 80 million rows (with 242 bytes per row) and 73 columns. There is a monthly batch update with millions of inserts, deletes, etc. There are nightly queries using QMF and ad hoc retrievals using DIS.

The purpose of this example is to convey a sense of sizing for the larger warehouse environments. Now, let's consider some of the key characteristics for a warehouse.

9.1.3 Some Characteristics

Embedded in the above anatomy are several key characteristics for a warehouse:

- business-oriented
- consolidates operational data
- manages transformations
- historical record
- packaged objects
- logically integrated

First, a warehouse is business-oriented. Almost all data kept within production systems is there to support one application or another. The way that data should be structured, indexed, coded, accessed, etc., is fundamentally different for consumption by an application, as opposed to a person. Hence, there is a need for the business orientation for a warehouse. This characteristic also implies that most of CASE tools for data definition, data dictionaries, and even the IBM repository are inappropriate for a warehouse.

Second, a warehouse consolidates operational data. Most writers state that operational data is copied to the informational database of a warehouse. This statement leads to two fallacies: The data is simply copied as is, and the copied data is redundant. In a well-designed warehouse, both statements should be false. Consolidation is a better term than copying since it implies significant value is added. The data needs "cleaning," in which the inconsistencies and inaccuracies in the operational data are minimized.

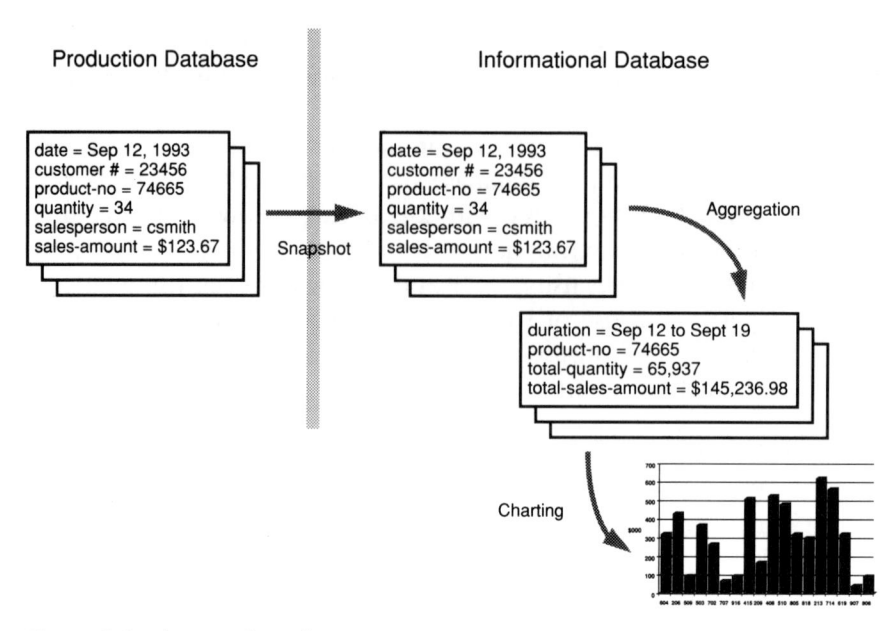

Figure 9.2. *Chaining of transformations.*

Third, a warehouse manages transformations. As detailed production (live) data is captured from the production databases, various transformations are applied to enhance its usefulness. Examples of these transactions are:

- *Snapshotting*: capturing a moment in time
- *Aggregating*: summing, averaging, etc.
- *Grouping*: collapsing rows into higher-level groups
- *Extrapolating*: filling in missing values
- *Forecasting trends*: filling in future values
- *Converting structures and formats*: to spreadsheets, charts, etc.
- *Sampling*: drawing an accurate subset for analysis
- *Expanding code fields into readable values*

Shown in Figure 9.2 is an example of chaining multiple transformations together. We start with a detailed record of a sale transaction within the production sales system. This detailed data is close to the point of capture and is used in many ways within the production system. At specific intervals (daily, for example), a snapshot is performed, copying the set of sales transactions for that time interval into the informational database of the warehouse. Typically this data is immediately aggregated with totals, counts, and other information into records, which are then used to forecast sales trends of various kinds.

Note that there is a chain of transformations which must be properly managed. All data within the warehouse is the product of transformation chaining, and the detailed history of this chaining should be maintained for each data element. An "algebra for data transformations" is needed to express and manipulate these transformation chains.

Fourth, the warehouse handles historical records. The majority of the data is historical. For example, the sales of products by the branch office would be captured from a production for the past week. This data would be keyed on the time period and accumulated with past sales data. Depending on limits of the technology, such data could usefully be kept for five to ten years, which is often mandated by legal requirements. Time-dependent data structures are complex to design properly. Further, the structures will change over long periods of time. In other words, think of a table containing sales transactions for a five year period. Depending on the date within these five years, the existence, typing, ordering, and naming of columns may change within the table. What does a simple SELECT against this table return? Each row may have a different structure. So much for normalized designs!

Fifth, a warehouse packages objects. The data is consolidated from various data resources and is then transformed; however, the final step is the packaging of this data into a form that is best consumed by the business community. Most warehouses package data into a relational table, which is accessed by an SQL query tool listing the data in rows and columns on the screen. Current desktop technology permits us to be much more creative. For example, the data could be delivered in the form of an Excel spreadsheet, complete with proper fonts, shading, summation formulas, headings, certified macros for sales trends analysis, and some "wizards" (i.e., user-guided procedures) to generate intricate graphs. As multimedia becomes viable, slow-motion video could show the sales histories in animated action!

Finally, a warehouse is logically integrated. This is probably the most difficult characteristic. Ideally, an integrated business model of the enterprise should be directing the data consolidation, transactions, and packaging of the warehouse. Otherwise, users will not receive a consistent and coherent view of the enterprise, regardless of the quality of the data.

9.1.4 Key Issues

Now that we have discussed what a warehouse is, let's broaden our discussion to warehouse management in general. This section touches on some issues in the design and operation related to warehouse management, in response to the following questions:

- Is a warehouse a place or an activity?
- Should a warehouse be separate from production systems?
- Is the relational data model sufficient?
- Is a directory a prerequisite?
- What is the right amount of granularity?
- Should a warehouse permit updates?
- How should data freshness be maintained?
- Can a warehouse handle semantic heterogeneity?
- What is the balance between the enterprise versus the workgroup?
- Should a warehouse support software distribution?
- Who owns warehouse management?

First, most consider a warehouse as a place where the activities of consolidation, transformation, and packaging occur. Is a warehouse more than just a large informational database? There is a another perspective: *warehousing as an activity*. We could have entitled this chapter "Warehousing Management" to emphasize that we may be managing process more than managing data. For instance, software distribution may be more important than data distribution for the warehouse. In many cases, the focus should be on the flow of data from production systems to warehouses to consumers, and then back as transactions to the production systems. The proper mechanism for scheduling, monitoring, and recovering these processes would be critical to warehouse management.

Second, should a warehouse be physically separate from production systems? Some industry observers (e.g., W. H. Inmon) strongly argue for the separation since the requirements for the two types of systems are totally different. Others blur the separation and, for example, allow a single DB2 subsystem to contain both production and warehouse tables. Conceptually in the definition or characteristics of a warehouse, there is not a requirement for separation, either in the platform or in the database engine. However, because of the complex nature of most production systems on a mainframe platform, it is probably prudent to operate the warehouse on a separate platform (perhaps one that is smaller).

Third, is the relational data model sufficient for a warehouse? As we applied complex transformations and package data into multimedia objects, a higher-level data model seems to be required to permit:

- flexible class hierarchies
- instances with varying structure within an object class
- intelligent inheritance rules
- refined models for time-dependent historical data
- object encapsulation for modularity
- multi-media data types

and so forth . . .

Can current relational database technology be extended to handle these new requirements? Or, should database technology be completely re-engineered? Or, will front-end tools allow the problem to go away for the database engine? This is the nub of a hot debate among vendors concerning object-oriented databases. And unfortunately, the basic tools for building good warehouses may become entangled in this debate.

Fourth, is a business directory a prerequisite for a warehouse? From the front office perspective, a business directory is needed to guide the consumer to the appropriate data. From the back office perspective, a business directory is needed to guide the acquisition and transformation of data into business information. But, must warehouse development wait for the availability of a suitable business directory for the enterprise? Such a business directory may take years to create, and whatever business directory may already exist may not be applicable to a warehouse environment. This is a tough issue! We must seek ways of allowing warehouse and directory development to evolve concurrently. In fact, one practical way for developing a good business directory may be by observing usage patterns in a functioning warehouse.

Fifth, seeking the right amount of granularity is a major design decision since it affects dramatically the volume of data maintained in the informational database. Because the usage patterns of this data are uncertain, it is ideally best to keep the data at the finest level of granularity (i.e., at the level maintained by the production systems). However, there are two hard limitations: the capacity to store the data; and the efficiency in retrieving and aggregating the data. A careful balance is needed.

Sixth, should a warehouse allow updates? Most industry observers strongly argue that the warehouse is strictly a read-only facility. Updates only occur when data is refreshed from the data resources, probably by a batch process in the evening. A read-only warehouse simplifies the concurrency controls for the database systems (no locking required), thus making the data more available. The only problem is that business decisions based on warehouse data must materialize as transactions are directed back into the production systems. It seems natural that new business processes (e.g., budget forecasting) will emerge from warehouse usage. Previously such processes were manual. Enhancements to the production systems should be quickly made to incorporate these new business processes; however, this is unlikely given the inability of production systems to cope with new requirements. Unfortunately, these new business processes will likely be bootlegged on personal workstations. The warehouse could assume a constructive role in bridging personal with enterprise systems by providing a fertile ground to incubate new business processes. If so, then the warehouse should be more than a read-only data store and actively solicit new business processes as a first step in the migration to production systems.

Seventh, how should a warehouse maintain data freshness? This question can be divided into two other questions: How new is new? And, how old is old? Recalling the discussion on data volatility in the last chapter, there are two distinct phases in the life of copied data, the knee and the tail. From a business perspective, a warehouse needs to recognize when the knee of data volatility occurs and automatically activate a refresh mechanism. Likewise for historical data, a warehouse needs to recognize when the tail of data volatility is reached and automatically activate an archive or purge mechanism. Note that data volatility may not be predictable. The challenge is to engineer the warehouse so that clues of volatility behavior can be captured and used to direct the refresh and archive mechanisms.

Eighth, the toughest task of warehouse management is handling the problem of *semantic heterogeneity*, which is described in the second chapter as a problem with SQL transparency. Sheth and Larson (1990) defined it as "a disagreement about the meaning, interpretation, or intended use of the same or related data." Let's examine a few examples of databases containing data about restaurants (from Sheth and Larson, 1990). Each contain a column called MEAL_COST for a specific restaurants. But, what does it mean? Is it the lowest cost meal, average cost, etc.? Does it include service and tax. Is its units in US dollars or Swiss francs? The second example shows different tables containing student grades. One class has grades on an A/B/C scale, while another class uses 1 to 10, and yet another uses a 100-point scale. How does one determine the grade point average for a student in all three classes? The third example comes from Goldring (1992), who considers the diversity among inventory databases at several different stores. In each database, there is a column called QTY_ON_HAND, but each database interprets this column differently:

- updated when shipments are received at the loading dock
- updated when restocking shelves at night
- maintained continuously as current level plus deliveries minus POS purchases

If you were manager of these stores, could you determine what your inventory really was? More pertinent, if we consolidated data from these various databases into our warehouse, could we draw valid business conclusions from this data?

Ninth, what is the balance between an enterprise warehouse and a workgroup warehouse? A warehouse is usually assumed to have an enterprise-wide scope. The business directory should cut across organizational units and business functions. Is there a need for a warehouse with a limited focus upon a workgroup? In Devlin and Cabena (1992), a workgroup warehouse was suggested to "ensure good query performance and improve security." As shown in Figure 9.3, workgroup warehouses can complement an enterprise warehouse, offering specialized data and transforms unique to that workgroup. It may be more practical to initiate warehouse development with a workgroup scope, rather than an enterprise scope, simply to manage the complexity (and funding, duration, etc.) of the project.

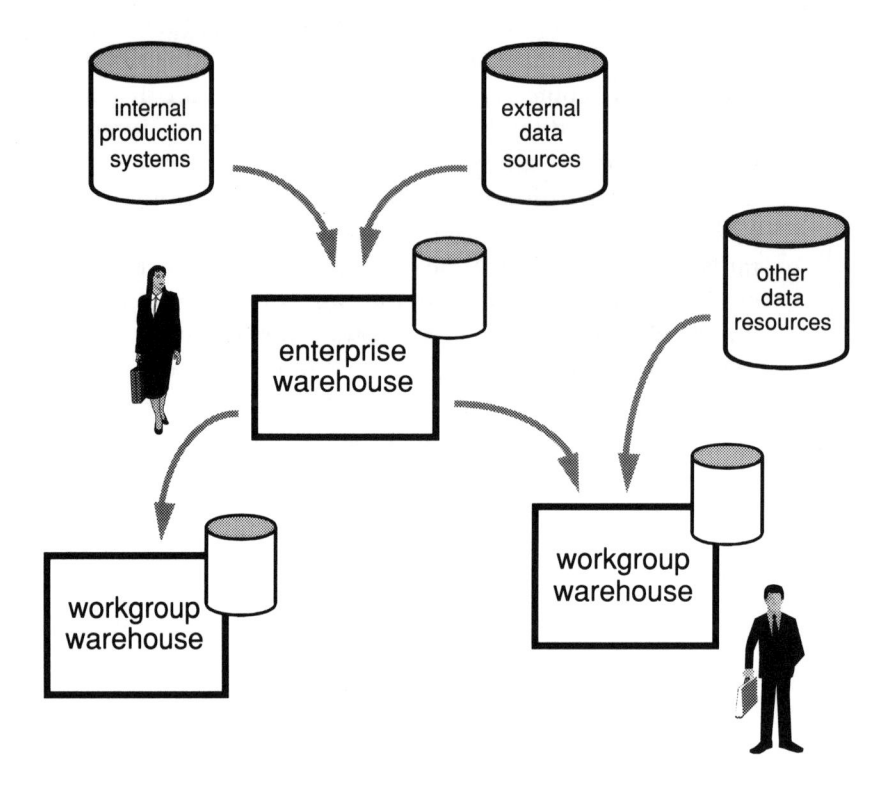

Figure 9.3. Enterprise and workgroup warehouses.

Tenth, should a warehouse support software distribution? Think for a moment about the requirements for a good software distribution system. Are they not identical to a good data warehouse? In other words, a good data warehouse should also be a good software, or process, warehouse. If a warehouse packages objects consisting of Excel spreadsheets with embedded certified macros, it is also supporting software distribution. Further, the infrastructure for the warehouse—access and copy management—should be equally applicable to software distribution.

Finally, who owns warehouse management? We may be able to take lessons from the experience and literature on Information Centers, those energetic teams commissioned to suppress the rising hoards of end users against the glass house! Please, let's try to avoid the mistakes of our past.

The ownership of warehouse management is particularly nasty because the ownership of data is highly political, striking at the heart of organizational autonomy within the enterprise. What incentive does a workgroup have to give up its data to an enterprise warehouse? To the workgroup, are the benefits greater than the costs and risks? To the workgroup, is its control of the data lost? The tracking of and sensitivity to data ownership should become a main feature in any successful warehouse.

Now, let's shift our discussion from the general concepts to a more practical look at IBM's approach to warehouse management.

▼ 9.2 INDEPTH: IBM INFORMATION WAREHOUSE FRAMEWORK

As stated in the IBM Programming Announcement 291-471 (dated September 11, 1991), IBM defined its Information Warehouse (IW) framework as "a set of database management systems, interfaces, tools, and facilities that manage and deliver reliable, timely, accurate, and understandable business information to authorized individuals for business decision-making." Products that support the IW framework "provide access to data wherever it is located in the enterprise . . ."

The IW framework consists of three main components: enterprise data, data delivery, and decision support. In IBM's terminology, the enterprise data component is "the heart of the warehouse and consists of full-function database management systems which provide data integrity, security, recovery, reliability, availability, and performance." Enterprise data for IBM emphasizes data managed by their DB2 and IMS/ESA products within MVS/390.

The data delivery component is "the means through which the right business data is delivered to knowledge workers . . . wherever it resides in the enterprise." Data delivery includes "data transfer, data transformation, data enrichment, and copy management tools and techniques." It is interesting to note IBM's distinction between data extraction and data propagation. Extraction is the copying of data for whatever purpose (retrieval only or update), while propagation is copying internally between two operational databases so as to maintain "one logical copy of the data" (e.g., between IMS and DB2). The key products for data delivery are: the DRDA-compliant products (i.e., DB2 2.3, SQL/DS 3.3, etc. as described in Chapter 7); Data Extract (DXT); Data Propagator; and the IBI EDA/SQL family of access tools (plus its call-level API).

264 ▼ Warehouse Management

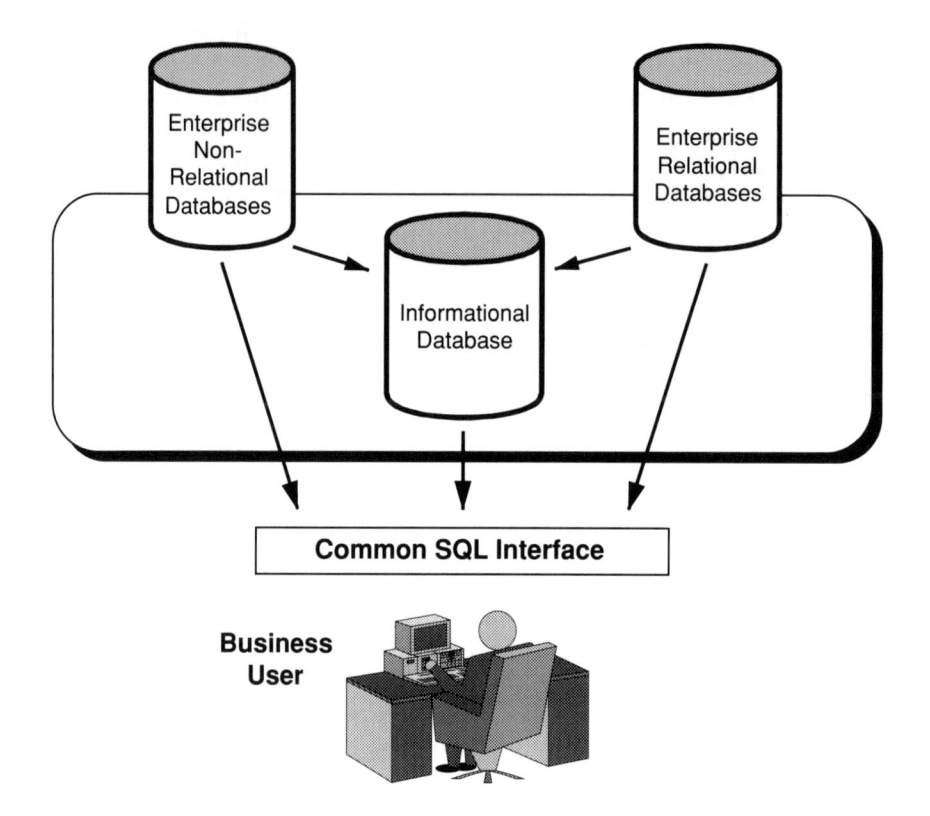

Figure 9.4. Focus of IBM Information Warehouse.

The decision support component "enables knowledge workers to transform data into information by formulating a request for selection of data, manipulating the data retrieved, and analyzing and presenting the transformed data in various information formats and graphical charts." The products identified by IBM for decision support are: SAA Personal Application System/2 (PAS/2); Application System (AS); Data Interpretation System (DIS); Executive Decisions (ED); Query Management Facility (QMF); SAA LanguageAccess; and Lotus 1-2-3/M.

What does this IW announcement mean to the industry?

The announcement was primarily a statement of direction by IBM to position the obvious decision support (i.e., warehousing) activities in most of IBM's large accounts as being synergetic to mainframe legacy systems. In the IW framework, the mainframe still has a role: supporting the enterprise-wide warehouse as a megaserver within the corporate network. This is illustrated in Figure 9.4. The two categories of existing data are the enterprise relational databases and the enterprise nonrelational databases (including VSAM data sets). In addition, there is a new informational database composed of copying data from the other two sources. The key point is that there is a common interface (i.e., SQL as a common access language) to any three of these databases. The implication is that the business user with the proper decision support tools can easily access either: (a) operational data directly; or (b) informational data that has been staged and transformed.

IBM clearly states that a business model is a prerequisite to developing a warehouse. The first step requires "a coherent business model" consisting of "a careful inventory of data currently held by the enterprise, determination of the value of new data that can be derived from this data, and evaluation of the security and systems management requirements to safeguard this data." Interestingly, the second step is "to install a relational database system if the enterprise does not currently have one."

The major criticism of the IW framework has been that it lacks adequate substance to give it credibility. Over a year after the IW announcement, there is still little information from IBM concerning many of the warehouse issues raised earlier in this chapter. For instance, there is no indication as to what an IW directory should be and how it relates to the IBM repository. Although good work on IW has been performed internally within IBM, the lack of solid material to the industry has caused many confusing ideas about what IBM's framework is and is not.

▼ ▼ ▼ ▼ ▼ ▼

For Further Information: The Devlin and Murphy (1988) article forms the basis for many of the IW concepts, and the work of IBM Europe on their EBIS architecture continues to point to future directions. *An Introduction to Information Warehouse* (IBM document GC26-4876) gives an overview. Scan recent conference proceedings of the International DB2 User Group for descriptions of IW developments.

▼ DISCUSSION QUESTIONS

1. What is new and different about the concept of a data warehouse?

2. Is the relational data model sufficient to support a data warehouse?

3. Is an information directory a prerequisite for a data warehouse? What should it consist of?

4. Should a warehouse permit updates to its data?

5. Should a data warehouse be designed for the entire enterprise or for a workgroup, or both?

6. In your company, who should own and/or manage warehouse management?

7. How would you explain to your top management the concept and benefits for the IBM Information Warehouse?

10

ADMINISTRATION ISSUES

This last chapter returns to the themes of the first chapter. Rising above the technology concerns of Enterprise Database Connectivity, this chapter addresses issues related to administration, including politics, economics, psychology, and so forth. The term "management" was considered instead of "administration," but the former term was used in previous chapters in a different sense. The technical discussions of access management, copy management, and warehouse management thus act as background to the really hard issues of this chapter. The topics in this chapter may seem unorganized, resembling a bizarre patchwork quilt. This, however, reflects the true nature of the unfinished work in this area.

In the first chapter, we raised concerns about the disintegration of enterprise systems and fragmentation of enterprise databases. Think for a moment about the last eight chapters of this book. Were there any solutions given that address either the disintegration of enterprise systems or the fragmentation of enterprise databases?

Unfortunately, current technology tends toward accelerating both disintegration and fragmentation in the short term, over the next one to three years. With the mainframe platform declining and exciting things happening on the desktop, our enterprise systems and enterprise data will gravitate towards smaller and more autonomous units.

The good news is that this new world of computing will foster creativity and responsiveness—qualities that have been sorely lacking. The bad news is that we lack the knowledge and skills for managing this new world of computing *in the large*. Small-scale systems will be extraordinary successes, while large-scale attempts will be striking disasters. For example, we are able to perform a schema change to one or two databases easily and reliably; we understand what is required, and we have the tools to assist. But, what about performing a schema change to five hundred LAN database servers that are dispersed worldwide? The problem is fundamentally different; it does not scale! And the knowledge accumulated over the years concerning change management for database administration is not as applicable as one would like. This dilemma suggests that enterprises may be forced to limit the size of their operations because of limits inherent in information technology.

This situation leaves the MIS professional of the future ill-prepared to cope with the demands of this new world of computing within the enterprise. In this chapter, we will outline a few major issues and glimpse a few potential solutions. As you will see, there are many bright spots amid this gloomy background.

▼ 10.1 THE SACRED SEVEN

The proper way to initiate this chapter on administration issues is to discuss the *Sacred Seven*—seven measures by which to evaluate any system. The Sacred Seven are:

- performance
- integrity
- security
- manageability
- availability
- recoverability
- flexibility

Let's briefly discuss each. First, *performance* is the measure of how quickly or timely the system performs its business function. Performance is different from efficiency. One would hope that good performance is caused by good efficiency, but that is not a requirement. Performance is a highly subjective measure. The criterion of good performance can vary significantly in the eye of the beholder. In the EDC area, performance is often very complex, since it depends on the interaction of autonomous systems over large networks.

Second, *integrity* is the measure of the quality of data or process for a specific business function. Much has been written in the database field on integrity constraints, which are quality filters for data entering a database. In the EDC field, integrity becomes broadened and takes on new significance in measuring whether the data or process is a valid representation of a specific business function.

Third, *security* is the measure of whether a user of the system is authorized to be involved with a specific business function. Security often is divided into authentication (determining who the user is) and verification (determining the user's privileges). Any distributed system has considerably greater threats to its security than a comparable centralized system. In particular, client-server systems have yet to deal with the difficult aspects of security.

Fourth, *manageability* is the measure of the effort required to operate the system over the scope and duration that it is intended. As mentioned earlier, managing one thousand database servers is a different problem than managing one or two database servers. Manageability has many aspects to it, from controlling configurations, balancing workloads, tuning performance to detecting problems, tracking changes, assigning personnel, and allocating resources.

Fifth, *availability* is the measure of the probability that the system is operating properly. In other words, when you want to use the system, is the system available for use? The industry often talks about 7x24 availability, meaning that the system should be available continuously, seven days a week and twenty-four hours per day. Many information systems were originally designed for batch processing: online during the day, batch at night, testing on weekends. Doing all of those activities continuously places high demands on the design and operation of a system. For databases, availability usually translates into concurrency limits. The number of active transactions (for either retrieval or update) against the same data element determines the availability of that data, rather than whether the system itself is functioning.

Sixth, *recoverability* is the measure of effort to recover a system from some failure. Remember Murphy's Law; every system fails sometime and somehow in ways that defy imagination. The ability of a system to recover easily from failure is critical.

Seventh, *flexibility* is the measure of effort needed to change the system in response to changing business requirements. There are many aspects to system flexibility, which have been discussed throughout the previous chapters, such as: scalability, portability, interoperability, permissiveness, transparency (between architectural layers), and openness.

Taken as a unit, the Sacred Seven represent a practical measuring stick to apply in any situation involving EDC. The Sacred Seven is balanced with the various costs incurred with design, development, and operation of systems. In the areas of our discussions, these costs could be:

- cost of hardware purchase, installation, and repair
- cost of software licensing, support, and maintenance
- cost of communication setup, leasing, and operation
- cost of development
- cost of personnel training, retraining, and hiring

and so forth . . .

Now that the obvious has been stated, let's consider the administration issues that move beyond the Sacred Seven.

▼ 10.2 HANDLING THE COMPLEXITY OF TECHNOLOGY

The most perplexing issue with EDC is properly handling the complexity of information technology (IT). Too few people understand the basics, and even fewer can employ technology wisely in our enterprises. Our IT world is sufficiently complex that there are no "silver bullets," no panaceas that will solve all of our problems, making life easy for us until our retirement days. The next few sections discuss some aspects of handling the complexity of technology, starting with our own feelings about it.

10.2.1 Riding the Technology Roller Coaster

Our feelings about technology in our professions are analogous to riding a super-triple-loop roller coaster. When you are grinding up the ramp, whether you like it or not, a sickening feeling swells up from the pit of your stomach. You have thoughts of how foolish you were to get on this contraption; your fingers firmly wrap themselves around the steel bar in front of you, seeking unconsciously the maximum grip. The true meaning of "white knuckles" becomes apparent. The fleeting thought of "let's try to have fun" seems as a distant weak voice in your mind as you hurtle over the top.

This is a true characterization of how we deal with the emotional impact of IT complexity. It often seems that the world is turning upside down on us. There are some who are thoroughly enjoying the ride, waving their arms midair as they swish through the loops. However, others are hanging on for dear life, concentrating on thoughts of how wonderful it will be when this ride is finished! Roughly speaking, we can divide people into two categories regarding their propensity towards IT:

- the white-knuckled people (technology fearing)
- the arm-waving people (technology loving)

10.2.2 Diversity of Technology

For the white-knuckled people, the motivations are to smooth the turns and eliminate the loops. Let's standardize; let's integrate; let's centralize. In other words, let's reduce our diversity of technology and adopt a specific IT profile that will be enterprise policy.

For the arm-waving people, the motivation is to fully experience the turns and rejoice in the loops. Let's learn from new technology; let's explore its limitations; let's grasp that next competitive advantage. In other words, let's increase our diversity of technology by continually evolving our IT profile. Where do we find this new technology? The arm-waving people simply go to the end of reality and turn left.

We know, however, that the actual situation is not black-or-white. Each of us is at times a white-knuckled person and at other times an arm-waving person. The stereotypes are to be avoided. A pure white-knuckled person will soon be obsolete, swept aside by the turbulence of change. Like living systems, minimal diversity implies maximal risk of extinction. IT diversity allows us to hedge our bets, its diversity gives us escape routes from unexpected glitches. On the other hand, maximal IT diversity implies chaos, particularly in terms of managing the IT. There are basic limits to comprehending changes and to applying properly new technology. There are basic limits to assimilating changes within the social fabric of our enterprises. We are limited in our ability to handle all of this complexity.

So, what is the balance? While this is an impossible question to answer in general, we can suggest reasonable guidelines:

- If it makes good business sense, try it. Adopt new technology if this specific IT adoption clearly meets basic criteria of the Sacred Seven. Adopt even if established policies are violated. On the other hand, remember that the adoption of a new technology carries an introductory price tag that can range from subtle to prohibitive.
- Then, learn from this IT adoption. Evaluate, probe, criticize, and analyze, with the perspective that this new technology may be incorporated into the IT profile of the enterprise. With our current technological diversity, these are not comfortable times for the faint-hearted.

10.2.3 Fads versus Concepts

At the same time, avoid fads! Just as in hiring a new employee, be sure to adopt technology that has some value to it. The noise level of our industry is very high, with glossy marketing brochures, high-power sales techniques, huge trade shows, and so on. We live in a time when FUD—fear, uncertainty, and doubt—is the norm. Seek that quieting feeling that comes when a technology, product, or vendor actually makes common sense.

Figure 10.1 shows the distinction between fads and concepts. A fad is content-free; a concept is content-rich. We need good concepts to build good technology. Both start as an interesting idea. The idea smolders for awhile, and then the idea either takes off or nose dives. The true nature of a new idea only materializes through hard thinking and the collective efforts of the industry. We need to understand new ideas by asking

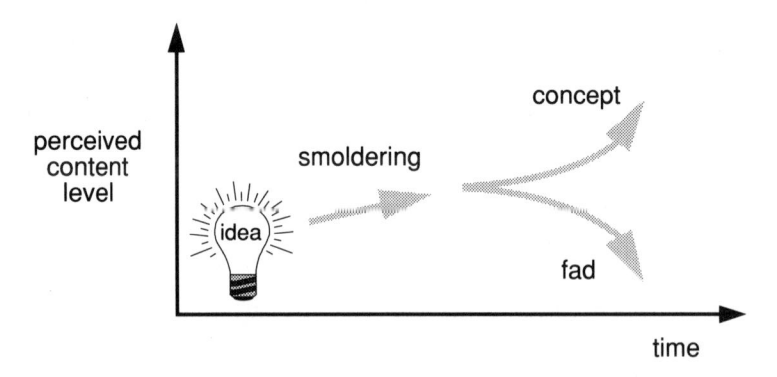

Figure 10.1. Fads vs. concepts.

questions. Concepts will explain other aspects of the technology. Concepts will lead to asking more refined questions.

The moral is: be aggressive in seeking good concepts that lead to good technology. Uncover the fads as soon as possible. And do not let others do this thinking for you. This includes consultants and vendors (book authors are exempted!).

10.2.4 Timing of Adoption

Realize that timing of adoption for a new technology is critical. The maturity of a new technology may have been weak two years ago; however, its maturity may be viable currently. Adopting a technology too early may lead to inappropriate evaluation. Adopting a technology too late may retard its natural assimilation by the enterprise. Other writers have used the analogy of surfing as applied to the timing of technology adoption. If you catch a wave too early, you are squashed; if you catch a wave too late, you will miss it entirely. Bad timing means that the benefits of the new technology will crush you or will pass you by, either of which is undesirable.

What is the proper timing? How do good surfers learn to catch the right wave at the right time? Good surfers spend a lot of time surfing. They test many waves before committing. Over time, they will say that there is almost a zenlike phenomenon of being one with the wave—blending their being into the dynamics of the water.

For some people, it may be difficult to be one with a new technology. Blending your being into a database server may be a bit disconcerting! However, that is the way that technology adoption has been successful. The principle from surfing is applicable.

The guideline is: live with the technology. Really understand the technology through its numerous layers of complexity. Know its limits; push it beyond the reasonable.

10.2.5 Assessing New Technology

A final word about technology: who should assess new technology? And how should it be done? Large enterprises often establish a technology assessment group whose responsibilities are to apply the above principles. However, this group runs the risk of being detached from the mainstream of the enterprise and could assess a technology from an inappropriate perspective.

The function of technology assessment should involve a cross-section of the enterprise. This function is too important to be secluded in a headquarter's back office. Line managers may be the best people to assess technology, since supposedly, they know the business and are the best at applying the Sacred Seven.

▼ 10.3 DEALING WITH LEGACY SYSTEMS

The previous discussion on adopting new technologies is nice, but the reality of most enterprises involves their legacy systems. Attached to a twenty-year lineage, these legacy systems supply critical services that are both a heritage and a burden. Legacy systems are a heritage since they embody twenty years of experiences accumulated in application software customized to the enterprise. Legacy systems are a burden since they embody twenty years of experiences accumulated in application software customized to the enterprise. If markets for the enterprise were stable, then legacy systems should be more of a heritage than a burden. However, markets are not stable in the 1990s. The basic businesses of most enterprises are undergoing radical changes, and legacy systems have thus become more of a burden in recent years.

Because of changes in basic business, the situation now is that most enterprises must migrate their legacy systems into the new world of computing—somehow, sometime. The issue is not whether, but how and when. The EDC situation is sufficiently complex that there are no panaceas.

What are we to do? Michael Stonebraker (1991) offers two succinct alternatives for dealing with legacy systems, the Cold Turkey approach or the Chicken Little approach. The Cold Turkey alternative is to junk completely the antiquated legacy system and rewrite everything in the best GUI development tool available. A few megaprogrammers with 100x productivity increases will whip this baby out in no time!

The Chicken Little alternative is to admit that eliminating the elderly legacy system is "too scary to contemplate" and, hence, do nothing—except for "normal" maintenance. With no debate, four million lines of "COBOL-CICS-VSAM-IMS" code is scary!

Neither of these alternatives is very appealing. But, Stonebraker points out that the most important asset of legacy systems is not the actual data or object code, but source code, test cases, bug reports, configuration, documentation, and data element directories. In other words, we must focus upon the assets that have accumulated in the infrastructure—an infrastructure that has evolved around our legacy systems over all those years. The issue is how can we migrate this infrastructure into the new world of computing.

Again, there are no panaceas for this issue, but some realistic but partial alternatives for migrating legacy systems are emerging. Here are a few suggestions:

- Kept the current legacy systems in place. Surround these systems with alternative ways of performing the same services and retrieving the same data, with the expectation that the new ways will replace the old ways over time.
- Retrofit the major legacy applications between the layers of presentation logic and business logic to act as mainframe-based application servers. In other words, offer a set of services, or action-object combinations, to LAN-based gateways and clients.
- Stage critical business-oriented data onto LAN-based informational databases in the style of data warehousing.
- Develop creative desktop applications using the latest GUI development tools. Drive the development with a clear rethinking of the ideal business function. Determine a *minimum* set of development standards for these applications, leaving open the ability to absorb new desktop technologies continuously. Unfortunately, the best available CASE technique may be to develop the application rapidly and allow it to be self-defining.
- Avoid developing the monolithic application. Rely on the emerging integration mechanisms in desktop presentation services, such as cut/paste, DDE, OLE, to evolve a comprehensive set of services.
- Stage onto LAN-based servers the production transactions that update the legacy systems from the desktop applications. Either batch or continuous, the LAN-based servers should move those transactions into the legacy systems. Over time, gradually retarget those transactions to new client-server systems. This allows a migration period in which the legacy system and a new client-server system can operate concurrently.
- Evolve a realistic information model of the business, based upon experiences with the desktop applications. This is a backwards, or grass-roots approach compared to conventional wisdom, since it is

bottom-up from the minute-to-minute business of the enterprise. This information model is critical in directing resources to new functionality for running tomorrow's business.

The final suggestion deserves a section to its own. This suggestion deals with allowing mutations to happen.

▼ 10.4 APPLICATION EXTENSIBILITY

A crucial issue is who designs and implements applications. The conventional wisdom is that the systems analyst knows best; that a well-crafted system life cycle will avoid big mistakes; and that large systems are necessary to preserve order and to conserve resources.

This wisdom was appropriate when one was able to state the information requirements for an application. When the business environment was stable and the technology was rigid, this was good wisdom, and it brought us through a thirty-year period of building successful information systems.

Times have changed. The person doing the business of the enterprise knows best because the business changes every day. We may make a lot of mistakes in any case, but the challenge is to learn from these mistakes rapidly and to convert the mistakes into the next version. Remember, small is beautiful because of the changing nature of new technology and our business environment. We can no longer afford large systems; at the same time, we cannot do without enterprise systems.

Consider the following as an alternative model to allow (good) mutations to happen:

1. Implement an initial version of the application, and deploy it to an active user community.
2. Allow for various extensibility mechanisms so that individual users can customize their applications.
3. Monitor customization efforts, and select the best application extensions to be promoted first to the workgroup version of the application and then to the enterprise version.

If these steps are performed correctly, the enterprise version of the application will evolve through user-driven mutations and will better track the changing application requirements and organizational constraints.

Figure 10.2 illustrates the flow of application versions.

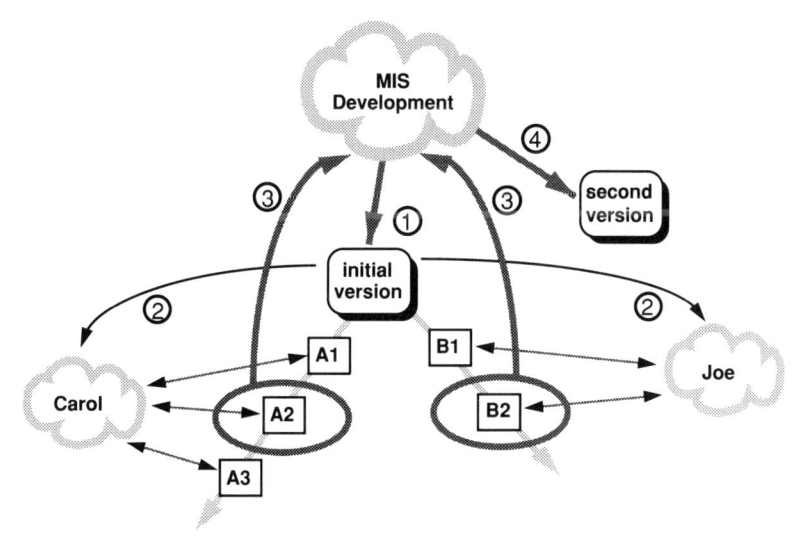

Figure 10.2. *Application extensibility.*

In Step #1, the MIS development group implements an initial version of the application and deploys it to the user community.

In Step #2, users work with the common initial version. Over time, some users extend their versions of the application. Carol has mutated her version in three stages (A1, A2, and A3). Joe has likewise extended his version in two stages (B1 and B2).

In Step #3, the MIS development group has monitored the extensions made by Carol and Joe. They have decided that some of the extensions of each user are desirable for other users. The extensions in Carol's A2 version and Joe's B2 version were selected to be merged into the common application.

In Step #4, the MIS development group deploys a second version of the common application. This second version might be deployed only to the workgroup of Carol and Joe, or it could become the common version for the enterprise. In either case, Joe should be happy because his B2 version is smoothly replaced with a common version supported by the MIS group. Carol is also happy because her A3 version is smoothly replaced with a common version plus her subsequent extensions, or differences from A2 to A3. Further, both get a $1,000 bonus in their next salary check.

The key issues with this approach of application extensibility are:
- Design extensibility mechanisms so that they are simple and intuitive for the user to extend; blend with the current version of the application; and compatible with the desktop environment.
- Limit the impacts of extensibility mechanisms. The mutations to the application should only affect the user who introduces those mutations. And for that user, an effective UNDO function is vital.
- Monitor the application extensions. As the user introduces extensions to his/her version of the application, those extensions are logged into a common database. Information should be collected about nature, usage, etc., of the user extensions.
- Analyze the extension logs. We need to determine whether the user is having difficulties and assist him/her. We also need to select the better extensions for promotion to versions of a higher level.
- Administer application versioning. Potentially there could be one standard enterprise version, plus standard versions for each workgroup, plus several more versions for each user. Efficient mechanisms for supporting thousands of versions must be established.

Note that this approach of application extensibility is equally applicable to "generic" products from software vendors.

▼ 10.5 INDEPTH: IBM DATAHUB

As an example of system management products, this section describes the IBM DataHub product that manages databases distributed across various IBM platforms from an OS/2 workstation. The core is the OS/2 workstation control point (called DataHub/2), giving a common presentation for database objects on any DRDA-compliant database (i.e., DB2, SQL/DS, SQL/400, DBM currently). In addition, DataHub can invoke system management tools on any of the database platforms. As shown in Figure 10.3, the common presentation for database objects uses a hierarchical outline consisting of one or more of the following:
- location or site
- subsystem or operating system
- database
- unit of work (active transaction)
- table and views

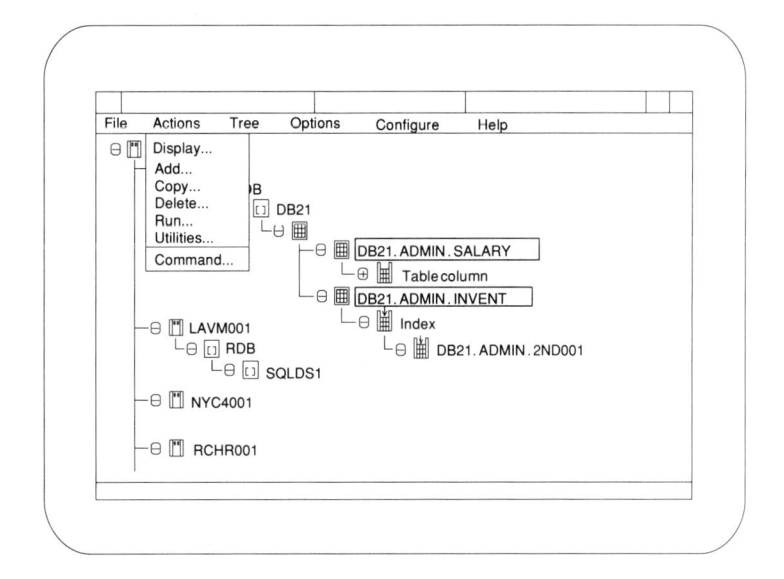

Figure 10.3. *DataHub presentation of objects.*

- table column
- table authorization
- index
- plan and package
- referential constraint
- lock status

The main menu has the usual pull-downs (File, Options, Configure, Help), along with one for Actions. Once specific database objects are selected, the Actions menu permits various tools to initiate processing on the respective platforms, such as:

- display of occurrences or status on objects
- add authorizations for objects, noting their implications
- copy database objects (definitions and content) to other databases
- copy authorizations to other databases
- delete authorizations
- run command statements, like SQL or JCL
- invoke utilities on remote databases
- enter commands manually and run

DataHub/2 at the OS/2 workstation interacts with database support modules on each host, or server, platform. Each support module can invoke various tools to provide database services, such as backup/load/unload/recover tables, reorganize tables/indexes, update statistics, load/unload views, copy tables, change authorizations, and display status on remote units of work.

DataHub complements the IBM SystemView structure. This structure consists of SystemView *dimensions* combined with SystemView *disciplines*. The dimensions are: end-user, which give a common presentation to the user; data, which has a standardized set of database objects; and application, which integrates tasks across environments. The disciplines for SystemView are: business management, change management, configuration management, operations management, performance management, and problem management.

DataHub performs the following specific functions within the SystemView structure:

- displays database objects across enterprise
- copies database objects
- manages database authorizations
- executes remote utilities
- displays status of remote units of work at each database

In addition, DataHub complements IBM Information Warehouse (described in the previous chapter) by:

- finding database tables/columns across enterprise
- copying data to an informational database
- managing privileges in relational databases

Several vendors have announced support for DataHub, presumably to integrate their database tools into the support modules. An important issue is whether these vendors will extend DataHub beyond the IBM platforms and databases, thus allowing the DataHub architecture to deal with enterprise-wide database administration.

▼ ▼ ▼ ▼ ▼ ▼

For Further Information: Review first *DataHub: General Information* (IBM document GC26-4874). The last section lists over ten additional manuals for DataHub. Of special note is the *DataHub Tool Builder's Guide and Reference* (IBM document SC26-3046).

▼ 10.6 ACTION PLANNING

The final section suggests a practical perspective and some concrete steps to formulate a viable EDC architecture that deals with the issues described earlier. Much of this section is common sense; it must be stated for the record, just like the Sacred Seven.

10.6.1 Hedge your Bets

Because of the complexity of architectures, technologies, and products, it is easy to lose perspective amid the numerous details. The key question is: What is really important for my company?

The best way to answer this question is to return to the basic motivations for using any information technology, as shown in Figure 10.4. This list of generic business actions is given in two orderings. First, the actions towards the top are more tangible to the enterprise than those on the bottom. In other words, the top actions are ones that we can understand, plan for, and even predict. Second, the actions towards the bottom have greater potential payoffs to the enterprise than those on the top. In other words, bottom actions are ones that, over the long term, can save our enterprise from extinction.

Closing a customer purchase
Cost displacement or reduction
Cost avoidance
Higher productivity
Improved decision making
Changed business function
New business product/service

tangible actions ↑

↓ potential payoffs

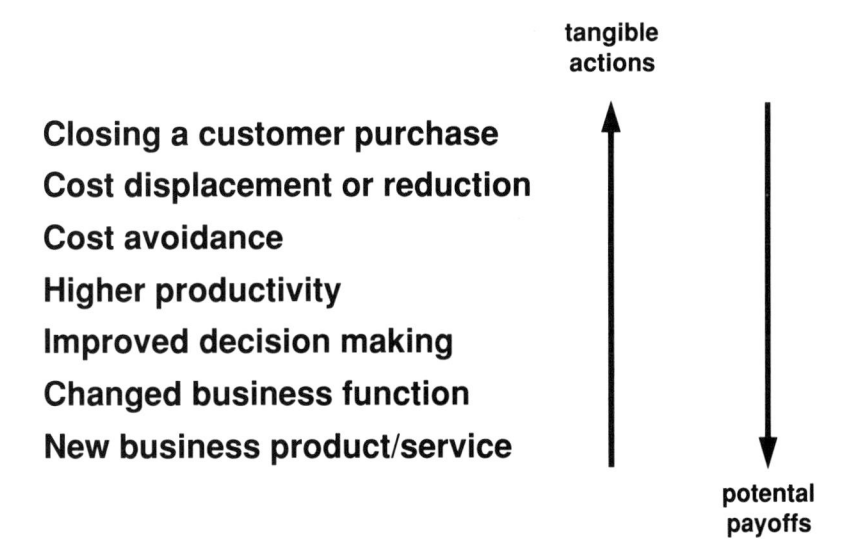

Figure 10.4. Back to basics.

The prudent business orientation is to *hedge your bets*. This is the classical case of diversifying a portfolio of risky investments. There should be a balance among certain, low-potential actions with risky, high-potential actions. This balance is determined by your available resources and by your propensity to absorb failures.

With respect to EDC architectures, there should be projects corresponding to "business as usual" and other projects aimed at "tearing the entire system apart." In all cases, there are several critical questions that we should continually examine:

- What is the real value of using any EDC product? There are penalties in performance and complexity relative to that of centralized database systems. Does the value (in terms of the Sacred Seven) clearly outweigh these penalties? In particular, is there sufficient database heterogeneity to warrant EDC products? Is the level of performance, transparency, etc. sufficient for the intended usage?
- Which EDC architectures and products will be accepted by the industry? In our industry, there are many sad stories of early adopters of the wrong architectures or technologies. Is there room for only one EDC architecture in the industry? Which EDC architecture may be enthusiastically adopted initially and then fade? Which EDC architectures will merge into more widely accepted EDC architectures?
- Can products based on several EDC architectures coexist independently or cooperatively? Is there sufficient functional differentiation among these products to offset the value of a common EDC architecture?

In summary, hedge your bets in formulating an EDC architecture and in initiating EDC projects.

10.6.2 Action Steps

Here are some concrete steps that can move us forward. For reasons cited earlier, we have no choice but to act. The problems will only grow worse. And, your retirement is not that close! Here are some suggested action steps:

10.6.2.1 *Formulate a game plan*

Identify precisely the needs of your enterprise for database connectivity by subject database and by application system. Factor in the variations and issues of access management, copy management, and warehouse management. Consider the suggestions relative to handling technological complexity, dealing with legacy systems, and application extensibility.

10.6.2.2 Ask the right questions
Probe vendors, consultants, standards people, and others about aspects of their approaches and products using the comparison criteria and questions described earlier.

10.6.2.3 Assemble the right team
Successful projects in the EDC area require a team of the right people. Skills from several disciplines may be required, including DB2, OS/2, Windows, Netware, UNIX, and even VTAM/NCP.

10.6.2.4 Get your hands dirty
There is *no* substitute for getting your hands dirty. Set up a prototype project, and take the time to perform a thorough assessment. Explore the available products, realizing that the appropriate product may not be available and that a close working relationship with a right vendor may be more fruitful.

Do that first application—When you feel confident in the technology, apply it to a real (but noncritical) application. Learn about the nontechnical aspects of applying this technology. For instance, does it integrate into the work culture surrounding the legacy systems?

10.6.2.5 Stay on top of it
This technology will evolve rapidly over the next few years. Devote the resources in a few quality people (and your own time) to learn and adapt the technology to your enterprise.

▼ ▼ ▼ ▼ ▼ ▼

Finally, have fun, and keep smiling through it all. These are exciting times. View the technology turbulence as an opportunity, rather than a problem.

▼ DISCUSSION QUESTIONS

1. From your perspective, is the Sacred Seven complete? What should be the priority among the Sacred Seven for your company?

2. Do you identify with the white-knuckled people or the arm-waving people? Does it make an actual difference in your system designs or in your product purchases?

3. What are your company's plans for its legacy systems? Are there formal discussions of this issue? Is there a formal plan?

4. In your company, is the extensibility of an enterprise application by end users an important issue?

▼▼▼ APPENDIX A
ODBC FUNCTION SUMMARY

The following table lists Microsoft ODBC functions, grouped by type of task. It also includes the level of Microsoft extension (i.e., conformance) and a brief description of each function. A conformance of 'core' implies that the function is compliant with the Call-Level Interface specification of the SQL Access Group. For more information about these functions, see the Microsoft ODBC API Reference manual.

CONNECTING TO A DATA SOURCE

FUNCTION NAME	CONFORMANCE	DESCRIPTION
SQLAllocEnv	Core	Obtains an environment handle. One environment handle is used for one or more connections.
SQLAllocConnect	Core	Obtains a connection handle.
SQLConnect	Core	Connects to a specific driver by data source name, user ID, and password.
SQLDriverConnect	Level 1	Connects to a specific driver by connection string or requests that the Driver Manager and driver display connection dialogs for the user.

| SQLBrowseConnect | Level 2 | Returns successive levels of connection attributes and valid attribute values. When a value has been specified for each connection attribute, connects to the data source. |

OBTAINING INFORMATION ABOUT A DRIVER AND DATA SOURCE

FUNCTION NAME	CONFORMANCE	DESCRIPTION
SQLDataSources	Level 2	Returns the list of available data sources.
SQLGetInfo	Level 1	Returns information about a specific driver and data source.
SQLGetFunctions	Level 1	Returns supported driver functions.
SQLGetTypeInfo	Level 1	Returns information about supported data types.

SETTING AND RETRIEVING DRIVER OPTIONS

FUNCTION NAME	CONFORMANCE	DESCRIPTION
SQLSetConnectOption	Level 1	Sets a connection option.
SQLGetConnectOption	Level 1	Returns the value of a connection option.
SQLSetStmtOption	Level 1	Sets a statement option.
SQLGetStmtOption	Level 1	Returns the value of a statement option.

PREPARING SQL REQUESTS

FUNCTION NAME	CONFORMANCE	DESCRIPTION
SQLAllocStmt	Core	Allocates a statement handle.

SQLPrepare	Core	Prepares an SQL statement for later execution.
SQLSetParam	Core	Assigns storage for a parameter in an SQL statement.
SQLParamOptions	Level 2	Specifies the use of multiple values for parameters.
SQLGetCursorName	Core	Returns the cursor name associated with a statement handle.
SQLSetCursorName	Core	Specifies a cursor name.
SQLSetScrollOptions	Level 2	Sets options that control cursor behavior.

SUBMITTING REQUESTS

FUNCTION NAME	CONFORMANCE	DESCRIPTION
SQLExecute	Core	Executes a prepared statement.
SQLExecDirect	Core	Executes a statement.
SQLNativeSql	Level 2	Returns the text of an SQL statement as translated by the driver.
SQLDescribeParam	Level 2	Returns the description for a specific parameter in a statement.
SQLNumParams	Level 2	Returns the number of parameters in a statement.
SQLParamData	Level 1	Used in conjunction with SQLPutData to supply parameter data at execution time. (Useful for long data values.)
SQLPutData	Level 1	Send part or all of a data value for a parameter. (Useful for long data values.)

RETRIEVING RESULTS AND INFORMATION ABOUT RESULTS

FUNCTION NAME	CONFORMANCE	DESCRIPTION
SQLRowCount	Core	Returns the number of rows affected by an insert, update, or delete request.
SQLNumResultCols	Core	Returns the number of columns in the result set.
SQLDescribeCol	Core	Describes a column in the result set.
SQLColAttributes	Core	Describes attributes of a column in the result set.
SQLBindCol	Core	Assigns storage for a result column and specifies the data type.
SQLFetch	Core	Returns a result row.
SQLExtendedFetch	Level 2	Returns multiple result rows.
SQLGetData	Level 1	Returns part or all of one column of one row of a result set. (Useful for long data values.)
SQLSetPos	Level 2	Positions a cursor within a fetched block of data.
SQLMoreResults	Level 2	Determines whether there are more result sets available and, if so, initializes processing for the next result set.
SQLError	Core	Returns additional error or status information.

OBTAINING INFORMATION FROM SYSTEM CATALOG TABLES

FUNCTION NAME	CONFORMANCE	DESCRIPTION
SQLColumnPrivileges	Level 2	Returns a list of columns and associated privileges for one or more tables.

SQLColumns	Level 1	Returns the list of column names in specified tables.
SQLForeignKeys	Level 2	Returns a list of column names that comprise foreign keys, if they exist for a specified table.
SQLPrimaryKeys	Level 2	Returns the list of column name(s) that comprise the primary key for a table.
SQLProcedureColumns	Level 2	Returns the list of input and output parameters, as well as the columns that make up the result set for the specified procedures.
SQLProcedures	Level 2	Returns the list of procedure names stored in a specific data source.
SQLSpecialColumns	Level 1	Returns information about the optimal set of columns that uniquely identifies a row in a specified table, or the columns that are automatically updated when any value in the row is updated by a transaction.
SQLStatistics	Level 1	Returns statistics about a single table and the list of indexes associated with the table.
SQLTablePrivileges	Level 2	Returns a list of tables and the privileges associated with each table.
SQLTables	Level 1	Returns the list of table names stored in a specific data source.

TERMINATING A STATEMENT

FUNCTION NAME	CONFORMANCE	DESCRIPTION
SQLFreeStmt	Core	Ends statement processing and closes the associated cursor, discards pending results, and, optionally, frees all resources associated with the statement handle.

SQLCancel	Core	Cancels an SQL statement.
SQLTransact	Core	Commits or rolls back a transaction.

TERMINATING A CONNECTION

FUNCTION NAME	CONFORMANCE	DESCRIPTION
SQLDisconnect	Core	Closes the connection.
SQLFreeConnect	Core	Releases the connection handle.
SQLFreeEnv	Core	Releases the environment handle.

APPENDIX B
COMPARISON OF DRDA AND RDA COMMANDS

The following table shows the commands defined for the DRDA (Level 1) protocol and the generic RDA protocol. It is instructive to analyze where the two protocol relate and where they differ.

CONNECTION MANAGEMENT

COMMAND	DRDA	RDA
Connect	Access Database	R-Initialize
Disconnect		R-Terminate

SQL BINDING

COMMAND	DRDA	RDA
Start Bind	Begin Bind	
Compile Stmt	Bind Statement	R-DefineDBL
Finish Bind	EndBind	
Rebind	Rebind Package	
Drop Bind	Drop Package	R-DropDBL

SQL LANGUAGE SERVICES

COMMAND	DRDA	RDA
Prepare	Prepare SQL	R-DefineDBL
Execute	Execute SQL	R-InvokeDBL
Execute Immediate	Execute SQL Immed	R-ExecuteDBL
Describe	Describe SQL	

CURSOR CONTROL

COMMAND	DRDA	RDA
Open Cursor	Open Query	
Fetch	Continue Query	
Close Cursor	Close Query	

TRANSACTION MANAGEMENT

COMMAND	DRDA	RDA
Begin Transaction		R-BeginTrans
Commit	Commit Transaction	R-Commit
Rollback	Rollback Transaction	R-Rollback

CATALOG INFORMATION

COMMAND	DRDA	RDA
	Describe Table	
	Describe Privileges	

CONTROL SERVICES

COMMAND	DRDA	RDA
Interrupt	Interrupt Request	R-Cancel
Status		R-Status

GLOSSARY

Abstract Syntax Notation One (ASN.1): ISO standard for encoding data values into a binary string.

access management: managing the architecture for the enterprise to support direct access from any client to any server.

access path: an efficient procedure to retrieve or update data within the database by an application.

ACID properties: properties of a transaction, which are: atomicity, consistency, isolation, and durability.

application: a set of software programs that support a specific business function by a user in a specific job position.

application extensibility: the ability of a user to extend a standard application into versions that are customized to his/her usage.

application programming interface (API): the specification for an application to invoke program functions.

application requester (AR): IBM DRDA client interface.

application server (AS): IBM DRDA server interface.

application support protocol: IBM DRDA protocol between a DRDA application requester and application server.

availability: measure of the probability that the system is functioning properly.

basic application structure (BAS): five layers that link a presentation object to a data object, consisting of: presentation services, presentation logic, business logic, data logic, and data services.

binding time: the time at which binding is performed, either at program preparation or at program execution.

binding: processing SQL statement by parsing the text, validating table names, etc. resulting in an access path.

call-level interface (CLI): an application programming interface consisting of a set of procedural calls to invoke program functions.

capability-aware: application code that is aware of the specific capability (not server type) to which it is connected.

Character Data Representation Architecture (CDRA): IBM DRDA architecture that defines 16-bit numbers to represent characters as code points, along with conversions to preserve the character meanings.

check-out replica: a copy for update usage that resynchronizes its updates with the primary database whenever the user is finished with updates.

chief information officer (CIO): An executive having line and staff responsibility for all enterprise-wide information processing activities.

client: a process that initiates requests for services from another platform.

client interface: an interface on the client platform that initiates requests via a protocol to the server interface on the server platform.

client-server architecture (CSA): an architecture consisting of two platforms having the roles of client and server.

commit: the database action that makes permanent any changes by a transaction to the database.

common gateway: an approach of using a database gateway between various clients and servers as the common element for connectivity among various client-server combinations.

common interface: an approach of using the client (or server) interface as the common element for connectivity among various client-server combinations.

common programming interface (CPI): IBM SAA framework of an interface used by a program for various services (e.g., SQL, communications).

common protocol: an approach of using the protocol between the client and server interfaces as the common element for connectivity among various client-server combinations.

Common Transport Semantics (CTS): component for IBM's new SNA blueprint that subsumes TCP/IP and OSI as alternative transport stacks.

concurrency: multiple transactions that are sharing resources at the same time.

concurrency control: the isolation of concurrency transactions so that they do not interfere with one another.

concurrent: execution of several processes during a unit of time but only one process is executing at the instant of time; see **simultaneous**.

connectivity: the technology to enable dissimilar systems to interoperate.

continuous replica: a copy for update usage that resynchronizes its updates with the primary database continuously as the updates occur to the copy.

conversation: a logical connection between two processes.

coordinator: a process that performs a two-phase commit protocol among multiple resource managers (such as a DBMS).

copy devaluation: the perceived decline in value of data that is copied.

copy management: managing the architecture to support copying of data (or process) from one database to another; emphasizes a server-server architecture.

copy request: a request to copy data from a source to a target.

copy set: the result of a copy request consisting of multiple result sets along with status information.

cursor: a position within a result set used by a program to process one row at a time.

data definition language (DDL): a language for defining the structure and characteristics of a database.

data flow: passing of a data structure from one system to another.

data manipulation language (DML): a language for retrieving and changing (insert, update, and delete) the contents of a database.

data object (DO): an object within a database linked to its corresponding presentation object.

data uncertainty: probability of knowing the real value or characteristic for a specific object instance that is being changed by other active transactions.

data warehouse: same as a **warehouse**.

database administration (or administrator) (DBA): a function or job position whose responsibilities are focused on maintaining the integrity and operation of one or more databases.

database engine: component of a DBMS that processes transactions against the database.

database gateway: a composite server/client component that adds a level to the client-server architecture, providing SQL dialect conversions and other services.

database management system (DBMS): collection of programs and utilities for organizing, storing, updating, and retrieving data as maintained in a database.

database support protocol: IBM DRDA protocol between a DRDA application server and database server.

de facto standard: a specification that was defined by one or more vendors and recognized by the industry as a viable standard.

de jure standard: a specification that was defined by a recognized governmental body, such as ISO or ANSI.

deadlock: two or more transactions that are permanently waiting for resources held by each other.

direct object manipulation (DOM): program interaction with an end user in which the user manipulates presentation objects through graphical images thereby causing changes in the underlying data objects.

dirty read: reading data that has been changed by another active transaction.

Distributed Computing Environment (DCE): OSF framework and product for a set of UNIX-based facilities for building distributed systems.

Distributed Data Management (DDM): IBM DRDA command set for conveying SQL statements to a server.

distributed database (DDB): a logical database consisting of one or more physical databases, acting as a single non-distributed database to the user or application.

Distributed Database Connection Services/2 (DDCS/2): IBM DRDA application requester for OS/2.

distributed join: a join from a SELECT statement whose tables are physically on different platforms.

Distributed Relational Database Architecture (DRDA): IBM architecture for database connectivity.

distributed request (DR): transaction consisting of multiple requests against multiple databases, and each request can act against more than one database.

distributed table: IBM term for a table that is partitioned and managed within separate databases.

distributed transaction monitors: a component of a distributed system that monitors transactions between applications and resources and insures proper transaction completion.

Distributed Transaction Processing model (DTP): X/Open framework for open mechanism to coordinate distributed transactions among various resources (not necessarily databases).

distributed unit of work (DUOW): transaction consisting of multiple requests against multiple databases, with the restriction that each request acts against only one database.

distributed update: a transaction consisting of multiple updates to more than one databases.

down-sizing: porting an application from a large platform (e.g., mainframe) to a smaller platform (e.g., personal computer).

dynamic data exchange (DDE): Microsoft Windows mechanism for exchanging data between executing applications.

dynamic link library (DDL): code modules that are linked efficiently at program execution, rather than during program preparation.

dynamic SQL: SQL statements that are parsed and bound at execution time, rather than at program preparation.

embedded SQL: SQL statements that are embedded in another language (e.g. COBOL) and must be precompiled during program preparation.

encapsulation: a clear distinction between the object specification and the internal mechanism of an object.

end-user computing: information processing for a single person performed by his/her own actions, rather than through an intermediary.

enterprise: a group of persons that are motivated by a common objective and utilize common resources to accomplish that objective.

enterprise application: an application whose business function or job position spans the enterprise, either in a vertical or horizontal sense.

enterprise database connectivity (EDC): concepts and practices of interconnecting federated databases.

enterprise database: the collection of any data that can affect decisions and be affected by decisions within an enterprise; or the database(s) that supports enterprise applications.

executive information system (EIS): an information system designed for use by a top executive.

extract chaos: wide-spread practice of extracting from various databases resulting in inconsistent comparisons among the data.

extract: a copy of data that is intended for read-only usage.

fad: a content-free idea.

fat cursor: a position within a result set used by a program to process more than one row at a time.

fear, uncertainty, and doubt (FUD): normal reaction to immature technology, unstable vendors, and poor products, usually promulgated by a competing vendor without sufficient evidence.

federated database (FDB): a collection of heterogenous databases with autonomous ownership.

flexibility: measure of effort to change the system in response to changing business requirements.

Formatted Data: Object Content Architecture (FD:OCA): IBM DRDA architecture to interchange formatted data, such as numbers and characters.

fragmentation: the degree of difficulty in partitioning the database design into appropriate pieces.

glass house: jargon for the machine room of a mainframe system.

graphical user interface (GUI): an user interface to an application using a graphical-based (rather than character-based) display and allowing direct object manipulation.

horizontal application: an application that deals with the coordination among different business functions.

horizontal partition: a partitioning that divides a table along subsets of rows.

information: data that has been assimilated by a person to aid in a decision-making activity.

information technology (IT): any technology that assists in the acquisition, processing, and communication of information.

Information Warehouse (IW): IBM trade-marked term for a warehouse.

informational database: a database constructed to support decision making in a flexible and broad manner; also known as a decision support database.

integrity: measure of the quality of data or process for a specific business function.

interprocess communication (IPC): mechanism for coordinating two independent processes, usually on different platforms.

legacy systems: critical enterprise applications built upon aging technology.

local area network (LAN): a communication network over a small area (e.g., within a building).

local server: a server that is connected to the client platform via a LAN.

long transaction: a transaction that does contain interaction with the application and even the user during its execution.

manageability: measure of the effort to operate the system over the scope and duration that it is intended.

management information system (MIS): a computer-based information system that is used in the operational management and decision-making of an enterprise.

message: data exchange with another platform without prior mutual establishment of a connection.

Multi-Protocol Transport Networking (MPTN): IBM's proposal to X/Open to integrate major networking transport protocols.

named pipe: a Microsoft process-to-process protocol either internal to a platform or external via LAN Manager.

node: an interchange point within a network that can generate or consume data.

object: the most basic unit of a database component.

object behavior: object specification that defines what an object can do.

object class: collection of object instances that have similar attributes.

object hierarchy: relationships among objects that are generalizations or specializations of each other.

object identifier: a system-assigned label that uniquely points to an object instance.

object instance: a specific object that represents a tangible thing or idea in the real world.

Object Linking and Embedding (OLE): Microsoft Windows mechanism for sharing complex objects among applications, either by embedding the object within the client data or by linking to that object residing elsewhere.

object method: object specification that defines the procedures that can affect the object.

object specification: the characteristics of the object class that are visible.

object-oriented data model (OODM): data model based on object-oriented concepts of class hierarchy, encapsulation, overloading, etc.

Open Data Services (ODS): Microsoft version of the Sybase Open Server that allows server applications to respond to requests from other client applications.

Open Database Connectivity (ODBC): Microsoft specification for connectivity of a Windows client application to a remote data resource using SQL.

open standard: a standard upon which all vendors have an equal opportunity to develop and market products.

open system: a system that is implemented with components adhering to specific standards.

Open System Interconnection (OSI): ISO reference model consisting of seven interconnection layers (physical, datalink, network, transport, session, presentation, application).

open systems approach: an architectural policy that maximizes the system components adhering to specific open standards.

organization: the policies and activities by which persons interact within an enterprise.

package: IBM DRDA binding output from SQL statements that is stored in the database to be used by the application.

partition: division of a table into subsets such that the union of all subsets is the original table and the intersection of subsets is null.

performance: measure of how quickly or timely that a system performs its business function.

periodic replica: a copy for update usage that resynchronizes its updates with the primary database at periodic intervals.

persistent SQL object (PSO): a set of bounded SQL statements stored within a database that exists beyond the execution of an application.

platform: a computing system with a specific operating system at a node in a network.

presentation object (PO): the image and a set of behaviors for an object appearing on a display.

primary database: the one (and only one) site of an object instance that is declared to be valid; also known as the system of record.

procedure driven interaction (PDI): program interaction with an end user that is driven by the procedure of the application.

process: the execution of a program consisting of an environment (e.g., initial parameters) and one or more execution threads.

production database: a database constructed to support efficiently specific business functions.

program preparation: the activity of generating an executable program involving code editing, precompilation, binding, compilation, and linking.

proprietary standard: a standard upon which only one vendor is able to develop and market products.

protocol: data structures and rules for interaction between two systems; also known as 'formats and protocol' or FAP.

RDA Dialogue: cooperative relationship between an RDA Client and an RDA Server; also known as **connection**.

RDA Transaction: a unit of work processed by one RDA Dialogue.

recoverability: measure of effort to recover a system from some failure.

refreshed extract: a copy for read-only usage that is refreshed a specific times.

relational data base management system (RDBMS): a DBMS using the relational data model.

relational data model (RDM): a model for defining and manipulating data proposed by Dr. Codd in the early 1970s.

remote commit: a commit or rollback requested by an application against a remote database.

Remote Database Access (RDA): ISO architecture for open connectivity among relational databases.

remote procedure call (RPC): a program call to a subprocedure that is not on the same platform.

remote request (RR): transaction consisting of one request against one database.

remote server: a server that is connected to the client platform via a WAN.

remote stored procedure (RSP): invoking a stored procedure in one database from code in a stored procedure (or trigger) in another database.

remote unit of work (RUOW): multiple requests against one database.

replica: a copy of data that is intended for update usage.

replicated table: IBM term for a periodic replica.

resource: data that enables a person to accomplish an objective.

resynchronization: an activity of ensuring that copied data is logically consistent with the primary version.

right-sizing: porting an application to a platform that is properly sized for that application.

rollback: the database action that removes any changes by a transaction to a database.

Sacred Seven: collection of seven system measures (performance, integrity, security, manageability, availability, recoverability, flexibility).

secondary database: other sites containing copies of an object instance.

security: measure of whether a user is authorized to be involved with a specific business function.

semantic diversity: database designs that are inconsistent among themselves.

server: a process that responds to requests and provides services to other platforms.

server interface: an interface on the server platform that accepts requests via a protocol from the client interface on the client platform.

server-aware: application code that is aware of the specific server type to which it is connected.

service access point: a function (or procedure) call across a defined interface.

Service Provider Interface (SPI): Microsoft WOSA component to interface with drivers that provide a specific service for Windows applications.

short transaction: a transaction that does not contain interaction with the application during its execution.

simple extract: a copy for read-only usage that is not refreshed by the primary database.

simultaneous: execution of several processes at the same instant of time by multiple processors; see **concurrent**.

single site update: a situation in which a specific object instance is updated at any time at only one site.

single-site update policy: the enforcement of only one update site at any specific time for any object instance.

site: an instance of a database engine at a node.

snapshot: copy of live data taken at specific time.

snapshot table: IBM term for a refreshed extract.

splintered transaction: a sequence of short transactions that an application program manages as a single transaction.

SQL Access Group (SAG): an industrial consortium whose objective is to strengthen and extend the ISO/ANSI standards work in SQL connectivity.

SQL transparency: effort to retarget SQL statements from one database to another.

standards: a set of specifications defining the proper interfaces and/or protocols for a system.

stored procedure (SP): a database object that contains code executed by the database engine.

Structured Query Language (SQL): language to define and manipulate a relational database; conceived as part of IBM System R project in the mid 1970s.

Systems Application Architecture (SAA): IBM framework for developing and operating applications across IBM platforms with cross-system consistency.

technology diversity: ability to handle dissimilar technologies within a coherent architecture.

think time: the time during a transaction when the user is thinking about an appropriate response.

thread: a single instance of a program execution.

timestamp extract: a copy for read-only usage that has associated with it the time at which the copy was performed.

transaction: a sequence of database actions that obey the ACID properties.

transaction boundary: the time duration between the start of a transaction and its end (either commit or rollback).

transaction program (TP): a program that executes transactions.

trigger: code that executes within a database engine when specific events occur.

two-phase commit protocol: a protocol to coordinate the use of multiple resources within a single unit of work.

ultra-long transaction: a transaction whose boundary spans days or months.

unit of work (UOW): same as **transaction**.

updateability: requirements to update specific object instances at various sites.

vertical application: an application that deals with multiple levels of a single business function.

vertical partition: a partitioning that divides a table along subsets of columns.

view: a relational table that is materialized when needed via a SELECT statement on other tables or views.

volatility: the degree to which data changes during normal usage.

warehouse: a collection of data objects that have been packaged and inventoried for distribution to a business community.

warehouse management: managing the architecture to support consumption of data (or process) by a business community; emphasizes a server-client architecture.

warehousing: the activity of flowing data from the point of capture through production database through transformation to its point of consumption.

wicked problem: a subtle problem with significant impacts late in the system life cycle; also know as 'I-gotcha'.

wide area network (WAN): a communication network over a large area (e.g., regions or countries).

Windows Open Service Architecture (WOSA): Microsoft framework to provide Windows applications with specific services from various drivers written to the Service Provider Interface.

workgroup: a small group of persons who perform the same business function for the enterprise requiring close cooperation.

workgroup computing: information processing for a workgroup.

ACRONYMS

3GL	Third Generation Language
4GL	Fourth Generation Language
ACE	Advanced Computing Environment
ACID	Atomicity, Consistency, Isolation, Durability
ACM	Association for Computing Machinery
ANSI	American National Standards Institute
API	Application Programming Interface
APPC	IBM Advanced Program-to-Program Communications
AR	IBM DRDA Application Requester
AS	IBM DRDA Application Server
AS	IBM Application System
ASCII	American Standard Code for Information Interchange
ASE	ISO Application Service Element
ASN.1	ISO Abstract Syntax Notation One — 8824:1989(E)
BAS	Basic Application Structure
BER	ISO Basic Encoding Rules — 8825:1989(E)
CAE	IBM OS/2 DDCS/2 Client Application Enabler
CASE	Computer Assisted Software Engineering

308 ▼ Acronyms

CDRA	IBM Character Data Representation Architecture
CICS	IBM Customer Information Control System
CIO	Chief Information Officer
CLI	Call-Level Interface
CMS	IBM Conversational Management System
CODASYL	Conference on Data Systems Languages
COS	Committee on Open Systems
CPI	IBM SAA Common Programming Interface
CSA	Client-Server Architecture
CTS	IBM SNA Common Transport Semantics
DAL	Apple Data Access Language
DB2	IBM Data Base 2
DBA	Database Adminstration (or Adminstrator)
DBC	Teradata Database Computer
DBL	ISO Database Language
DBM	IBM OS/2 ES/2 Database Manager
DBMS	Data Base Management System
DCE	OSF Distributed Computing Environment
DCS	IBM OS/2 DDCS/2 Database Connection Services
DDB	Distributed Database
DDCS/2	IBM Distributed Database Connection Services/2
DDE	Microsoft Dynamic Data Exchange
DDL	Dynamic Link Library
DDL	Data Definition Language
DDM	IBM Distributed Data Management
DG	MDI Database Gateway
DIS	IBM/Metaphor Data Interpretation System
DML	Data Manipulation Language

DO	Data Object
DOM	Direct Object Manipulation
DOS	Microsoft/IBM Disk Operating System
DP	Data Processing
DR	Distributed Request
DRDA	IBM Distributed Relational Database Architecture
DS	IBM DRDA Database Server
DTP	X/Open Distributed Transaction Processing model
DUOW	Distributed Unit of Work
DXT	IBM Data Extract
EBCDIC	IBM Extended Binary Coded Decimal Information Code
EDA/SQL	Information Builder Enterprise Data Access/SQL
EDC	Enterprise Database Connectivity
EDI	Electronic Data Interchange
EHLLAPI	IBM SNA 3270 Enhanced High Level Language API
EIS	Executive Information System
FD:OCA	IBM Formatted Data: Object Content Architecture
FDB	Federated Database
FUD	Fear, Uncertainty, and Doubt
GUI	Graphical User Interface
IBM	International Business Machines
IDUG	International DB2 User Group
IMS/DC	IBM IMS/Data Communications
IMS/DB	IBM IMS/Data Base
IMS	IBM Information Management System
IPC	Interprocess Communication
ISAM	Index Sequential Access Method
ISDN	Integrated Services Digital Network

ISO	Internation Standards Organiation
ISV	Independent Software Vendor
IT	Information Technology
IW	IBM Information Warehouse
IXF	IBM Information Integration Format
LAN	Local Area Network
LU6.2	IBM SNA Logical Unit type 6.2
MDI	Micro Decisionware Inc.
MIPS	Million Instructions Per Second
MIS	Management Information System
MPTN	Multi-Protocol Transport Networking
MQI	IBM SNA Message Queuing Interface
MVS	IBM Multiple Virtual Tasking System
NCP	IBM Network Control Program
NCS	Hewlett-Packard/Apollo Network Computing System
NIST	USA National Institute of Science and Technology
NT	Microsoft Windows New Technology
ODBC	Microsoft Open Database Connectivity
ODS	Microsoft Open Data Services
OEM	Original Equipment Manufacturer
OLE	Microsoft Object Linking and Embedding
OMG	Object Management Group
OODM	Object-Oriented Data Model
OS/2	IBM/Microsoft Operating System/2
OSF	Open Systems Foundation
OSI	ISO Open System Interconnection reference model
PDI	Procedural Driven Interface
PM	IBM OS/2 Presentation Manager

PO	Presentation Object
PSO	Persistent SQL Object
QMF	IBM DB2 Query Management Facility
RDA	ISO Remote Database Access
RDBMS	Relational Data Base Management System
RDM	Relational Data Model
RDS	IBM OS/2 ES/2 Remote Data Services
RISC	Reduced Instruction Set Computer
RPC	Remote Procedure Call
RR	Remote Request
RSP	Remote Stored Procedure
RUOW	Remote Unit of Work
SAA	IBM Systems Application Architecture
SAG	SQL Access Group
SDK	Software Development Kit
SDLC	IBM SNA Synchronous Data Link Control
SNA	IBM System Network Architecture
SP	Stored Procedure
SPI	Microsoft WOSA Service Provider Interface
SQL	Structured Query Language
SQL/DS	IBM Structured Query Language/Data System
SQL2	SQL Version 2 (now called SQL-92)
SQL3	SQL Version 3
SQLCA	SQL Communication Area
SQLCLI	SQL Access Group Call-Level Interface
TCP/IP	Transmission Control Protocol/Internet Protocol
TDS	Sybase Tabular Data Stream
TIC	IBM Token-Ring Interconnect

TP	Transaction Program
TSO	IBM Time-Sharing Option
TSQL	Sybase Transact-SQL
TSR	Terminate and Stay Resident
UAE	Microsoft Windows Unrecoverable Application Error
UI	UNIX International
UOW	Unit of Work
UPM	IBM OS/2 User Profile Management
VM	IBM Virtual Memory
VMS	DEC Virtual Memory System
VSAM	IBM Virtual Storage Access Method
VTAM	IBM Virtual Telecommunications Access Method
WAN	Wide Area Network
WOSA	Microsoft Windows Open Service Architecture
WYSIWYG	What You See Is What You Get
XPG	X/Open Portability Guide
YAA	Yet Another Acronym

REFERENCES

American National Standards Institute. *Database Language SQL with Integrity Enhancement.* Document ANSI X3.135–1989, 1989.

Astrahan, M.M., et al. "System R: Relational Approach to Database Management." *ACM Transactions on Database Systems*, 1(2), 97–137 (1976).

Atre, S. *Distributed Databases, Cooperative Processing, & Networking.* New York: McGraw-Hill, 1992.

Bachman, C.W. "Data Structure Diagrams." *ACM Data Base*, 1(2), 4–10 (Summer 1969).

Barghouti, N.S., and G.E. Kaiser. "Concurrency Control in Advanced Database Applications." *ACM Computing Surveys*, 23(3), 269–317 (September 1991).

Bernstein, P.A., V. Hadzilacos, and N. Goodman. *Concurrency Control and Recovery in Database Systems.* Reading, MA: Addison-Wesley, 1987.

Codd, E.F. "A Relational Model of Data for Large Shared Data Banks." *Communications at the ACM*, 13(6), 337–387 (January, 1970).

Couger, J.D., M.A. Colter, and R.W. Knapp. *Advanced System Development/Feasibility Techniques.* New York: John Wiley & Sons, 1982.

Date, C.J. *An Introduction to Database Systems.* Volume I. 5th ed. Reading, MA: Addison-Wesley, 1990.

Date, C.J. *A Guide to the SQL Standard.* 2nd ed. Reading, MA: Addison-Wesley, 1989.

Date, C.J. "What is a Distributed Database?" *InfoDB*, 2(2–3), 2–7 (1987).

Date, C.J., and C.J. White. *A Guide to DB2.* 3rd ed. Reading, MA: Addison-Wesley, 1990.

Davis, S., and B. Davidson. *2020 Vision*. New York: Simon & Schuster, 1991.

Devlin, B.A., and P. Cabena. "Data Warehouse Implementation Experience in IBM Europe." *Proceedings of the IDUG Conference*. New York City, May, 1992. 388–399.

Devlin, B.A., and P.T. Murphy. "An Architecture for a Business and Information System." *IBM Systems Journal*, 27(1), 60–80 (1988).

Dow, C., J. Rizner, and D. Stacy. "Distributed Relational Database Architecture: What's It All About?" *IDUG Globe*, 4(1), 1+ (January, 1992).

Fosdick, Howard. "What is IBM's Information Warehouse?" *Enterprise Systems Journal*, 10–13 (June, 1992).

Goldring, R. "Delivering Data to the Information Warehouse." *InfoDB*, 6(4), 29–37 (Summer, 1992).

Goldring, R. "Distributed Database Snapshot Issues." *InfoDB*, 5(3), 20–27 (Fall, 1990b).

Goldring, R. "The Long Road to Heterogeneous Distributed DBMS." *Database Programming and Design*. 33–35 (July, 1990a).

Goodman, N. "Concurrency Control in Complex Transactions." *InfoDB*, 5(3), 28–40 (Fall, 1990).

Goodman, N. "The Object Data Model in Action." *InfoDB*, 6(2), 2–12 (Fall, 1991).

Gray, J., and A. Reuter. *Transaction Processing: Concepts and Techniques*. San Mateo, CA: Morgan Kaufmann, 1992.

Hackathorn, R.D. "Emerging Architectures for Enterprise Database Connectivity." *InfoDB*, 6(1), 11–19 (Summer, 1991).

Hackathorn, R.D. "Managing the Distribution of Enterprise Data." *Relational Journal*, 3(1), 2–3+ (February-March, 1991).

IBM. *DataHub: General Information*. IBM Publication GC26–4874, October, 1992.

IBM. *DataHub Tool Builder's Guide and Reference*. IBM Publication SC26–3046, 1992.

IBM. *Information Warehouse Framework*. IBM Programming Announcement 291 171, September 11, 1991.

IBM. *An Introduction to Information Warehousing*. IBM Publication GC26–4876, September, 1991.

IBM Distributed Data Library. *Concepts of Distributed Data*. IBM Publication SC26–4417, December, 1988.

IBM Distributed Data Library. *Distributed Remote Data Architecture*. IBM Publication SC26–4651, August, 1990.

IBM ITSC. *Client/Server Computing Application Design Guidelines*. IBM Publication GG24–3727, September, 1991.

IBM ITSC. *Data Integrity in a Cooperative Processing Environment*. IBM Publication GG24–3769, November, 1991.

IBM ITSC. *Distributed Relational Database: Using OS/2 DRDA Client Support with DB2*. IBM Publication GG24–3771, May, 1992.

IBM ITSC. *Introduction to Distributed Data*. IBM Publication GG24–3200, September, 1988.

IBM System Application Architecture. *Common Programming Interface, Database Level 2 Reference*. IBM Publication SC26–4798, April, 1991.

IBM System Application Architecture. *An Introduction to SystemView*. IBM Publication GC23–0576, 1991.

Inmon, W.H. *Developing Client/Server Applications in an Architected Environment*. Wellesley, MA: QED Technical Publishing Group, 1991.

Inmon, W.H. *Effective Data Base Design*. Englewood Cliffs, NJ: Prentice-Hall, 1981.

Inmon, W.H. *Information Systems Architecture: A System Developer's Primer*. Englewood Cliffs, NJ: Prentice-Hall, 1986.

Inmon, W.H. *Integrating Data Processing Systems: In Theory and in Practice*. Englewood Cliffs, NJ: Prentice-Hall, 1984.

"Inside IBM's Database Strategy." *DBMS Magazine*. Special supplement to DBMS. IBM Publication G520–8051, September, 1989.

ISO, Information Technology, Abstract Syntax Notation One (ASN.1). ISO 8824: 1989(E), 1989.

ISO, Information Technology, Open Systems Interconnection. Basic Encoding Rules for ASN.1. ISO 8825: 1989(E), 1989.

ISO, Information Technology, Open Systems Interconnection. *Remote Database Access, Part 2: SQL Specialization Protocol*. ISO JTC1/SC21/WG3 N996, DIS 9579-2, February 28, 1990.

ISO, Information Technology, Open Systems Interconnection. *Remote Database Access, Part 1: Generic Model, Service and Protocol*. ISO JTC1/SC21/WG3 N995, DIS 9579-1, March 24, 1990.

Khoshafian, S., and R. Abnous. *Object Orientation: Concepts, Languages, Databases, User Interfaces*. New York: John Wiley & Sons, 1990.

King, P. "Dancing with the Enemy: A Guide to Vendor Alliances and Consortia." *Uniform Monthly*, 41–48 (January, 1992).

Lyman, N. "Implementing Large DB2 2.3 Information Warehouse Applications." *Proceedings of the IDUG Conference.* Geneva, September, 1992.

Martin, J. *Application Development Without Programmers.* Englewood Cliffs, NJ: Prentice-Hall, 1982.

Martin, J. *Computer Data-Base Organization.* Englewood Cliffs, NJ: Prentice-Hall, 1977.

Martin, J. *Data Communication Technology.* Englewood Cliffs, NJ: Prentice-Hall, 1988.

McGoveran, D., with C.J. Date. *A Guide to Sybase and SQL Server.* Reading, MA: Addison-Wesley, 1992.

Micro Decisionware. *Stored Procedures Programmer's Guide for CICS/DB2.* Document Number 507-B01201-10-01, January, 1991.

Micro Decisionware. *CICS/DB2 Server Host Installation Guide.* Document Number 501-B01201-11-01, July, 1991.

Micro Decisionware. *Database Gateway Reference and Installation Guide.* Document Number 501-G01211-20-01, July, 1992.

Microsoft. *Microsoft Open Database Connectivity Software Development Programmer's Guide.* Version 1.0. Microsoft, 1992.

Newman, S., and J. Gray. "Which Way to Remote SQL?" *Database Programming and Design*, 4(12), 46–54 (December, 1991).

Özsu, M.T. and P. Valduriez. *Principles of Distributed Database Systems.* Englewood Cliffs, NJ: Prentice Hall, 1991.

Peters, T. *Thriving on Chaos.* New York: Alfred A. Knopf, 1987.

Pu, C., and A. Leff. "Replica Control in Distributed Systems: An Asynchronous Approach." *Proceedings of the 1991 ACM SIGMOD International Conference on Management of Data*, 20(2), 377–386 (June, 1991).

Reinsch, R. "Distributed Database for SAA." *IBM Systems Journal*, 27(3), 362–369 (1988).

Ross, R.G. "Interview with William H. Inmon." *Data Base Newsletter*, 20(4), 1+ (July/August, 1992).

Sheth, A.P., and J.A. Larson. "Federated Database Systems for Managing Distributed, Heterogeneous, and Autonomous Databases." *ACM Computing Surveys*, 22(3), 183–236 (September, 1990).

Shneiderman, B. *Software Psychology.* Cambridge: Winthrop Publishers, 1980.

Stallings, W. *Data and Computer Communications.* New York: Macmmillan Publishing, 1985.

Stonebraker, M. "The 10 Megatrends of the 1990's." *Proceedings of Database World*. Chicago, D2/1–D2/25, November, 1991.

White, C.J. "Client/Server Computing in a DB2 Environment." *InfoDB*, 5(1), 18–22, (Spring/Summer, 1990).

White, C.J. "Distributing and Accessing Corporate Data." *InfoDB*, 6(4), 14–28 (Summer, 1992).

INDEX

Abort, *see* ROLLBACK
Access management, 24–25, 167–220
Access path, 44
ACID properties, *see* Transaction
Advanced Computing Environment (ACE), 23
Aggregating, 256
American National Standards Institute (ANSI), 20, 22
Append mode, 224
Apple Data Access Language (DAL), 152
Application, 11–12
   extensibility, 276–278
   horizontal, 12
   portability, 21, 28
   vertical, 12
Application programming interface (API), 40–46, 183
   call-level, 42–43, 182, 186
   embedded, 41–42, 59
Application server, 121, 122
ASN.1, 217
Autonomy, 263
   server, 117
Availability, 15, 107, 269. *See also* Sacred seven

Bachman data structure diagram, 101
Back office, 253–254
Basic application structure (BAS), 95, 118–123, 137
   slicing, 118–123
   structure linkage, 97–98
   value linkage, 97, 98
Bind. *See also* Application programming interface
   function, 195
   processing, 197–198
   SQL, 44
Business directory, 259
Business logic, 275

Capability-aware, 148
Centralized database, 230, 241
Centralized system, 89–103
Check-out replica, 237–239
Checked extract, 233–234
Client, 102–103
   interface, 142–143, 169, 172
   platform, 169, 170–172
Client-server architecture (CSA), 112–118. *See also* Peer-to-peer architecture; Server-server architecture; Server-client architecture
   bilevel, 113–114
   client-centric, 113

319

Client-server architecture *(continued)*
  client-to-server ratio, 113
  database, 120, 122
  enhanced, 128, 122
  enhanced database, 120
  gateway, 114. *See also* Database gateway
  in the large, 268
  multilevel, 114–115
  routing gateway, 114
  server-centric, 113
  server-to-client ratio, 113
Collating sequence, 57
COMMIT, 62–64
Common-gateway approach, 27, 137, 147, 152–155
Common-interface approach, 27, 137, 147–152
  client-owned, 149
  client-side, 149
  server-owned, 149
  server-side, 149
Common-protocol approach, 27, 137, 147, 155–157
Common Transport Semantics (CTS), 180
Competitive advantage, 271
Competitive pricing, 22
Complexity, 109, 270–274
Computer-assisted systems engineering (CASE), 14
Concurrency control, 15, 69–80. *See also* Transaction
  granularity, 259–260
  isolation level, 75
  optimistic, 78–79
  pessimistic, 72–78
Concurrent, 69
Consolidation, 255. *See also* Warehouse
Continuous replica, 236, 246
Converting, 256
Copy, 125–126
  request, 223
  set, 223

Copy management, 24, 25, 221–248
  blending, 225
  create mode, 224
  full-image, 235, 237, 241–243
  incremental image, 235, 244
  placement, 149, 223, 224
  primary copy, 223
  push/pull copies, 226
  replace mode, 224
  routing, 225
  secondary copy, 223
  source, 223
  target, 223
  update mode, 224
Corporation for Open Systems (COS), 23
Cost reduction, 108. *See also* Sacred seven
Custom development tool, 171
Custom services, 118
Customization, 276

Data-centric, 90
Data definition, 30
Data encoding, 56
Data independence, 10
Data integrity, 19
Data logic (DL), 96, 120
Data manipulation, 30
Data model, 33–34. *See also* Object-oriented data model, Relational data model
  hierarchical, 34
  network, 34
Data object (DO), 91–94
  protected, 93–94
  shared, 93, 127
Data resource, 210
  external, 252–253
  internal, 252–253
Data semantics, 57–58
Data service (DS), 96, 120
Data sharing, 30. *See also* Information sharing
Data space, 95

Data transformations, 257
Data uncertainty, 79–80
Data volatility, 227–229, 249, 260
  business value, 227
  copy devaluation, 228
  nonvolatile data, 125, 228
Data warehouse, *see* Warehouse
Database administrator, 51
Database gateway, 147, 152, 157–158. *See also* CSA gateway
Database management system (DBMS), 30–33
Database platform
  autonomous, 16
  heterogeneous, 16
Database privileges, 81–82
Database uncertainty principle (DUP), 80
Davis and Davidson, 2–3
DB-library, *see* Sybase/Microsoft SQL Server
Deadlock, 76–78
Decision support, 31–33, 263, 264
Departmental computing, 9
Desktop, 1, 94, 108
  integration mechanisms, 51–53
Digital Equipment Corp
  VAX Data Distributor, 247–248
Direct object manipulation (DOM), 8, 91
Dirty read, 70
Distributed database, 16–18, 120, 123–124
Distributed join, 132
Distributed Remote Database Architecture (DRDA), *see* IBM DRDA
Distributed request (DR), 129
Distributed system, 105–135
  advantages, 107–108
  disadvantages, 108–111
Distributed table, 126, 232
Distributed transaction monitor, 128, 134–135

Distributed unit of work (DUOW), 129
Distributed update, 130–132
Down-scaling, 118
Down-sizing, 7
Driver, 149. *See also* Common-interface approach; Microsoft ODBC
Duality, 10, 34
Dynamic Data Exchange (DDE), 52
Dynamic Link Library, 183
Dynamic SQL, 44–45, 188. *See also* Bind

End-user computing, 6
Enhanced presentation, 121
Enterprise, 11. *See also* Warehouse
Enterprise application, 12–13, 33
  consistency, 12–13
  deployment, 14–15
  development, 13–14
  uniformity, 12–13
Enterprise database, 13–14
  fragmentation, 5, 267
Enterprise database connectivity (EDC), 1, 24–27
Enterprise server, 117
Enterprise system
  disintegration, 4–5, 267
Enterprise-to-workgroup distribution, 17–18
Event-dependent copy, 228–229
Exclusive locks, 74
Expanding, 256
Extract, 25, 125, 221. *See also* Copy management
Extract chaos, 91, 126, 232–233
Extracted table, 126, 232
Extrapolating, 256

Fads, 272–273
Fear-uncertainty-and-doubt (FUD), 20, 272
Federated database (FDB), 16–18, 19
File access method, 34

Flexibility, 270. *See also* Sacred
    seven
Forecasting, 256
Formats and protocol (FAP), *see*
    Protocol
Fragmentation, 226
    horizontal, 226
    vertical, 226
Front-end tool, 47–53
    API, 51
    categories, 50–51
    development power, 49–50
    GUI development, 275
Front office, 254
Full-image copy, *see* Copy
    management
Function logic (FL), 96, 120

Game plan, 282–283
Generic interface, 149
Generic service, 118
Generic tool, 171–172
Glass house, 7
Global optimization, 132
Graphical user interface (GUI), 7. *See
    also* Desktop
Grouping, 256
GUI development tool, *see* Front-end
    tool

Hedge your bets, 281
Hidden SQL, 168
Historical copy, 228
Historical records, 257
Host variable, 201

IBM Corporation
    Character Data Representation
        Architecture (CDRA), 196
    Client Application Enabler (CAE),
        209
    Database Manager (DBM), 54
    DataHub, 278–280
    Distributed Data Management
        (DDM), 196–197

Distributed Database Connection
    Services/2, 154–155, 207–210
Distributed Relational Database
    Architecture (DRDA), 156,
    193–210
    DRDA Application Requester (AR),
        193–194
    DRDA Application Server (AS),
        193–194
    DRDA Application Support Protocol,
        193–194
    DRDA Database Server (DS), 194
    DRDA Database Support Protocol,
        194
    Formatted Data: Object Content
        Architecture (FD:OCA), 196
    Information Warehouse (IW),
        263–265
    Message Queuing Interface (MQI),
        180
    Remote Data Services (RDS), 208
    SAA Distributed Data Architecture,
        128
    SystemView, 280
Incremental-image copy, *see* Copy
    management
Industry consortium groups, 22–24
Information sharing, 1, 5
IBI EDA/SQL, 152, 263
Information model, 275
Information technology (IT), 2, 19
Informational database, 254
Informationalization, 3
Integrated business model, 257
Integration mechanisms, 275
Integrity, 15, 222, 269. *See also* Sacred
    seven
Interface, *see* Layered architecture
Interface definition language (IDL),
    133
International Standards Organization
    (ISO), 20, 22, 139
Interoperability nirvana, 219
Interprocess communication (IPC),
    122, 127

Interprocess communication *(continued)*
  asymmetric, 127
  connection, 127
  data, 127
  direct, 127
  execution, 127
  indirect, 127
  message, 127
  symmetric, 127
IS-A hierarchy, 38. *See also* Object
  generalization, 38
  specialization, 38
Isolation, *see* Concurrency control

Join path viewing, 101–102

Layered architecture, 138–140
  interface, 138
  service access point, 138
Layering, 138
Least common denominator, *see* Permissiveness
Legacy system, 110, 274–276
  infrastructure, 275
Local area network (LAN), 7, 175–177
  transport, 169
Local autonomy, 18, 107, 123
Local server, 115–118, 176
Lock manager, 74. *See also* Concurrency control
Locking duration, 75–76
Locking granularity, 74–75
Lost update, 72
LU6.2, 196, 216

Machine efficiency, 33
Mainframe system, 9. *See also* Legacy system
Manageability, 15, 162–163, 269. *See also* Sacred seven
Memory protection, 177
Micro Decisonware Inc.
  Database Gateway for DB2, 155, 186, 189–193
  TRANSFER feature, 221, 239–247

Microsoft
  Access, 98–102
  Object Linking and Embedding (OLE), 52–53
  Open Data Services (ODS), 154–155, 190
  Open Database Connectivity (ODBC), 152, 182–188
  Service Provider Interface (SPI), 183
  Windows Open Service Architecture (WOSA), 183–184
MIS development, 277
Multi-protocol transport networking (MPTN), 180
Multimedia, 257, 259
Multiversioning, 79
Mutations, 276

National Institute of Science and Technology (NIST), 22
Network plumbing, 25, 168–169
Nonrepeatable read, 70–71

Object, 34, 37. *See also* IS-A hierarchy
  behavior, 37
  class, 224
  encapsulation, 10, 38
  identifier, 37
  instance, 37, 224
  method, 37
  representation, 37–38
  specification, 37
Object Management Group, 23
Object-oriented data model (OODM), 35, 36–38. *See also* Data model
  inheritance, 38
  overloading, 38
Open Software Foundation (OSF), 23
Open system, 20–21
Open systems interconnection (OSI), 140
Openness, 161–162
Organization, 11
Ownership
  data, 263

Ownership *(continued)*
    driver, 149
    server, 117

Package, 198, 204
Partition, 124–125, 226, 230–232. *See also* Copy management
    horizontal, 83, 231
    vertical, 83, 231
Peer-to-peer architecture (PPA), 115. *See also* Client-server architecture
Performance, 160–161, 222, 268–269. *See also* Sacred seven
Periodic replica, 245–246
Permissiveness, 164
    least common denominator, 148, 164
    maximal approach, 164
    minimal approach, 164
Persistent SQL object (PSO), 46–47. *See also* Stored procedure
Peters, Tom, 2
Phantom row, 71–72
Placement, *see* Copy management
Point-and-click, 8
Preemptive multitasking, 177
Presentation logic (PL), 95, 121, 275
Presentation object (PO), 92
Presentation service (PS), 95, 121
Presentation space, 94–95
Procedure driven interaction (PDI), 7, 90–91
Process coupling, *see* Interprocess communication
Process transparency, 84–87
Production application, 31–33
Production system, 258
Program-centric, 90
Program execution, 198
Program preparation, 198
Proprietary interface, 144
Protocol, 139, 143. *See also* Layered architecture

RDA
    dialogue, 211
    services, 211
    transaction, 211
Recoverability, 15, 269–270. *See also* Sacred seven
Refreshed extract, 234–235, 244–245
Relational data model (RDM), 35–36, 259. *See also* Data model
    integrity rules, 36
    language, 36
    structure, 36
Reliability, 107, 109, 163
Remote commit, 129–130
Remote Database Access (RDA), 156, 210–215
Remote procedure call (RPC), 121, 122, 128, 133–134, 137
    called procedure, 133
    calling procedure, 133
    stub, 133
Remote request (RR), 129
Remote server, 116, 176
Remote unit of work (RUOW), 129, 194, 229
Replica, 25, 126, 221. *See also* Copy management
    synchronization, 235–236
Replicated table, 126, 236
Request, 65, 141
Result, 141
Resynchronization, 235
Retargeting, 145, 161, 275
Retrieval, 223
Right-sizing, 7
ROLLBACK, 63–65
Row viewing, 100

Sacred Seven, 268–270, 281
Sampling, 256
Scalability, 22
Schedule, 248
Security, 15, 109, 222, 269. *See also* Sacred seven

Index

Security control, 80–84
Semantic heterogeneity, 261
Server, 103
  interface, 143, 169
  platform, 169, 172–173
Server-aware, 148
Server-client architecture, 251. *See also* Client-server architecture
Server-server architecture, 221. *See also* Client-server architecture
Service access points, *see* Layered architecture
Shared locks, 74
Simple extract, 232–233, 241–245
Simultaneous, 69
Single-site update policy, 130, 229, 233, 235. *See also* Copy management
Snapshot, 126, 256, 257
Snapshot table, 126, 235
SQL, 38–40
  connectivity language, 39, 53
  SQLCODE, 57, 201
  transparency, 25, 53
SQL Access Group (SAG), 23, 212–215
  SQL Call-Level Interface (SQLCLI), 182, 214
Stability, 22, 163
Staging, 222
Standards
  de facto, 20
  de jure, 20, 22
  proprietary, 21
Static SQL, 44–45, 195, 216–217. *See also* Bind
Status code, 56–57
Stored procedure, 47, 83–84, 96, 134
Sybase
  Open Server, 155
  Tabular Data Stream (TDS), 156, 186
Sybase/Microsoft
  DB-library, 42, 189
  ISQL, 53–54
  SQL Server, 53

System catalog procedure, 189
System catalog table, 55–56
System interoperability, 21–22
System management, 278

Table viewing, 98–100
Technology. *See also* Information technology
  assessment group, 273–274
  diversity of, 271–272
  fearing (white-knuckled), 271
  loving (arm-waving), 271
  roller coaster, 270–271
  timing of adoption, 273
Tennant, Rich, 3, 4, 19
Terminal emulation, 121
Think time, 65
Timestamp extract, 233
Timestamp ordering, 79. *See also* Concurrency control
Transaction, 15, 61–68, 131
  ACID properties, 62–63
  atomicity, 62
  boundary, 64
  chained, 63
  consistency, 62–63
  durability, 62–63
  isolation, 63
  linkage, 97
  long, 66–67
  short, 65
  splintered, 68
  ultralong, 68
Transformation, 224–225, 256
  chains, 257
Transparency, 161
Transport, 133
Two-phase commit, 130–132

Unit of work, *see* Transaction
UNIX International, 23
Up-scaling, 118
Updateability, 226
User efficiency, 33
User identification, 87

View definition, 82–83

Warehouse, 232, 251–252
   enterprise, 261
   ownership, 263
   packaging, 257
   updates, 260
   workgroup, 261
Warehouse management, 25–26, 251–265
Warehousing, 258
Wicked problem, 54, 55

Wide area network (WAN), 7, 175–177
   transport, 169
Workgroup, 6. *See also* Warehouse
   computing, 6–7
   server, 117
Workgroup-to-enterprise distribution, 18

X/Open, 23–24, 182, 213
   Distributed Transaction Processing model, 134